IMITATIVE FLY TYING

IMITATIVE FLY TYING

Techniques and Variations

IAN MOUTTER

The Countryman Press
Woodstock, Vermont

Library of Congress Cataloging-in-Publication Data
Moutter, Ian
    Imitative fly tying: techniques and variations/Ian
    Moutter.—1st ed.
        p. cm.
    ISBN 0-88150-574-9
    1. Fly tying. I. Title.
SH451. M67 2002
688.7'9124   dc21

                                        2002019288

Book design by Sharyn Troughton

Published by The Countryman Press, P.O. Box 748, Woodstock, Vermont 05091

Distributed by W.W. Norton & Company, Inc., 500 Fifth Avenue, New York, NY 10110

Published in the UK by Swan Hill Press, an imprint of Quiller Publishing Ltd.

Printed in Hong Kong

10 9 8 7 6 5 4 3 2 1

DEDICATION

When in the midst of writing this book, I was interrupted by a telephone call from a flyfisher who wished to take the Scottish casting instructor qualification. The caller was someone I had met on a couple of occasions and although our previous meetings were brief, I liked him, he's called Willy. As we talked on the telephone Willy suddenly burst into an expletive, which seemed out of character and out of synch with the subject of our conversation 'Jesus! A plane's just flown into one of the twin towers of the World Trade Centre in New York'. At the time I had no concept of what he was talking about. 'Look, Ian I have got to watch this, I will have to call you back OK!' were his words as he put the telephone down. This was the first indication that something terrible had been perpetrated, the first indication that a senseless act of terrorism on a scale never seen before had taken place. Those who acted to create such suffering, are those who believe they can steal that most precious gift, the gift of life. An attitude appropriately summed up in the words of their so-called leader 'we value death as much as those in the west value life'. This act of barbarism had nothing to do with west, east, south or north, it was simply that, an act of barbarism. There will be many who died in those collapsing towers who enjoyed casting a fly for a rising trout, many who loved to swim a deep nymph or streamer in search of steelhead and many who just liked to be by the waters with a rod in hand. This book is dedicated to all those fishers who died in the events of 11 September 2001. I cannot see those responsible for ending these lives as ever having cast a fly upon the water.

CONTENTS

PREFACE

I have attempted within the pages of this book to describe some of the methods I use when tying fly patterns designed to imitate specific natural flies. The book assumes that the reader has at least a basic knowledge of fly tying. That said, however, each procedure is explained in what I hope is a clear and easy to understand manner, allowing tyers of limited experience to complete and enjoy the patterns and techniques described. Experienced tyers should have little or no trouble at all in mastering the various techniques.

This is not a book of fly patterns, although there are many different patterns described throughout the following pages. It is primarily a book of methods and techniques and each fly pattern included is there as a vehicle with which to demonstrate a particular tying technique or combination of techniques. The patterns used in this way have been chosen not just for the fact that they allow a particular method to be explained, but that they are tried and tested patterns in their own right. To this end I hope that readers will not only tie the fly patterns described, but, more importantly, use the techniques and apply them to their own favourite patterns, or use them to design their own imitative fly patterns. The tying sections are designed to be used as a manual to accompany the tyer at the tying bench and include full tying sequences.

The writing of this book has been a labour of love and I hope that the enjoyment I have experienced, will be shared by the reader. Books on fly fishing and fly tying generally come in two very distinct guises. There is the 'how to do it' reference type and there are those that stir our hearts in narrative form. I have attempted to place this book in both camps, writing each chapter in two parts. The first part of each chapter is a relatively short narrative and the second part, a practical bench top fly tying manual.

I would think that many of the techniques described will be unfamiliar to readers and some are variations of well established methods, my hope is that every reader will find things that will interest them and inspire them to wind some thread around a hook.

The title *Imitative Fly Tying – Techniques and Variations* accurately sums up the contents of this book, as the techniques described are used to tie specific natural insects. Of more importance, the techniques are applied to imitate a specific insect at a particular stage of its life cycle, which is, I believe a more precise and accurate description of imitative fly fishing. To 'Hatch a Match' at the tying vice is, for me, and many other tyers, an important factor in the total enjoyment of fly fishing, resulting in, what I refer to as, a complete experience. *You see the insect that the fish are feeding on – you tie, better still design and tie, a fly pattern to imitate that particular insect – you fish with that pattern – you catch a fish using that pattern.* A complete experience! Each technique described within this book gives the fly tyer a method by which this can be approached.

Tying my own flies is a vital part of my enjoyment of fly fishing, that is not to say that I am above using fly patterns tied by anyone else. Far from it, if a pattern sitting in someone else's fly box attracts my eye, I have been known to borrow it, on what usually becomes a permanent basis. I have an enthusiasm in seeing fly patterns that are designed by other tyers and in learning the methods by which they were tied, I hope that readers will find the same enjoyment in the ideas provided by this book.

Today it is possible to pick up any of the many magazines on fly fishing or fly tying and find fly patterns advertised for sale at what often seems to me to be paltry sums of money. The fly patterns on offer through the pages of any such magazine can vary from the beautifully tied to the distinctly dubious. For those fly fishers who have neither the time nor the inclination to tie their own fly, what is offered by these advertisers is an incredibly diverse source of fly patterns. Most fishers will learn whose fly patterns they like and they will tend to stay with that source. I see tying and designing my own fly patterns as an important part in the world of fly fishing, a part that adds an extra kick to the overall experience, a part that I would not choose to be without.

Keeping fly tying simple is something that I continue to learn as the years go by. By simple I don't mean not taking the time to learn or develop new techniques to solve a problem or to allow a fly pattern to be presented in a particular way. What I mean by simple is only applying to the fly pattern that which is necessary to produce the required impression when the pattern is in or on the water. I am not a lover of highly realistic fly patterns, seeing them as more the field of the model maker than the fly fisher. I would go as far as to say I would prefer to fish with an old chicken feather tied to a hook than use a pattern that almost exactly reproduces the form of a particular insect. My reason for this is that such models lack the impression of life and this is especially so when they are in or on the water. A simple spider pattern will, in my opinion, look more alive in the water than any realistic looking pattern and as such will catch more fish. Having said that I can but admire some of the realistic patterns I have seen, but I prefer them behind glass hung on the wall than tied upon my own tippet.

Of the six chapters contained in this book, the first four are aimed at specific stages of the life cycle of particular insects. The first of these chapters highlights the emerging fly. The following three chapters cover the adult upwinged fly, the spent spinner and nymphs, larvae and pupae respectively. Each of these chapters offers a variety of ways in which the natural insect can be imitated successfully. The fifth chapter is based on the magic of small stream fishing and the fly patterns I use when fishing such small waters. The sixth chapter delves into my own experiences with the third hand of the fly tyer, the fly tying vice and my experiences with the many different models I have used over the years.

The measure of a successful fly pattern is not solely based on the fact that it can catch fish. It is a little like fly fishers who cast with all the skill and dexterity of an armless, plastic, garden gnome, but who refuse to improve their skills on the basis that they can catch fish. Big deal, in my experience anyone who wants to can catch fish, just so long as they go fishing, what really counts is how you do it. Satisfaction, regarding designing, tying and fishing your own fly patterns, does not come solely from a pattern catching fish, but by it catching fish in the way that you intended the pattern to catch fish. For example if a pattern is designed to imitate a natural fly in the surface of the water, struggling at the final stage of emerging and it does not sit within or on the surface of the water, but sinks. Then, even if its underwater guise inspires a fish to take, it cannot be considered a successful emerger pattern, because the fish has not been tempted in the way intended. I have met a lot of anglers who would not agree with this, their attitude being so long as it catches fish, who cares. As far as I am concerned this misses the point by a long shot and, while they are welcome to their opinion, I do not have to agree with it.

This is the main difference between imitative fly fishing and other forms of fly fishing. Some forms of fishing a fly make no demands on the pattern used imitating anything in particular and certainly not an insect at a specified point in its life cycle, the patterns used are attractors, lures designed to grab the attention of a fish and prod it into action. This is a very different approach to the imitating of a natural fly by applying materials in such a way that they allow the hook to be presented to a fish in a very particular way, providing an impression of the real thing.

The final part of the book, the Appendix, contains sections on the techniques, methods and materials employed when tying the fly patterns described in the actual chapters. There is also a section on suppliers. Naming fly tying material suppliers can be hazardous from a writer's point of view. The market can be fairly volatile with wholesalers falling out of favour with manufacturers and retail outlets discontinuing to deal with certain wholesalers. There are also the

Shadowed Waters

unfortunate cases of businesses occasionally closing down. The market place is far from fixed. I have, however, tried to make the list as up to date as possible, but betwixt pen and final copy of a book, many a change can take place.

I hope that those who read this book enjoy it and find something of value amongst its pages. Tight lines and may your thread never break.

Ian Moutter

1. AIR'S APPARENT

Part I

As the years pass so my interest and fascination with the fly life, which constitutes the basis from which my passion is formed, increases. As a boy the relationship between that tied upon my tippet and those pesky and annoying insects that flew around my head whilst I was fishing, was non existent. In fact it would be true to say that if a mayfly had jumped off the water, flew through the air and hit me right square between the eyes, I would have had no idea what it was and I may even have suspected that it might sting me. It took time for the void between reality and imitation to contract and for me to realise the importance of duping the fish with fly patterns designed to play the role of some specific natural insect on which the fish were feeding, tended to feed on or could be tempted to feed upon. In those early years it would never have occurred to me that the fly tied upon my tippet was meant to copy, even vaguely, those actual flies I could see on or near the water. The slow realization of what was really happening was more an evolution than a sudden understanding or enlightenment and for this I am very grateful. My easy, slow seduction into the realm of true fly fishing took many years, with only little bits and snippets being revealed to me at any one time. Looking back it was probably beneficial and completely appropriate that things progressed in this particular manner. If I had thought at the time that I may be required to learn about all those different flies, I would more than likely have never bothered continuing in my vain attempts at presenting a fly carefully to some, hopefully, unsuspecting fish. The great god of fly fishers, however, knew best, his secrets and mysteries were revealed to me gradually one at a time and only ever as they were needed and never any more. Let's face it there are so many flies of use to the fly fisher and each one has its own life cycle and each specific part of that cycle can be important. In those early days, if the thought had ever occurred to me, that it may be necessary to learn all the ins and outs of fly life in its myriad forms, I would have, perhaps, continued my fishing by fixing a worm or maggot on to the hook at the end of my line.

To me the natural flies that I come across when fishing are like wrinkles, they get more attractive the older I get and the more familiar they become to me. Now by older I mean in terms of fly fishing years not necessarily in overall years, although this often adds up to the same thing. Then again you never want either wrinkles or familiarity to completely take over. Enough wrinkles to add a mature elegance to a face, but not enough to resemble a dried-up passion fruit and enough knowledge and information regarding flies, to enable you to fish successfully in all the situations you find yourself in, is more than adequate

Lately I have found myself suffering from what, for me, is an unusual affliction. The symptoms of this disease involve me crouching over the water. Sometimes even hanging off or over rocks, often on my belly, or balanced precariously one hand desperately holding on to some tree branch or tuft of grass. At these times my eyes are locked on to the surface of the water and my prayer is that the branch or tuft is sufficient to hold my weight and prevent a ducking. Or even on the odd occasion it has been reported that I have been seen running and jumping along the banks of the local stream cupping my hands together in the air, much to the consternation of those persons watching. I have been, as you may well suspect, bearing up to an acute attack of entomologia.

Entomologia, by its nature, apparently comprises of different stages and levels of acuteness. The stage I am currently experiencing appears to be centred on those flies undergoing the transition from a watery domain to one of the air. These emerging insects are an important food source for trout and as such of serious interest to people who hunt for trout using the artificial fly. I am one of these anglers and whilst understanding the fatal nature of such a pursuit, or perhaps disease would be the better word, I can accept that the hands of fate, hold and guide me and trust in its wisdom. In doing so I will, hopefully, become a beneficiary of the generous nature, which at times, fate bestows on those of us who attempt to catch a fish with the fly.

All insects which spend part of their life cycle in the water and a later part as flies, have what is commonly referred to as an emergence. This emergence regards the transition from a water-based insect to one of the air. It is a transition that can take place in many different ways, some of which are useful to the fly fisher and some not so useful or indeed totally useless. Take for example the damselfly, as a nymph the imitation is particularly profound as a tempter of trout, with fish feeding on them avidly and as fly tyers recognize this attraction, many such fly patterns exist to imitate it. It has got to such a point that it is difficult to open a magazine without another so-called new damselfly nymph imitation being described. Most of them are pretty much the same and as such worthy of ignoring with as much enthusiasm as the trout shows for the real thing. The sequence of emergence adopted by the damselfly nymph, however, effectively takes them out of the reach of the fish. The damselfly nymph normally uses bankside vegetation, or any other convenient route, to crawl out of the river, lake or pool. The transition from nymph to adult fly takes place here, away from the water and beyond the threat of being eaten by a fish. So for all practical purposes the damselfly nymph makes a first class fly pattern to use, but any other stage in the life cycle, including the point where the adult emerges from the nymph, is unimportant from a fly fishing point of view. I know of a few adult damselfly patterns, but on the whole I would not be inclined to use them, except perhaps as a novelty or to tie as a showy, pretty fly pattern. Incidentally if you have never seen a damselfly changing from the drab dun colour when newly emerged, to the bright metallic colours we normally associate it with, try and take the time out to do so. It is not difficult to find

a dull grey brown newly emerged fly by the water, watching it dry out and changing to colours electric may take some minutes, but it is well worth the wait. The damselfly's method of emerging effectively takes it out of that list of flies, which I would include as emergers at least as far as fishing is concerned.

Another example would be the stonefly. On the rivers I fish the stoneflies are much loved by trout but again usually in the form of the nymph. Looking under just about any stone or rock will reveal why this is the case, the stonefly nymphs are in abundance. My own observations would seem to indicate that the stoneflies, especially the larger species, tend to crawl out of the water onto stones and rocks to complete the transition from nymph to adult. Anyone who walks along the banks of a river or stream with a population of these flies, at the right time of year and taking the time to look carefully, will find the discarded nymph exoskeletons, empty but perfect effigies of the real nymph. I hesitate to be completely definite about all stoneflies exiting the water in this way, there being so many different species, of vastly differing sizes and it is possible some may emerge differently to those I am familiar with. My own experience being what it is, I only ever use nymph imitations when fishing the stonefly and personally do not consider stoneflies as belonging to that group of flies which fly fishers refer to as emergers. That is not to say that a fly pattern designed and tied to imitate the adult fly would not catch fish, let's face it just about anything tied on to a hook will catch a fish at times and sometimes very successfully, but that doesn't make it fly fishing

To be included as emergers, flies must fulfil certain criteria. The first of these is that the early part of their life cycle must be spent within the water as aquatic creatures, the nymphs, larvae and pupae, which play such an important part in the life of the fly fisher. The second criterion is that the emergence must take place on the water, this allows the fish access to the emerging fly as a food item during the transition from water to air. It is this transition time that has lately so fascinated me and stirred my curiosity, resulting in the strange bankside behaviour previously mentioned. Watching flies emerge is totally fascinating and it is surprising how each emergence can differ. Sometimes the fly can be almost clear of the shuck before reaching the surface of the water, at other times a monumental struggle takes place in the water surface as the fly attempts to break free of the shuck, not always successfully. At times the process is so quick it is over before there is anything to observe. At other times it is leisurely, dangerously so, giving the fish plenty of time to mop up the stragglers. Sometimes the emergence is only partially successful and these crippled flies become a ready

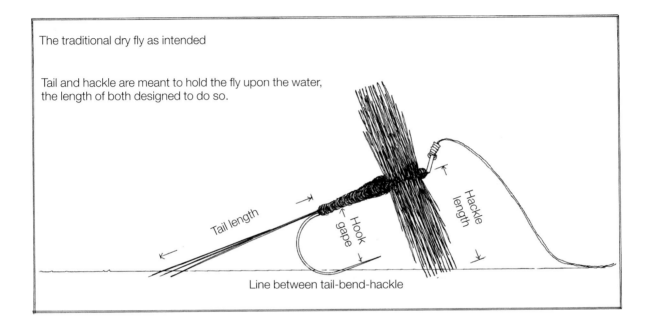

The traditional dry fly as intended

Tail and hackle are meant to hold the fly upon the water, the length of both designed to do so.

Tail length

Hook gape

Hackle length

Line between tail-bend-hackle

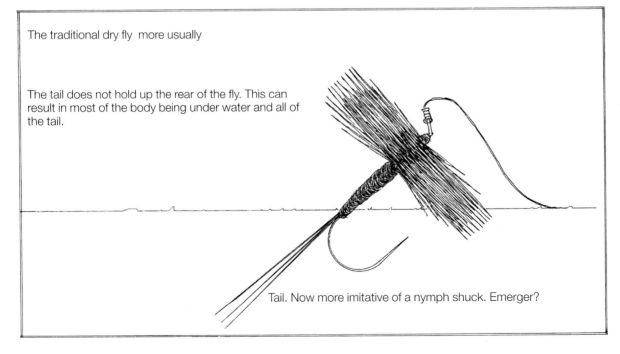

The traditional dry fly more usually

The tail does not hold up the rear of the fly. This can result in most of the body being under water and all of the tail.

Tail. Now more imitative of a nymph shuck. Emerger?

supply of convenience food for the fish. I have seen some flies that have emerged from the nymph well before they reach the surface of the water and, in the case of these flies it could be said that they emerge twice, once from the nymphal skin and then from the water itself. The physical transition takes place deep down in the depths, with the adult fly floating upward to the surface of the water. In these cases the transition from water to air is separate from the change of nymph to adult and I call these flies, sub-emergers.

Those flies that fulfil these criteria include upwinged flies, caddis (sedge) and the midge. Not all types of upwinged flies can be counted as useful emergers for fly fishers, but most can. In fact it would be fair to say that, historically, much of the interest in and progress of fly fishing, especially that of the dry fly, was centred on the upwinged flies to the greater degree and to a lesser extent the caddis. When I look at this history and the development of dry fly fishing, it becomes clear that the emerging fly, especially in the early years, was not clearly recognized and on the whole ignored, with the majority of floating flies being tied as so-called adult patterns. Looking through the catalogue lists of fly patterns from the late eighteen hundreds through to the early nineteen hundreds would seem to confirm this. There are, however, celebrated exceptions to this found within these lists and the Gold Ribbed Hare's Ear is probably the most notable, but only when it is tied with a rough fur hackle. This makes an excellent surface emerger pattern, particularly useful in an olive or sedge hatch, but I am unclear what it was originally intended to imitate.

These days I seldom fish using an adult fly pattern when there is a hatch of flies on the water, preferring to use a fly designed to imitate the emerger. The thinking behind this is that for every adult fly floating gracefully down the river, or taking to the air the instant it is free from the shuck, there must have been an emerger. There is also my belief that, in most circumstances, the classic adult dry fly pattern is more often taken by trout as an emerging fly rather than the fully emerged adult fly. The classic dry fly, with traditional wound hackle, was and con-

tinues to be tied following a particular formula, with the hackle and tail designed to hold the hook out of the water as much as is possible. But how often do they act exactly as planned? As far as I can see not that often. Classic trout flies tied using wool, animal furs and other materials available at the time of their creation do little to enhance floatability and seldom will the body of the fly remain completely out of the water. Usually the hackle supports the front half of the fly, but the tail is not substantial enough to hold up the rear of the fly, hook bend et al. The result of this being that the rear of the fly breaks through the surface of the water, a position more allotted to the role of the emerger than the adult dry fly. Add a little water absorption and this will compound to the point where it becomes the normal state of affairs. So far from being a relatively recent innovation, emerger fishing has, at least to my way of thinking, been practised since the dawn of dry fly fishing.

I love fishing emerger patterns, to be quite honest I love fishing just about anything, but given the chance to fish the emerger I will. A fly pattern that sits part under water and part above, seems to be a fitting and appropriate way to present a fly and there can be no doubt that flies tied to do this are very successful at attracting the attention of fish. I love watching the confident way fish rise to emerger patterns – half-heartedness plays little part in such rises. Creating flies to imitate emergers adds another dimension compared to when using the latest pattern found in the tackle shop or described in the monthly fly fishing magazines. Not that these should be completely ignored, but taking the model from what is actually observed on the water and then tying a pattern to imitate it, gives me the greater satisfaction. Approaching fishing this way contributes an additional dimension and depth to when I am on the water, with my intent not being solely on the pursuit of the fish, but also being immersed in all that surrounds and is within the water. It is a completeness that I have found is in short supply elsewhere, something that I treasure and value. It is also something that allows me to pursue, even when off the water, my interest and pleasure in the fly life and the imitation of that life at the tying bench.

Searching out the likely places with the fly

Part II

I may not have evidence other than that of my own eyes to prove it, but the impression I have gained during the time that I have fished using the fly, is that trout take the emerging fly with more gusto than at any other stage of the life cycle. That is not to say that the newly emerged dun floating down the river with wings upright or the skating sedge with pupae shuck left behind are not an attraction to the trout, far from it. But I have little doubt that the natural fly is in the most danger from becoming additional protein during the emerging process and that fish are at their most enthusiastic when feeding upon them. The only other time that I find trout show such enthusiasm is when the spinners return to the water to lay the eggs and finally die. Patterns designed and tied to imitate emerging flies will always prove successful for as long as trout swim within the waters we fish. More consistent success comes my way when fishing the emerging fly compared to fishing the adult.

I have named this section Air's Apparent because that is exactly the situation with emergers. Up to the time of emergence the element in which these insects have spent the whole of their lives has been water, the transition into the adult fly takes them from this watery world into the air. It is one of the many miracles of life that go on around and about us every day and of which fly fishing makes us aware. This second part of Air's Apparent will describe many of the methods I employ when tying my own flies to imitate the natural emerging insect. Much of what follows is, as far as I am aware, an alternative approach to that usually taken and the methods used are, for the greater part, original or a development of a recognized method or technique. When I see techniques with which I may not be familiar, I often ignore them on the basis that they are too much trouble to apply to my own flies and unnecessary for my fishing. I would like

to vouch for each of the techniques described in the following pages, they are all easy to complete. An initial view may give the impression that some of the techniques, for example the furled hackles, are over-complicated. This is not so and practised once or twice it is to be hoped that they will join the ranks of the many well established and simple methods used effectively by fly tyers.

When designing and tying flies I like to ask myself, what am I imitating? It is not enough to name a particular natural fly or group of natural flies. Tying flies is not just a matter of imitating a particular fly, what we are actually doing is imitating a natural fly at a specific stage in the life cycle of that fly. So a fly pattern will be a specific nymph, larva or pupa, a specific emerger, or a specific adult fly and in the case of the mayflies, it can also be a particular spent spinner. The recognition of the natural flies that are on the water does not mean that fish will always limit feeding to those flies that, to all intents and purposes, would appear to be the dish of the moment. But for consistent success when fly fishing for trout it is not a bad idea to let nature make the decision about which fly pattern you are going to tie on to your tippet. If the fish are rising to a hatch of olives its quite a good idea to follow suit, and present an olive emerger pattern. Equally if the mayfly spinners are returning to the water to lay their eggs and the spent spinners are littering the surface of the water much to the delight of the local trout, it makes sense to use the appropriate spent spinner pattern. Now please don't get me wrong, I am well aware that what I am saying is basic stuff and well understood by most fly fishers. Personally I see it as the essence of fly fishing for trout, however, it is surprising how often this generous guidance is not followed and the generosity of nature with its many pointers is ignored. There is no doubt that closely observing what is happening on and around the water has improved my fishing skills, my resulting catches and, perhaps best of all, it has increased the depth of my pleasure considerably, much more so than having the best of tackle and bulging fly boxes.

When I go fishing for trout I carry very few fly patterns, but each one has been chosen to cover a specific job or circumstance. Many of them can be used to represent more than one type of natural fly. Take the olive dun as an example, imitative patterns tied in three or four different sizes will cover a multitude of other flies. Spinners are the same, a few different sizes tied with reddish brown bodies and a whole host of natural insects are successfully covered. Sedges and midges can be imitated in the same way, with one specific pattern tied in different sizes and colours serving to act as imitations for many different insects.

The materials and the techniques used to tie the patterns described in the following sections can be applied to any number of different fly patterns. That I decided to use a specific pattern says only two things, first the pattern is suitable for describing the particular technique being described and second it is a fly pattern that I have used and the pattern has proved a successful tempter of fish. I hope that you will also find this to be the case. In essence, as mentioned in the preface, this book is about techniques and methods, rather than an additional collection of fly patterns. Having said that, the patterns that follow are all good fly patterns to use at the right place and at the right time.

Sub-Emergers

At one time I thought that all flies emerged either in the surface of the water or crawled out of the water to complete their emergence in the air. I know now that this is not true. I have witnessed the event on many occasions and have seen, at least with some upwinged flies, that emergence can take place subsurface and by subsurface I mean deep down not just below the surface of the water. I have seen the fully emerged fly rising up from a great depth of water, nymph skin left far behind. In the case of the large upwinged flies, like the true mayfly, this can be quite a sight. My own experience of this has been

limited to the large mayflies and the sulphur coloured yellow may dun and I suspect that this is due to the relatively distinct colours displayed by these flies, making it easy to witness such an event. Although I am not in the position to demonstrate that it is the case, I strongly suspect that other flies emerge deep subsurface but that their camouflaged colours make it extremely difficult to observe.

The fact that some flies emerge subsurface presents me with a descriptive dilemma. Are the emerged flies that float slowly up from the depths to be considered, at least in a fly fishing sense, real emergers? Or, as stated in part one of this chapter, 'to be considered a candidate for the name emerger in fishing terms, a fly must undergo the transition in or just below the surface of the water'. Put simply, is the emergence considered the transition from the nymph or pupa to the adult fly, or from water to air? My inclination would be to maintain that handy definition described in part one of this section and treat these apparently impatient flies separately. That said these deep underwater emergers are extremely attractive to trout and as such are well worthy of being recognized, understood and utilized by fly fishers. I have presumed to give these particular flies a name and have called them 'sub-emergers'. Many well established fly patterns, which on the face of it would not appear to clearly imitate any particular natural fly, are very good impressions of the 'sub-emerger' rising up to the surface of the water with legs, tails and body creating a mêlée of colour and movement. It is no surprise to me that many of the traditional Irish lough style wet flies, tied using soft feather overhackles taken from game birds, imitate the 'sub-emerger' very accurately. It was while fishing on the large Irish loughs that I first became aware of this phenomenon. Since the time I became aware of 'sub-emergers' I have made the effort to observe more closely anything that may resemble such flies and I have seen plenty of evidence to suggest it is fairly widespread. This evidence, however, has been limited to bright coloured flies. Logic denies me the luxury of limiting deep 'sub-emergers' to those few brightly coloured species I have seen. I am fairly sure that at sometime in the future it will be

An adult damselfly newly emerged. The author does not consider the damselfly as a true emerger in fly fishing terms as emergence takes place off the water.

proven that subsurface emergence is commonplace with most if not all upwinged flies and perhaps even other flies such as the caddis.

The following pattern has been designed as a tribute to such adventurous flies and in this particular case the Mayfly Dun Sub-Emerger. Contrary to the airborne dun the colours of this fly are quite vivid in the water and the use of orange and brown/olive combine to imitate the colours I have seen displayed. These colours may be different on the waters you may fish and, accordingly, they can be changed to suit local variations. The overall impression given by this fly when in the water is of a straggly mess, which more than adequately describes how the natural fly looks when rising up slowly through the water. There is nothing particularly unique in this tying, it is more interesting in what it imitates and how it is fished.

Tying the Mayfly Dun Sub-Emerger

This fly is tied on a short shank hook and is weighted at the rear of the hook, just at the start of the bend. The purpose of weighting the fly in this way is linked to the way it should be fished. The fly is allowed to sink after being cast. It is then retrieved using a steady long pull on the line. After each pull the fly is allowed to sink again by waiting a generous few seconds before commencing with the next pull. Being weighted to the rear draws the fly downwards, leading by the rear, which opens out the hen hackle and the soft game hackle. It is this action that imitates the 'sub-emerger' best of all, a complete mess of legs, wings and body. It can be fished either on its own or as the top fly pattern in a team.

Materials Required

Hook	Wet fly hook, medium to heavy size 6 or 8 e.g. Kamasan B175.
Body	Brown and olive dubbing with a little Lite Brite dubbing mixed thoroughly together.
Underbody	At the start of the hook bend four turns of heavy lead wire wound towards the hook eye.
Hackle	The main body hackle is a soft long-fibred hackle dyed orange, doubled, hen or cock.
Over-hackle	Partridge flank, olive or natural dyed brown.
Rib	Stainless steel wire.
Thread	Of own choice 8/0.

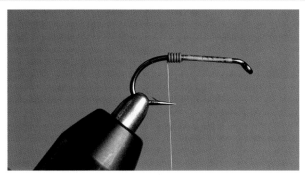

Photograph 1 Place the hook into the jaws of the vice and test the hook for soundness. Attach the waxed tying thread and wind using flat thread to the start of the hook bend. Wind on five turns of medium lead wire, ensuring that both ends are under the hook shank, cut off the excess lead wire.

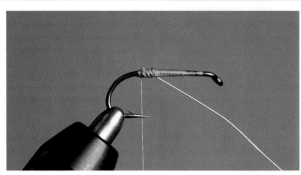

Photograph 2 Wind the tying thread around the lead wire in random open turns finishing with the tying thread on the hook eye side of the wound lead wire. Now tie in the wire rib on the underside of the hook shank using the 'loop over the thread method' and return the thread to the other side of the wound lead wire, making a few turns of thread directly against the wound wire.

Photograph 3 Dub the thread with the body dubbing and wind over the wound lead.

Photograph 4 Take the main body hackle and tie it in on the hook shank by the tip with the good side facing you. Cut off any excess hackle tip and double the hackle using the technique described in the diagram opposite.

Doubling the hackle can prove to be a problem for many fly tyers, although I don't know why because the techniques used are quite simple, no matter which method is used. Doubling the hackle can often make the difference between a fly tied to an average standard and the fly that stands out as being tied well. The best method of doubling I know of and use to the exclusion of all others was shown to me by Ally Gowans, of Ally's Shrimp Fame one evening at the National Sports Centre in Largs, Scotland. Ally and I were working on an Instructors' assessment course and relaxing one evening tying flies in the bar. He showed me the following method.

First tie the tip of the hackle in place on the hook and pull the feather fibres downwards so they sit at ninety degrees to the hackle stalk. Now holding the hackle taut with the good side facing you, run the outer edge of a pair of scissors along the upper edge of the hackle stalk pushing the fibres backwards. Repeat on the other side of the hackle stalk. Repeat if required. The effect of doing the above is that the position of each hackle fibre is changed and rather than sitting out at ninety degrees from the hackle stalk, they are now angled backwards as a doubled hackle should. A brief setting with the thumb and fingers will complete the exercise. Once mastered this method is excellent and to be preferred to all others.

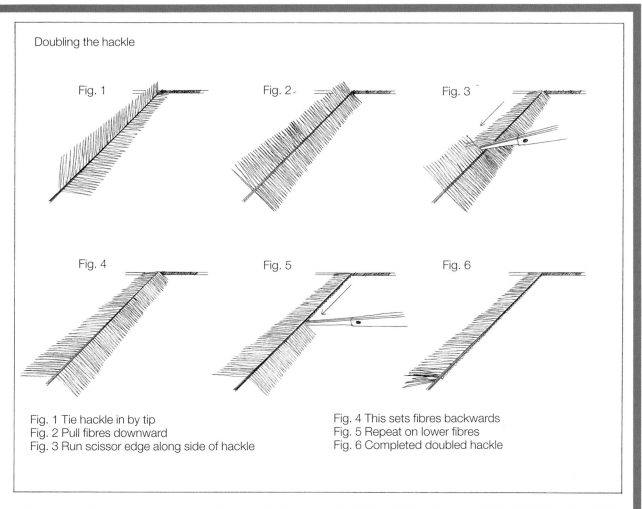

Doubling the hackle

Fig. 1

Fig. 2

Fig. 3

Fig. 4

Fig. 5

Fig. 6

Fig. 1 Tie hackle in by tip
Fig. 2 Pull fibres downward
Fig. 3 Run scissor edge along side of hackle

Fig. 4 This sets fibres backwards
Fig. 5 Repeat on lower fibres
Fig. 6 Completed doubled hackle

Photograph 5 Dub the thread and wind the dubbed thread to just behind the eye of the hook, remembering to leave plenty of space to tie in the remaining materials and to form a small head. The thread should be lightly but thoroughly dubbed with the body material and the turns of dubbed thread should be close together and tight.

Photograph 6 Wind on the wire rib and tie in on to the underside of the hook shank and remove the excess wire by wiggling it to break. Five turns of rib are ideal.

Photograph 7 Wind on the doubled hackle so that the stalk sits directly behind the wound wire rib, following behind the windings of the rib exactly. Tie in the hackle on to the underside of the hook shank. When the doubled hackle is wound on, ensure that the hackle fibres are leaning towards the rear of the hook. Cut off the excess hackle.

Photograph 8 Now tie in the partridge hackle by the tip, again with the good side facing you. Now double the fibres on this hackle. I find that on short game hackles the easiest method to double the hackle is to use the thumb and first finger, squeezing the hackle fibres into position.

Photograph 9 Make three or four turns of the partridge hackle and again tie in on the underside of the hook shank, directly behind the hook eye. Cut off the excess partridge hackle. Form a small head using the tying thread. When forming the head do not be tempted to force the hackle fibres too far back over the hook, ideally they should be sticking out fairly straight from the hook. Finish the fly pattern with a whip finish.

Photograph 10 The completed fly.

That completes the tying of the Mayfly Dun Sub-Emerger. The tying is not particularly different from many of the other patterns that imitate the mayfly. The inclusion of the lead in the rear combined with the soft hackle does produce a very attractive profile in the water, a profile, which, while looking messy, imitates the sub-emerging natural fly fairly accurately. If the pattern is fished in the way described, it can be deadly in both still and flowing water. The trick is to add as much movement as possible. As well as stopping and starting the retrieve, the rod tip can be used to impart the impression of life especially when fishing in rivers and streams. Most of my success with this fly pattern has been on lakes and lochs, given the right circumstances though, it has proved to be a useful additional trick up the sleeve when fishing a rise of mayflies on a river.

Detached Hackles

Over the last couple of years I have become very interested in the creation of pre-formed, detached hackles. This interest can be traced back to when writing the book *Tying Flies the Paraloop Way* and my involvement with the USA based tyer Jim Cramer of Bodega Bay, California. Jim's excellent contribution to 'the Paraloop Way' included a small section on detached hackles and how to create them. I included one of his flies, the Scardy Cat, as the last fly in the gallery of flies at the end book and maintain that it is a form of Paraloop fly, although some tyers may disagree. It was from this brief involvement with Jim, that I first felt inspired to investigate the possibility of detached, pre-formed hackles. Initially this was as an alternative method for producing Paraloop flies, but has now evolved into a completely separate subject in its own right.

The work on pre-formed detached hackles has resulted in two very different forms, both of which I have found very useful for tying certain types of fly. The first of these to be developed was what I called the Perfect Furled Hackle and the second the Crumpled Furled Hackle. Hans Weilenmann the Netherlands based tyer, all round fly fishing aficionado and good guy, was kind enough to come up with the name Crumpled Furled Hackle after I sent him samples and the name has stuck. The Crumpled Furled Hackle was initially developed in an attempt to provide a hackle with a very buggy look to it

Initially, the creation of each hackle may appear to be a bit fiddly and time consuming, with each one taking a couple of minutes to complete. This time is more than made up for in the fact that each detached hackle can be used to provide the hackling for up to a dozen flies, and applying each hackle can take just a few seconds to tie in. The speed and ease of application more than makes up for the time taken to create them in the first place. The use of these pre-formed detached hackles is ideal when applied to emerger patterns, due to it being possible to apply the hackle to only the topside of the hook shank, allowing the completed fly to sit low in the water.

Much more use could be made of these pre-formed hackles than I have attempted to date, but for anyone willing to experiment, the possibilities are endless. I think that pre-formed detached hackles, in various forms, will become a regular addition to fly tying techniques in the future. The use of such hackles is very much in its infancy, but once the idea gets out into the mainstream of fly tyers I believe that a whole new world of applying a hackle to a fly pattern will be available.

How to tie a Perfect Furled Hackle

This particular pre-formed, detached hackle was produced originally as an alternative to tying the normal Paraloop hackle. It was christened the Perfect Hackle because it is the only method that I have come across, or have been able to devise, that allows a detached hackle to be formed where the hackle fibres sit straight and in order. The overall effect is one of a long sinuous caterpillar and a completed hackle placed on the hand seems to be almost alive. When tying Paraloop flies I call the finished hackle, prior to tying in, the Hackle Brush and the Perfect Furled Hackle is, for all intents and purpose, a detached, extra long hackle brush.

The process of creating this hackle is very straight forward, but to some eyes it may appear fiddly and complex. I can assure any reader that it is extremely simple to form and even simpler to apply to a fly pattern. I find each hackle formed can be used to tie up to a dozen completed flies.

After I have produced the finished article, more often than not I allow the completed hackles to be soaked overnight in a product such as Watershed or some other silicon based liquid floatant and then left to dry out thoroughly. I find it is more convenient to do this at this early stage rather than after the fly patterns have been tied. Hackles treated in this way float far longer and more efficiently than those hackles that remain untreated. This adds to their attraction in my eyes, as they require far less attention and maintenance to allow them to float in the manner desired.

The illustration clearly describes how to create a Perfect Furled Hackle. The materials required are:
1. A good quality, genetic cock saddle hackle, the longer the better. I use some that are in excess of 12 in (30 cm) in length. The hackle fibres should be fairly even for the whole length of the hackle and the stalk reasonably thin and pliable. For most of my detached hackle tyings I use saddle capes from Hoffman, Whiting Farms. They are perfect for the job, the uniformity of the hackle fibres results in a detached hackle that is very even throughout its length.
2. A 20 in (51 cm) length of thin GSP floss, kevlar thread or polypropylene floss. This provides the material for the furled core of the detached hackle. I prefer to use thin GSP floss, it has a stiffness that allows it to be easily manipulated and the ends can be melted and bonded together. Polypropylene floss does not have the strength of GSP and kevlar will only burn and not bond at all when a flame is applied close to it, although both can be used as an alternative to GSP, as can many other materials.

The first part of the procedure produces the double furled core around which the hackle will be wound. This process will be familiar to many readers, but to assist those unfamiliar with double furling the procedure is explained and illustrated in detail.

Fig. 1

Fig. 1 Form a loop with the GSP or any suitable alternative material and tie a non-slip knot at the loose ends. Place the loop over a barbless hook fixed upside down in a vice, or alternatively make one of the 'furling points' (as illustrated opposite), place this in a vice and place the loop over the point. Now take a weighted hook or one hook of a dubbing spinner and place it into the other end of the loop. Make sure that the knot is at either the top end of the loop or the bottom and not in between the dubbing spinner hook and the vice hook. The reason for this is that you do not want the knot to be a part of the final hackle.

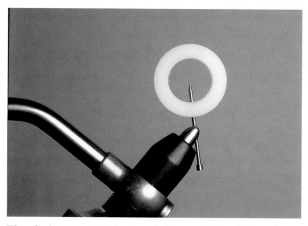

The furling point designed by my friend Ron from Edinburgh. Ron designed it after seeing me almost spear my head at a demonstration when using a needle fixed in a vice as a furling point. Thanks Ron my life is now a lot safer.

Both a weighted hook or a dubbing spinner can be used to spin materials prior to furling.

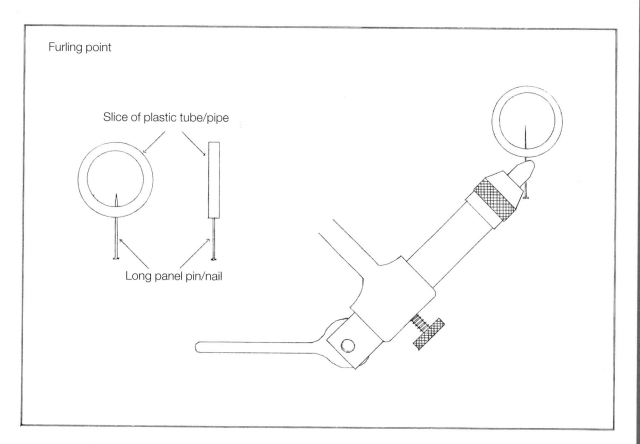

Furling point

Slice of plastic tube/pipe

Long panel pin/nail

The furling point developed by Ron Harvey of Edinburgh

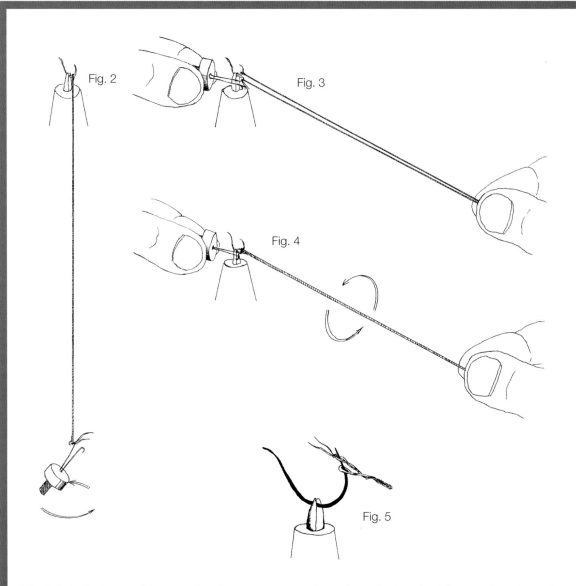

Fig. 2

Fig. 3

Fig. 4

Fig. 5

Fig. 2 Spin the loop making sure that the turns are even throughout the length of the spun loop. Running your finger and thumb up and down the spun material can help to even out the turns. Continue spinning until the material can be spun no more without jeopardizing evenness throughout the whole length of the spun loop.

Fig. 3 Now bring the lower end of the spun loop up to the upper end, whilst holding the centre of the spun loop between your thumb and finger. Make sure that everything is kept tight at this stage.

Fig. 4 Release the centre of the spun loop and allow the material to furl on itself. This process is best completed using the thumb and finger to control the furling process, this helps to ensure that the result is even throughout the whole length of the furled loop. It is beneficial to add a few twists using finger and thumb at the end of the furling to ensure furling is complete and to run the thumb and first finger along the furling to ensure it is even.

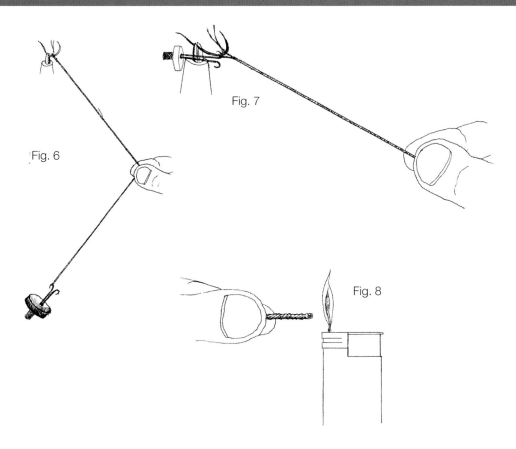

Fig. 7

Fig. 6

Fig. 8

Fig. 5 Unhook the weighted hook or dubbing spinner and attach the loose end to the hook in the jaws of the vice. The removal of the hook will leave a space in the material to place over the hook fixed in the jaws of the vice.

Fig. 6 Place the weighted hook or single hook from the dubbing spinner into the end of the furled material and spin following the same twist as exists in the single furled material. Spin as tightly as possible until evenness can no longer be maintained.

Fig. 7 Now repeat Fig. 3 and Fig. 4 using the already furled GSP. This will double furl the core. When the double furling is completed make a few twists, using thumb and finger to ensure the process is complete.

    The result of this is a length of material that has been double furled. Furled materials have a quality that allows them to maintain their shape, the main constituent of this quality is that the material is always under tension. It is this quality that allows the second part of the process to be completed successfully and to maintain the shape of the furled material.

Fig. 8 Take the completed core off the vice hook and singe the loose ends together using a flame from a cigarette lighter, and squeeze the melted ends together. This will bond the loose ends together. If kevlar is used this will not melt so this part of the procedure is impossible, this is one of the reasons why I prefer to use GSP.

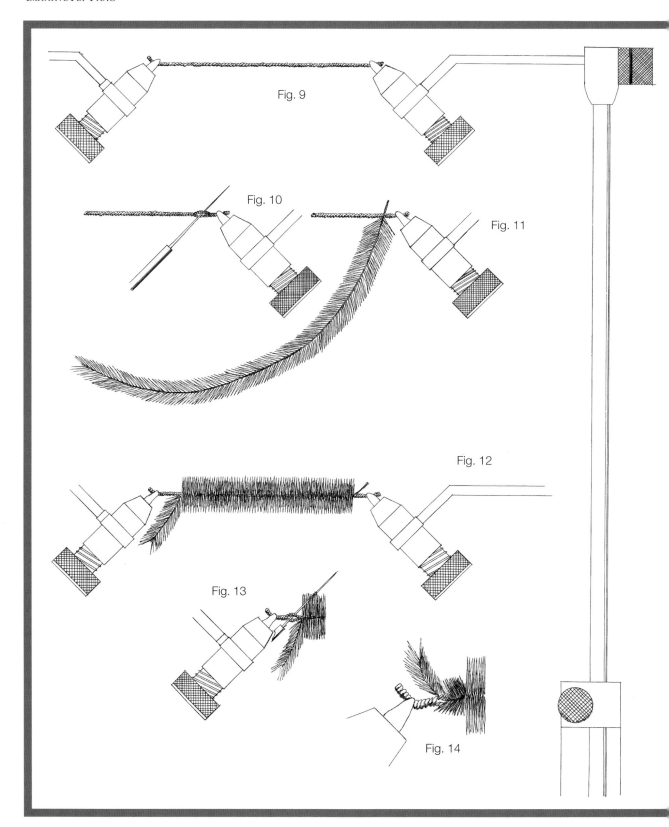

Fig. 9

Fig. 10

Fig. 11

Fig. 12

Fig. 13

Fig. 14

Fig. 9 Place each end of the core into the jaws of two separate vices, as per the illustration and adjust so that the core is brought under tension.

Fig. 10 Take a dubbing needle and open up a gap in the core material at one end. I usually open up at the right end rather than the left.

Fig. 11 Feed the base of the hackle through this gap, pushing it through for about ½ in (13 mm).

Fig. 12 Now wind the hackle along the core in the opposite direction to which the core has been furled. It is the tension in the furled core that allows this winding to take place successfully. In effect each turn made around the core is against the tension of the furling.

Fig. 13 When all but the last inch (25 mm) or so of the hackle has been wound on in even equal distanced turns, use a dubbing needle to open up a gap in the core at the position where the turns of hackle end.

Fig. 14 Now feed the tip of the hackle through the gap and pull it through completely.

A Perfect Furled Hackle.

This completes a Perfect Furled Hackle. The completed hackle can be removed from the vices and it will not unwind. The uses of this hackle are described after the instructions on how to tie the Crumpled Furled Hackle. I sent Jim Cramer in the USA examples of this detached hackle. Now Jim doesn't like to use a gallows tool when he is tying, so he came up with a technique whereby the hackle is initially fed into the core as described in Fig 10, but without attaching the ends of the furled core to the gallows tool. Hackle pliers are then attached to the end of the hackle and the core pulled tight using the hands. The hackle is then wound around the core by spinning the hands, the weight of the hackle pliers allows the hackle to be spun around the core. When completed the end of the hackle, where the pliers were attached, is feed through the core as in Fig. 12. Now that's what I call a neat technique!

How to tie a Crumpled Furled Hackle

I really like this method of forming a detached pre-formed hackle, its uses are many, but I find it ideally lends itself to emerging patterns. The method, like the Perfect Furled Hackle has not to my knowledge been published before and I initially developed it as an alternative to providing a top of the hook shank hackle. I also wanted a hackle that had a very buggy look. The resulting hackle has this effect and initially appears to be a bit of a random mess, each fibre being twisted and bent, which lends itself to providing a hackle on such flies as the Gold Rib Hare's Ear emerger. If you want a very buggy looking hackle then the Crumpled Furled Hackle is for you. Without treating the hackle with silicon prior to tying in, the hackle fibres will quickly revert to being straight after wetting them. Used either treated or not treated, this method provides a very useful way of applying a hackle to a fly pattern.

It may seem strange that I bother to crumple the hackle fibres prior to furling but crumpling the fibres produces a more even hackle after furling than if the hackle is left uncrumpled. Try it and see the result for yourself if the hackle is not crumpled first. If you require all the hackle fibres to return to being straight, then soak the finished product in water and allow it to dry prior to any silicon treatment.

Just like the Perfect Furled Hackle, the Crumpled Furled Hackle can be formed using more than one hackle. I use up to three depending on how dense or bushy the hackle is required to be, or what size of hook is being used, which often comes to the same thing. When using more than one hackle, complete the following procedures with the hackles placed together as one, making sure you use hackles of the same length. Mixing different colours of hackle together can be a very useful method to enhance the overall look of a fly. If there is a need to strengthen the completed hackle, a length of GSP or kevlar can be run down the whole length of the hackle prior to furling and included in the spinning.

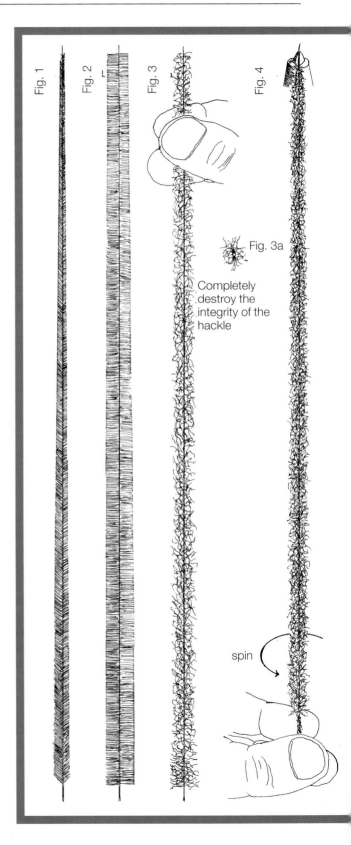

Fig. 1

Fig. 2

Fig. 3

Fig. 4

Fig. 3a

Completely destroy the integrity of the hackle

spin

These illustrations describe how to create a Crumpled Furled Hackle. The materials required are:

1. A genetic saddle hackle is ideal but the technique can be used with any hackle of choice. The hackle should be long, the longer the better, with even fibres throughout its length. The same hackles that are suitable for creating the Perfect Furled Hackle are ideal.

2. If a strengthening core is required, a length of GSP or kevlar that is slightly longer than the length of the hackle or hackles. This material is laid along the whole length of the hackle prior to spinning. As when tying the Perfect Furled Hackle I prefer to use fairly thick GSP thread as this allows me to melt the ends together giving a solid bond.

Fig. 1 Take a long genetic saddle hackle.

Fig. 2 Holding the top of the hackle, draw all the fibres, both sides of the stalk, downwards so that they sit at ninety degrees to the hackle stalk.

Fig. 3 Squeeze and roll the hackle fibres between the thumb and two first fingers, moving up and down the hackle until the integrity of each fibre has been compromised and they sit in a random manner around the hackle stalk. Continue this until a cross section of the hackle resembles **Fig. 3a**. I find wetting my fingers with saliva every now and then can assist in this procedure.

Fig. 4 Now fix the top of the hackle, or tops if more than one hackle is being used, into the jaws of a tying vice, making sure that the tip is not too close to the position where the hackle is secured. I find that an inch (25 mm) of hackle tip extending beyond the vice jaws is ideal. The reason for this is that the stalk becomes extremely thin the closer it approaches the tip of the hackle and is liable to break easily. Now spin the hackle from the base end using your thumb and first finger. Take care not to over-spin as this will break the hackle, however, you will be surprised at how much spinning the hackle stalk will take. Use a dubbing brush to brush the hackle fibres up and down during the process of spinning, this helps to keep the fibres at ninety degrees to the hackle stalk. Initially there is an element of trial and error involved in how much the hackle should be spun, the saving grace if you do break the hackle is that it will inevitably break at the top, usually at the point it is held by the jaws of the vice. Therefore if the hackle does break it can be re-fixed into the vice jaws and spun again.

Fig. 5

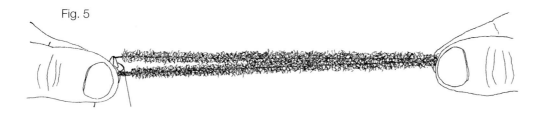

Fig. 5 Now grip the base of the spun hackle, or hackles, with your left thumb and finger and the centre of the spun hackle with your right thumb and finger. Bring the base of the spun hackle up to the top of the hackle to where it is held by the vice jaws.

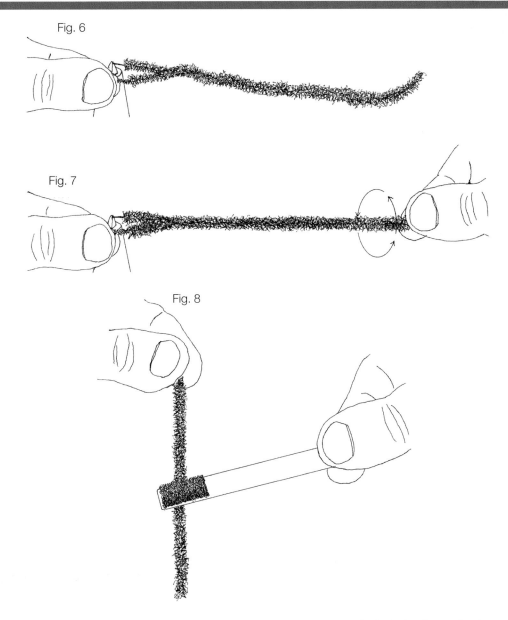

Fig. 6

Fig. 7

Fig. 8

Fig. 6 Let go of the right thumb and finger, whilst maintaining grip with the left. This will release the hackle and it will automatically furl upon itself.

Fig. 7 Complete the furling by giving the furled hackle an additional twist in the direction of the furling. Only do this procedure to the point that when released the hackle will not unfurl to any degree. Continue holding the loose end of the hackle whilst twisting.

Fig. 8 Now take a dubbing brush and brush the furled hackle in both directions to release any fibres caught up in the furling process. This completes the Crumpled Furl Hackle.

A furled hackle locked by hackle pliers.

Experience has shown me that it is usually unnecessary to bond the loose ends of the completed hackle. To be on the safe side, however, I use a pair of hackle pliers to lock the loose end until the hackle is required for use. As an alternative to the use of hackle pliers, I sometimes tie the loose ends with a short length of thread. It is at this stage that I would normally soak the hackle in silicon waterproofer overnight, allowing it to dry off completely before applying it to a fly pattern. Adding a core of GSP or other material will definitely make the hackle stronger, but I have had no problem to date with this hackle breaking without a core being added, even after landing several relatively large fish on the same fly.

How to apply the Perfect and Crumpled Furled Hackles to Fly Patterns

Both detached hackles can be used in the same way, but each will produce a different effect, the result of which will influence how the fly will act when on the water. I like to use the Crumpled Furled Hackle for the more buggy-looking patterns and the Perfect Furled Hackle for patterns designed to float well in most water conditions including those that are very rough. Both hackles can be applied to the hook shank at any position and can extend in length from the start of the hook bend through to the hook eye, providing, if required, hackling along the whole length of the fly. Where the hackle is positioned and how long it is, will depend on the pattern of fly being tied.

I use two basic methods when applying the hackle to a fly and both methods can be applied to either hackle. The first of these methods is what I call 'Normal' and the second 'Reverse'. Of the two I find the Reverse method the most useful and effective. The illustration explains both methods. My preference for the Reverse method is that it does away with any head to the fly and the excess material can be used to help form the body of the fly. When using the Reverse method the thread is tied off either behind the hackle or immediately before the tail. The Normal method can either incorporate the section of the hackle that is tied in to help form the body or, alternatively, the material used to initially tie in the hackle forms part of the thorax. In both cases the hackle is pulled over the thorax and tied in behind the eye and a head formed as is the case with most fly patterns.

To illustrate the application of the above detached hackles to a fly pattern I have chosen a general Olive Emerger imitation. I have used the same pattern of fly for both the 'Normal' and the 'Reverse' method and the Perfect Furled Hackle is used in the first example and the Crumpled Furled Hackle in the second. By using the same pattern of fly, the differences in applying the hackle and in the choice of detached hackle will be far clearer than if different patterns were to be used.

Applying a Detached Hackle 'Normal' Style to a General Olive Emerger Pattern

Materials Required

Hook Partridge Klinkhamar hook size 14.

Hackle Pre-formed detached perfect hackle blue dun cock.

Body Olive polypropylene dubbing mixed with a little pinch of Lite Brite.

Thorax Olive and brown mixed polypropylene dubbing.

Thread Of own choice 8/0.

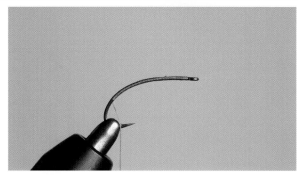

Photograph 1 Place the hook into the jaws of the vice and test the hook for soundness. Attach the waxed thread and wind using flat turns of thread to a point around the bend of the hook, as in the photograph.

Photograph 2 Dub the tying thread with the body dubbing and wind on to the hook shank forming a slightly tapered body.

Photograph 3 Take the detached hackle and pull one end through your thumb and first finger to expose a clear end of the central core. Tie this end on to the top of the hook shank as shown in the photograph. The main body of the hackle should be facing back over the hook.

Photograph 4 Now dub the thread with the olive and brown polypropylene dubbing and then wind on to the thorax area forming a shaped thorax. The thorax should be wider in the centre than at either end.

Photograph 5 Pull the hackle over the thorax and brush the fibres away from where the hackle will be tied in behind the hook eye. I use a dubbing brush to brush the fibres away. Then tie in the hackle behind the hook eye.

Photograph 6 Cut off the remaining detached hackle and lock the loose end of the removed hackle with hackle pliers. Then form a small head directly behind the hook eye using the tying thread and complete the fly pattern with a whip finish. Cut off the tying thread.

That completes a general Olive Pattern using a Perfect Furled Hackle in the 'Normal' style. The next pattern is the same general Olive Pattern but this time the Crumpled Furled Hackle is used in the 'Reverse' style.

Photograph 7 The completed fly.

Applying a Detached Hackle 'Reverse' Style to a General Olive Emerger Pattern

The materials are the same except that in this case the hackle is a Crumpled Furled Hackle using two hackles to form the furled hackle.

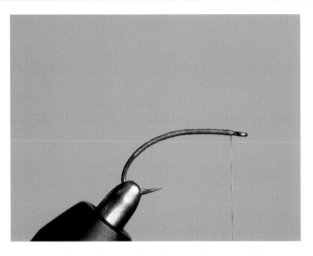

Photograph 1 Place the hook into the jaws of the vice and test the hook for soundness. Attach the waxed thread and wind using flat turns of thread to a point around the bend of the hook, as in the photograph. Now wind the thread, again using flat turns of thread, back to behind the hook eye. This forms the thread foundation of the fly pattern.

Photograph 2 Take the detached hackle and tie in directly on top of the hook shank, behind the hook eye. The main body of the hackle should extend beyond the eye of the hook. Take the tying thread to where the hackle is first tied in directly behind the hook eye. Now dub the tying thread with the thorax dubbing.

Photograph 3 Wind on the dubbed thread forming a shaped thorax that is thicker in its middle than at both ends.

Photograph 4 Now pull the detached hackle over the top of the thorax and tie in on to the top of the hook shank. Cut off the remaining detached hackle and lock the loose end with hackle pliers. Continue the tying thread around the hook bend to the point as shown in the photograph.

Photograph 5 Dub the tying thread with the body dubbing and wind back along the hook shank forming a tapered body. Wind the dubbed thread right up to the hackle.

Photograph 6 Remove any excess dubbing from the tying thread and complete a whip finish directly between the body and the hackle. Cut off the tying thread and pull out the dubbing from the thorax with a dubbing brush.

Photograph 7 The completed fly.

That completes the Olive Emerger using a detached hackle tied in reverse. I like this particular tying, finding it a neat way to apply a hackle and complete the fly pattern.

Normal methods of applying pre-formed detached hackles

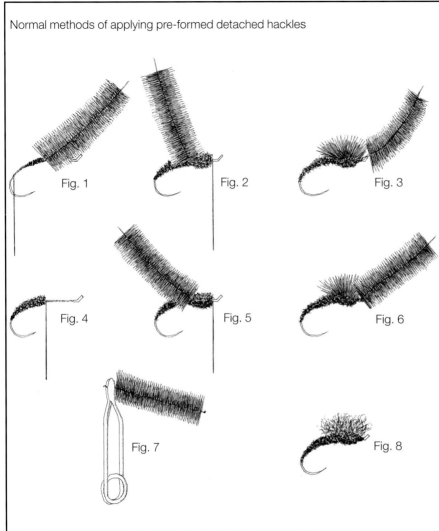

This illustration shows two of the methods used when attaching a detached hackle.

Fig. 1 Attaches the hackle by tying it into the body area of the fly pattern.

Fig. 2 The thorax is then formed.

Fig. 3 Then the hackle is pulled over the thorax and tied in behind the hook eye.

Fig. 4 Shows the body formed prior to the hackle being tied in.

Fig. 5 The hackle is then tied into the thorax area and the thorax formed.

Fig. 6 The hackle is again pulled over the thorax and tied in behind the hook eye.

Fig. 7 Shows the cut end of the detached hackle locked by hackle pliers.

Fig. 8 Shows a furled crumpled hackle tied using the second method.

Two examples of crumpled furled hackles.

Crumpled hackles compared to the perfect hackle in the centre.

Various detached hackles.

Hooks and Tying in Positions for Emerging Flies

The choice of hook is very important when tying many forms of emerging fly patterns. For flies emerging in the surface of the water I prefer to use two basic shapes of hook. The first has a continuous bend and is often marketed as a shrimp or buzzer cum midge pupa hook. I usually use the Kamasan B100, but many other manufacturers make suitable continuous bend hooks. The other shape of hook I like to use are hooks suitable for the tying of Klinkhamar style flies and are what I consider to have an elegant bend. The hook suitable for tying the Klinkhamar style flies is not, in my opinion, as versatile as the continuous bend hook, but for those flies that require the front of the fly to be horizontal to the water and the rear submerged, it is ideal. The illustration shows clearly the difference in the two styles of hook.

The continuous bend hook, as the name implies, has the bend starting from directly behind the hook eye. Whilst the hooks suitable for Klinkhamar style tyings have a relatively level section of shank behind the hook eye, initially the bend is less pronounced, becoming more pronounced further down the hook shank.

Why is the hook choice so important when tying emerging flies? The answer to that is that the hook choice is important when tying most flies, but where a fly is required to float and more importantly to float in a very specific way, the choice of hook can be the difference between success and failure. It is not only the shape that is important, the weight of the hook is an important factor. There is no sense in tying a surface emerging fly pattern using floating materials, on to a hook of a weight that will ensure that the fly will sink. So for most of the emerger patterns I tie, light weight wire hooks are used. There is no doubt that very successful emerger patterns can

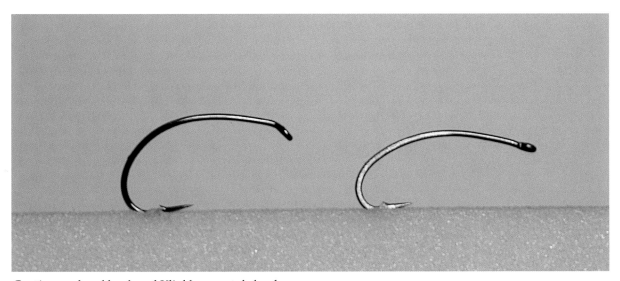

Continuous bend hook and Klinkhamar style hook.

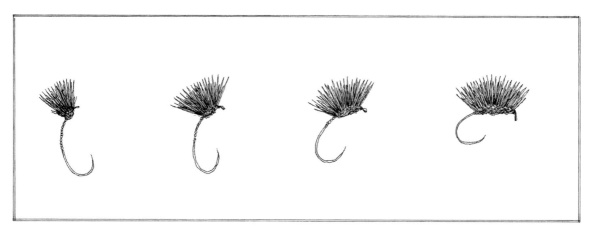

This demonstrates how the length of the hackle effects the way in which a fly pattern sits in or on the water surface. This can range from vertical to horizontal.

and are tied on hooks different to the two I have highlighted, but on the whole to present the flies in the positions on the water that I prefer, the two hook shapes described more than adequately fulfil the requirements.

Although it appears to be generally accepted that the position of the pupa or nymph, immediately prior and during emergence, is to the greater extent horizontal to the water surface, I am convinced that this is just one of the many positions effected by the emerging insect. As mentioned earlier in this chapter, many nymphs are fully emerged well before they reach the surface of the water and also nymphs or pupae can be well into the emerging process by the time they reach the surface. This being the case I do not believe the position of the fly in the surface of the water needs to be limited to any one position, but can be successfully imitated in whatever manner you may fancy. The continuous bend hook allows this flexibility to a far greater degree than any other shape of hook, which is why it is my favourite hook for tying emerging flies.

The continuous bend hook allows the fly pattern to sit in the surface of the water in whatever position you may prefer. The application of materials allows almost complete control of this positioning. The diagram above illustrates this far better than I can explain in words and demonstrates how the length of the hackle applied to the hook, will influence the way that the fly pattern will be presented when on the water.

Running from left to right, the first fly has a small hackle placed on the top of the hook shank. This will have the effect of floating the fly pattern almost vertically. Moving to the second fly the hackle has been extended down the hook shank for a small distance. This has the effect of tilting the fly pattern off the vertical. The third fly has the hackle extended further and accordingly the fly will sit more inclined towards the horizontal. The final fly has the hackle increased to the extent that it sits horizontally in the water.

This effect can be achieved not only by extending the hackle but also by where the material, which allows the fly to float, is applied. The diagram opposite illustrates this. Running from left to right, the first fly has the floating material applied directly behind the hook eye and the hook will sit to the vertical in the surface of the water. The second and third flies have the material positioned further along the bend and will sit progressively off the vertical heading towards the horizontal. The floating material is positioned in the centre of the bend in the final fly, resulting in the fly sitting at the horizontal and both the point and the eye of the hook submerged, a very tasty option when applied to emerger patterns.

As can be seen the continuous bend hook allows the fly to sit in the water in any way you want it to, it is this flexibility that makes such a hook so useful.

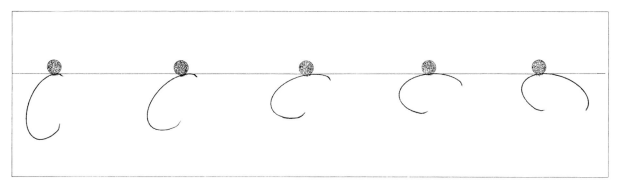

The placement of material will also effect how the fly pattern will float on or in the water. Again this will range from vertical to horizontal.

Front and Rear Shucks

Most emerger patterns imitate the natural insect by placing a shuck imitation at the rear of the fly. There are exceptions to this, the excellent Shipman's Buzzer is one of these. This most simple of fly patterns imitates the shuck at both ends, at the hook bend and at the hook eye and the main body is tied between. To my mind this is a more accurate depiction of what really takes place during emergence, with the insect breaking out of the top of the shuck rather than, as most emerger patterns depict, coming out of the shuck like toothpaste out of the nozzle of a tube. The emergence would be more accurately illustrated if the top of the toothpaste tube were left screwed on, then squeezed and the paste allowed to burst out from the upperside. Emergence on the whole occurs out of the upper thorax section of the natural fly, with the shuck splitting open the top of the thorax and at times on into the body

section. While this produces a predominantly rear shuck, the head and thorax of the nymphal skin form a significant part of the overall shuck.

Using a continuous bend it is possible to imitate this most effectively. The main body of the fly is tied to allow both the rear and the front of the hook to sit under water. This is highly suggestive of the emerging fly and I have found it extremely useful when fishing slow moving or still water. The following fly pattern illustrates how to tie a fly this way. I call fly patterns tied this way 'Front and Rear' emergers and the following pattern is a Front and Rear Red Midge Emerger. The method can be applied to any number of different flies and I have them imitating mayflies, midges and many different sedge/caddis patterns. This particular pattern incorporates a full Paraloop hackle.

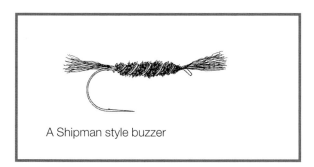

A Shipman style buzzer, note the filaments at each end of the body.

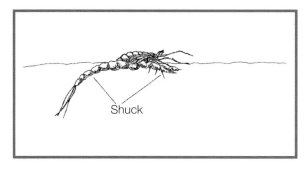

A fly emerging in the surface of the water from the shuck of the nymph.

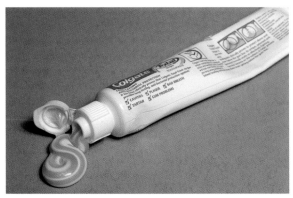

The above photograph shows how most emerger patterns are tied. The toothpaste coming from the end of the tube is like a fly pattern tied with a rear shuck tied as a tail.

In this case the tube is split along the top and the toothpaste bursts out of the split. This illustrates the way in which a fly escapes from the nymphal shuck more accurately than the toothpaste coming out of the end.

Tying the Front and Rear Red Midge Emerger

Materials Required

Hook	Continuous bend hook e.g. Kamasan B100.
Hackle	Light blue dun cock hackle.
Post	GSP or kevlar.
Underbody	Polypropylene floss cream or white.
Body	Red/claret polypropylene dubbing mixed with a little light SLF or pearl Lite Brite.
Shuck	Red holographic tinsel.

A Front & Rear Red Midge Emerger

Fig. 1 Wind the tying thread using flat turns of thread right around the hook bend as shown in the diagram. Tie in the red holographic tinsel on to the underside of the hook shank and wind the tying thread back along the hook shank for a distance approximately just less than one third of the way back to the hook eye. Wind on the holographic tinsel to the thread and tie in. Cut off the excess tinsel and take the thread back to where the tinsel was tied in. Keep the excess holographic tinsel for later in the tying.

Fig. 2 Tie in the prepared hackle with the good side facing mainly towards you and slightly upward. Tie in the post loop and then the underbody floss. Cut off the excess materials and return the tying thread to where the post is tied in.

Fig. 3 Wind on the underbody floss, using flat turns of floss, to a point approximately halfway towards the hook eye. Form a body with a shape wider in the middle than at the ends. Wind the tying thread in open turns to the other side of the floss underbody and tie in the floss on the underside of the hook shank. Cut off the excess floss.

Fig. 4 Now wind the thread back over the underbody to the post, using open turns and with the thread spun tight. Unwind the thread and dub with the mixed body dubbing.

Fig. 5 Wind on the dubbed tying thread to the other side of the underbody in tight, close turns. The tight spun thread previously wound over the underbody will assist in allowing the dubbed thread to grip the underbody. Remove any excess dubbing from the tying thread.

Fig. 6 Place the post loop into the hook of a gallows tool, ensuring that it is held taut. Now wind the hackle up the post in close touching turns, for a distance equal to that of the length of the body. Open up the loop above the turns of hackle and feed the tip of the hackle through the loop, pull all the unwound hackle through the loop and let the loop close. This will lock the hackle tip and prevent the hackle from unwinding.

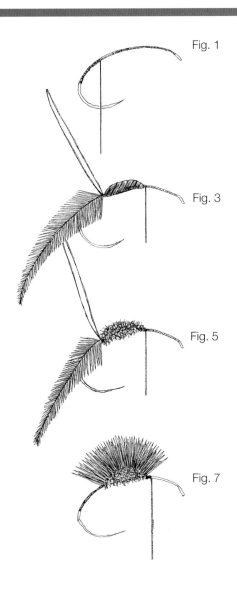

Fig. 1

Fig. 3

Fig. 5

Fig. 7

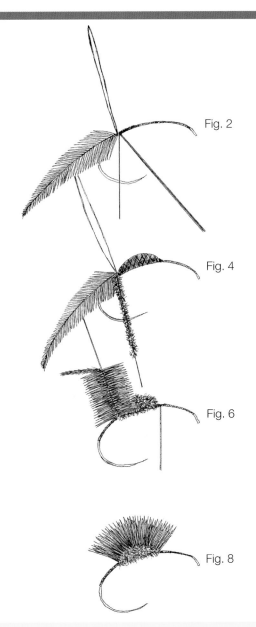

Fig. 2

Fig. 4

Fig. 6

Fig. 8

Fig. 7 Double the hackle slightly by brushing the hackle fibres towards the rear of the hook, using your thumb and first finger. Then pull the hackle over the body and tie in on the top of the hook shank directly against the body. Cut off the excess hackle and post loop.

Fig. 8 Wind the thread to the hook eye and tie in the remaining red holographic tinsel on to the underside of the hook shank. Take the thread back to where the hackle was tied in and wind the holographic tinsel to the thread. Tie in the tinsel and cut off the excess then complete a whip finish under the front of the hackle.

That completes the Red Midge Emerger Front and Rear style. As you can see both ends of the fly pattern will be submerged under the surface of the water, with the main body of the fly pattern floating in the surface. This method can be used to imitate any form of emerger you require. This particular tying is very simple but wings and other bits and pieces can be applied if you so wish.

Foam and the Emerging Fly

The use of foam is highly effective when applied to surface emerging and dry fly patterns. It allows very lightly dressed patterns to float ad infinitum. When tying imitative fly patterns the tyer is not only attempting to provide an impression of a particular fly, but rather a particular fly at a specific stage in its life cycle. Fly patterns should, in my opinion, be able to fulfil their allotted role at all times, not only when conditions are favourable or when they are first tied upon the leader at the start of a fishing session. It is in the choice of materials used and how they are applied that this can be achieved. The materials provide not only the shape and impression of the fly, but also how it acts when on or in the water. Fly patterns will not act as intended or desired if the materials used in their construction do not allow them to do so. If a fly is designed to float then the materials used in its construction must ensure that this happens. If part of the fly is intended to float and part to sink below the surface, then again the materials used, including the choice of hook, must allow this to happen. It is the choice and manipulation of materials that ensures that a fly, designed to fish in a certain way, does so.

I do not use floatants when on the water, I will often treat my hackles and other materials with silicon-based products prior to applying them to a fly pattern or treat the hackles of the completed flies the day before I go fishing. But I refuse point-blank to use floatants when on the water. I find it all too fiddly and messy, besides the fact that I would never find the bottle when I needed it (I also refuse to have things dangling from my clothes). There is also the problem of everything that comes within my reach being generously doused with the wretched stuff, especially those things you least want covered in an oily mess. I have found that if thought and preparation is put into the tying of fly patterns, its use is totally unnecessary. This approach to fly tying is what I often refer to as holistic tying, more than likely because it sounds good, is a little mysterious and appeals to a side of my character that must have an element of the pretentious built in.

It appears that many anglers assume that flies need to be treated regularly with floatants to allow the fly pattern to fulfil its role effectively. In the past this was probably true, the materials available for tying fly patterns benefited greatly with the use of some form of liquid floating aid. In this day and age, the preparation and judicious use of materials make adding floatant to a fly pattern when actually fishing, more often than not, unnecessary. Put simply, I like to build the floatant within the fly itself, the use of foam in its many guises helps to provide this. Adding foam not only provides floatability to a fly pattern, but if done properly and with a little thought, it can enhance the overall look. Many tyers I know do not like using foam as they say it spoils the look of a fly. The shattering of their aesthetic values is not due to the foam itself, but by the way foam is applied to a fly. Applying foam can enhance the look of a fly both from the angler's point of view and, I believe, from the viewpoint of the fish.

Use of the most suitable type of foam for a particular task is essential and can result in a fly that is durable, floats forever and requires minimum maintenance for continuous fishing. Use the wrong type of foam for a particular task and you may well be better off not having bothered to use it in the first place. Emerger and dry fly patterns will often require to be replaced after a fish has taken them. The slime from a fish is a very effective sinking agent and once it is absorbed into the body of the fly there is little that can be done at the time to allow it to continue fishing effectively, that is until it has been cleaned and dried off completely. Drying off and using a few false casts will help; however, in my experience it is best to change the fly. Incidentally if you ever find that your leader insists on floating and you want it to sink, try using fish slime on the leader as it works very well. Fly patterns sensibly incorporating foam and other suitable materials will only require a quick wash through in the water and dried in tissue or on a handkerchief, for them to be up and active and fulfilling their duty effectively as if it was the start of the day.

There are many different types of foam available for fly tying, some of it marketed and purchased specifically for that purpose and some that can be salvaged form everyday items. There are different names and trade names for different types of foam and plastazote, ethafoam, and expanded polystyrene are just a few that come to mind. From a fly tying/fly fishing point of view, one of the most important factors when using these materials is whether they are what I refer to as flexible, or what I call hard. Both flexible and hard foam have their uses when tying flies, but there are important differences and it is these differences that influence what foam is the best to use on any particular fly. Using flexible foam obviously allows greater manipulation than hard foam and it will not break no matter how much it is bent. Flexible foam will also revert to its original shape when released after being bent. Hard foam, an example of this would be expanded polystyrene, will break if it is bent beyond a certain point. There is also a tendency for hard foam to retain the shape of any manipulation, at least up to a certain point. These very different qualities allow foam to be used in many alternative ways and to achieve very specific results. There is also the question of whether foam is closed or open cell. For obvious reasons the foam used to tie floating flies should be closed cell, as this will limit any water absorption. You do not want the foam applied to the fly pattern to act as a sponge and suck in and absorb water, as this will have the opposite effect of what is required. It is also useful to use foam that is resistant to the effects of ultra violet light (UV) as there is no point in tying flies that will effectively disintegrate in the not too distant future. If you take these factors into consideration the best foam I have found available for tying flies is:

Flexible foam: Expanded polyethylene and expanded polyolefins (plastazote)
Hard foam: Polystyrene in various forms

The flexible foams I use when tying flies floats better than the hard foams (expanded polystyrene and various others) and I can only conclude that this is due to the amount of air, within the structure of the flexible foam being greater than in the harder foams. I am aware of hard foams that float as well as the flexible foams I use but I do not currently use these foams in my tyings. I also have come across flexible foam that does not float as efficiently as some of the hard foams I use, but again, I do not currently tie with these foams. This being the case, a smaller amount of flexible foams that I use is required to keep a fly afloat than would be required if hard foam were to be used. This difference can be very important when designing a fly. Then again expanded polystyrene is better able to retain its shape when compared to flexible foam, when materials, such as dubbed thread, are wound around them. It comes down to what the inclusion of foam is expected to do that decides which type of foam should be used.

A very important point to bear in mind when applying foam to a fly is that it is not always necessary that the application of the foam is in sufficient quantity to make the hook float. I look on it like a floating aid, which, when combined with the other materials used, make the fly pattern a more efficient floater than one tied without the inclusion of foam. This is especially noticeable when using hard foam as an underbody. In this case the foam forms the greater bulk of the body and as such will not absorb water, unlike other materials. Although the foam is not sufficient to keep the hook afloat completely by its own qualities, the underbody, tail and hackle all combine to make a most efficient floating fly pattern, with no more than the occasional couple of false casts being required to keep the fly afloat indefinitely. I like to keep this factor in mind when designing and tying my own flies as it effects the amount of foam applied to the hook.

For the emerger and dry fly patterns that incorporate foam described in this book, I use the following different forms of this most useful material. Whilst I am no expert on foam regarding its manufacture or even from what they are exactly made from, the following is, I believe, correct. The sources described are correct, they being where I obtain my own stocks.

Flexible Foam

Flexible foam is used in the majority of the flies I tie which incorporate any type of foam. By flexible I mean that you can bend it at will and it will not break. It can also be stretched to a certain degree without breaking. Foams of this type are readily available from fly tying material outlets in various forms, for example: sheets of varying thickness, blocks and cylinders. It is available in various colours and when the required colour cannot be found, it can be coloured easily using permanent ink pens. Foams of this type are expanded polyethylenes and expanded poly-olefins and the flexibility is achieved by the inclusion of a plasticizer during manufacture. Without the inclusion of plasticizer the foam would be rigid and would not provide the flexibility required when tying certain fly patterns. My local fishing tackle shop markets expanded polyolefin under the name Plastazote.

Hard Foam

Whilst most of the foam I use is flexible foam, I am increasingly including what I refer to as hard foam within my own fly patterns. I normally incorporate this foam as an underbody, its rigidity allowing other materials to be easily wound around it, while maintaining the ability of the foam to retain air within its structure. Although I refer to this type of foam as rigid, there is an element of flexibility and it is this that allows it to be used effectively. The best source of this material is the white cups in which coffee and tea is so

The sources of the foam used, including polystyrene cup and burger box.

often served in take-away food outlets. They can also be bought in most supermarkets. This is a completely different form of foam to polyethylene and polyolefins and is formed from small balls of expanded polystyrene bonded together. In its expanded form polystyrene contains ninety-five per cent air, so even when bent and shaped it is still a very efficient way of making a hook float or to assist in its floatability. This type of foam is unsuitable for many fly tying purposes due to its tendency to break easily and this is one of the main reasons why I generally only use it as an underbody or under-thorax. It appears that poly-styrene is a very versatile material, not only does it provide the source material for foam, in its non-expanded forms it is used for much of the hard food packaging like yoghurt containers and for items such as plastic cutlery and other rigid products for example cabinets for electrical items, toys and disc cases.

There is another form of foam I like to use and this is found in the clamshell containers used to serve food like burgers etc. My local baked potato take-away is kind enough to supply me with all my needs of this material. This foam is different to the expanded polystyrene described above and could best be described as flexible with a hard coating. It can be bent easily, but will not recover like flexible foam. The surface is sealed and has a shiny appearance. This sealed surface is extremely useful, as it does not absorb any water, although when cut there appears to be slight water absorption along the cut edge, although this appears to have very limited penetration. It is, however, very useful in some areas of fly tying for example when adding wing cases to a pattern. This material is also polystyrene but in a different form.

Pre-Formed Hard Foam Underbodies

How you apply foam to an emerger fly pattern depends upon the effect required by its inclusion, when the fly is on or in the surface of the water. In the section in this chapter entitled 'Hook and Tying Positions' it is clear that the application of foam at specific positions on the hook effects how the completed fly pattern will float. Placed at the front of the hook behind the eye, the fly pattern will sit vertically and placed in the centre of the hook, the fly pattern will tend to sit horizontally. When applying foam as an underbody the same principles will apply. The different positions of the fly pattern when in the water being controlled by where the underbody is applied on the hook, how long the underbody is and what other materials are used in conjunction with the foam in the construction of the fly.

When applying foam as an underbody I like to use hard foam cut from an expanded polystyrene cup. The following describes how this can easily be achieved, while at the same time allowing pre-formed foam underbodies to be made quickly and simply. I am sure everyone has seen the pre-formed lead underbodies used to add weight to and create nymphs. These are nor-

mally sold in bags of a dozen and are marketed by many fly tying material outlets and they make the application of lead, to a nymph pattern, easy, slipping around the hook shank, requiring only a squeeze with pliers to fix them in place. They also help to form the basic body shape. The following will show how this can be done with foam to achieve the same result as the lead underbodies regarding shape. It will, however, have the opposite effect in that their application will make the fly pattern float rather than sink, or at least assist in allowing the pattern to float well.

The method for creating these hard foam underbodies requires a polystyrene cup, a long strong dubbing needle and a sharp craft knife. The illustration clearly shows how to proceed.

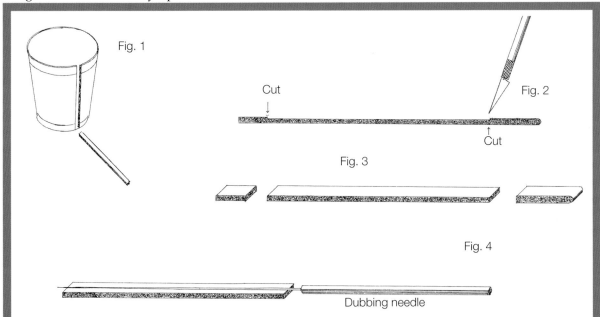

Fig. 1 Take an expanded polystyrene tea/coffee cup and cut a strip out of it from base to top. This strip should be approximately 3 to 5 mm wide depending on the size of hook you are using.

Fig. 2 Cut off any ridges in the polystyrene at the base and top end.

Fig. 3 This will provide a strip of polystyrene of equal width throughout its length and around 4 to 6 in (10 to 15 cm) long, depending on the size of the cup being used.

Fig. 4 Take a long, strong dubbing needle and place the needle in the centre of the strip, length ways. Do not worry if the needle is too short to cover the whole length, as it can be reversed to complete the next stage.

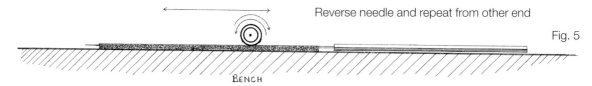

Roll pen case pushing needle into polystyrene strip

Reverse needle and repeat from other end

Fig. 5

BENCH

Fig. 5 Now press the needle lengthways into the foam, making sure the needle is in the centre throughout the length of the foam. This is best done by placing the foam on a solid surface like a tying bench or table. If the needle is too short, place it at the other end of the strip and repeat making sure the indentations in the foam meet in the middle. Rolling a pen case along the needle will enhance the trough formed in the foam.

Fig. 6

Fig. 6 The result will be a length of foam indented with a shallow channel.

Fig. 7 Now squeeze the foam around the needle and then repeat Fig. 5.

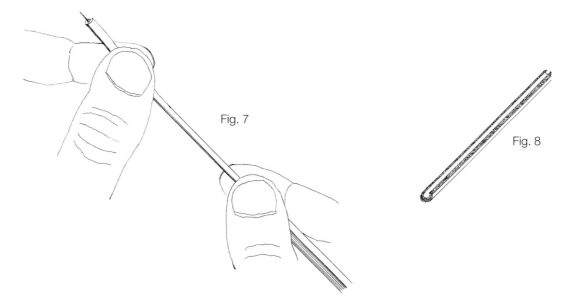

Fig. 7

Fig. 8

Fig. 8 You will now have a trough-shaped expanded polystyrene foam strip.

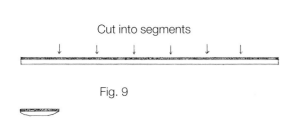

Cut into segments

Fig. 9

Fig. 9 Depending on the size of hook you are tying on, cut a section from the trough of foam and using a pair of good fine pointed scissors taper one end or both ends, depending on the pattern the underbody will be applied to.

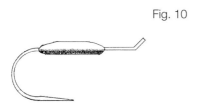

Fig. 10

Fig. 10 The trough of the foam underbody is applied around the hook shank prior to tying in.

That procedure produces a single pre-formed foam underbody. They take only a few seconds to make and any number of different sizes can be made and stored for future use. When tying emerger patterns I usually taper both ends. When using these underbodies for true dry flies and some emergers I often only taper one end, the tapered end is fixed at the tail end and the non-tapered end butts up to the thorax area.

The beauty of this system is that the material used is fairly rigid and once placed on a hook, materials can be applied over it. Even traditional dry flies can utilize these underbodies and they are ideal for producing the bodies on Adams and Wulff patterns (see section titled 'Floating Down the River'.)

Tying an Emerger Pattern using a Pre-Formed Foam Underbody

To demonstrate the use of the hard foam underbody when tying emerger patterns, I have chosen to imitate the emerging March Brown. This fly is a large upwinged fly and can be found on the waters I fish from the start of the trout season through into June and sometimes even July. They are the first of the large upwinged flies to show themselves in the year and in some areas they herald the start of the season, although in most of the streams I fish, a little more time needs to elapse before they decide to take to the air.

A hook of size 14 is suitable, sometimes even a size 12 is not out of place.

Tying the March Brown with foam underbody

Materials Required

Hook	Continuous bend hook size 14 Kamasan B100 or similar.
Body	Fine brown polypropylene dubbing.
Underbody	Pre-formed polystyrene foam underbody tapered at tail end only.
Hackle	Red cock or furnace hackle.
Wing	Blue dun cock hackle tips, kept short.
Shuck	Ivory Antron floss mixed with a little Lite Brite.
Thread	Own choice 8/0.

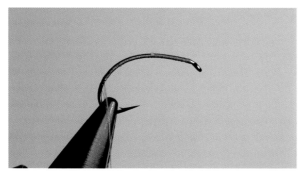

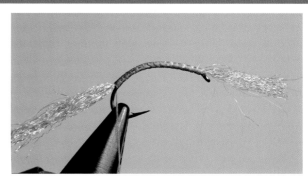

Photograph 1 Place the hook into the jaws of the vice and test the hook for soundness. Attach the waxed tying thread and wind, using flat thread, to the position on the hook shank as shown in the photograph.

Photograph 2 Take the ivory Antron floss mixed with a little Lite Brite and lay it along the top of the hook shank so that it extends over the front and rear of the hook. Now wind the thread back along the hook shank, tying in the mixed floss on to the top of the shank as you go. Return the tying thread to where the floss was first tied in.

Photograph 3 Take the pre-formed polystyrene underbody and offer it to the hook. The tapered end should extend to the point where the floss was first tied in. Tie in the underbody using fairly random open winds of tying thread, make sure the underbody is secure at each end. The underbody should not extend far beyond the halfway point along the hook shank. Return the thread to the tapered end of the underbody.

Photograph 4 Dub the tying thread with the brown body dubbing and then wind over the underbody, making sure that the whole of the underbody is covered. It is wise to dub lightly and use tight touching turns of dubbed thread. When the wound dubbed thread reaches the end of the underbody, remove any excess dubbing and continue the thread to where the floss is tied in.

Photograph 5 Prepare and tie in the blue dun hackle tip wings. This is best done by preparing the hackle tips as shown in the sequence on page 75. Return the thread to the start of the body and cut off any excess hackle stalks.

Photograph 6 Tie in the hackle with the good side facing you. Cut off any excess stalk.

Photograph 7 Wind the hackle to the point where the hackle tip wings are tied in. Lift up the hackle tip wings and tie in the hackle on to the underside of the hook shank. Cut off the excess hackle.

Photograph 8 Form a small head with the tying thread, while at the same time fixing the hackle tip wings into position. Complete a whip finish and cut off the tying thread.

Photograph 9 Cut the shuck floss to length at each end and using a cigarette lighter, singe each end of the shuck, ensuring that the melted ends are pressed together using thumb and first finger.

Photograph 10 The completed fly.

Flex and Foam

Another method that I find extremely useful when tying emerger patterns is what I call 'Flex and Foam'. The method was developed when I was looking for a way in which to fix foam firmly to a hook at any position required and combines flexible foam with Flexifloss, Superfloss, Supafloss or what any other name is used to market this lycra-based product. In fact foam and Flexifloss go very well together as Flexifloss will not cut foam when tied around it, no matter how tightly this is done, unlike many other products.

The method is extremely simple and can be used in many different ways. To illustrate its use I have chosen the parachute method of 'Flex and Foam'. The method not only applies foam to a fly but also provides a useful sight aid for when the fly pattern is on the water, an advantage not to be sniffed at as eyesight slowly deteriorates with time.

Most of the fly patterns that I tie using this method, make use of the sections of cylindrical foam available through fly tying material suppliers and used to tie the likes of Boobies. If they are not available to you then obtain an old telescopic car aerial and separate the various sections. By doing this you will have three or four tubes of various diameter. Now sharpen the edges of each tube at one end, using a wet stone or fine metal file. You are now the proud owner of a set of foam punches, specifically designed to provide foam cylinders of various sizes. All you need to do now is push the sharpened end of a tube slowly through a block of flexible foam, turning the tube back and forth as you do so. Once through the foam, a section of cut cylinder will normally protrude out of the end of the tube, pulling this out carefully will reveal a perfect cylinder of foam ready to be applied to your next fly, just cut to length.

Parachute fly patterns like Klinkhamar style flies benefit greatly from the application of this technique. What is interesting and very useful is that more turns of hackle can be placed around the post than usual and the Flex and Foam method will automatically result in the hackle fibres being compressed together. Also, when applied to parachute flies, Flex and Foam will reset the angle of the hackle fibres so that they are angled downwards. It is good to have a technique that achieves this as it adds a little extra to some fly patterns, a little extra that enhances the overall effectiveness of the fly. Some highly experienced and successful fly fishers and tyers I am acquainted with do not use parachute flies, claiming that the horizontal hackle is not to their taste. They prefer a hackle to be angled downward. The use of Flex and Foam will allow the hackle on a parachute fly to angle downwards, especially if the base of the foam is cut with a slight curve inwards, giving it a concave shape.

When tying emerging flies using this method, I find Front and Rear style flies, as described earlier in this section, are especially effective. So the following fly is in effect a 'Front and Rear, Flex and Foam, Parachute Emerger' a real mouthful. The fly being imitated is the Yellow May Dun. I hope you enjoy this tying, the fly is extremely effective in both still and running water and one thing is for sure, it will not sink. The Yellow May Dun is one of the most attractive and noticeable upwinged flies on the water. Its bright yellow, almost sulphur colouring make it stand out against the water and the surrounding bushes and trees. This colour provides its Latin name of *Heptagenia sulphurea* and makes the fly unmistakable. Saying that, many anglers mix up this fly with the Stonefly, the Yellow Sally, which has a similar distinct colouring. These are two very different flies, requiring imitation to be approached from a separate viewpoint. This is one pattern that cannot really be used to imitate any other natural fly, the colour limits its use to when the Yellow May Dun is on the water. At the right time and place, however, this particular pattern can be extremely effective. While the rises of the Yellow May Dun can never, at least in my experience, be described as large, when compared with many other upwinged flies, they do tend to be consistent. Where the fly is common the fish will take them with enthusiasm. The procedure used in the following tying can be applied to just about any imitation. Change the hook size, colour of materials etc. and you have an olive, mayfly or whatever else you choose to tie.

Tying the Yellow May Dun Parachute 'Flex and Foam' Style

Materials Required

Hook   Continuous bend hook e.g. Kamasan B100.

Hackle   Grizzle cock hackle dyed light yellow.

Body   Yellow polypropylene dubbing mixed with a little pearl Lite Brite dubbing.

Thorax   As per the body with a little brown dubbing mixed in.

Post   Flexifloss.

Foam   Slice of a yellow foam cylinder.

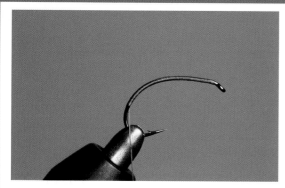

Photograph 1 Place the hook into the jaws of the vice and test the hook for soundness. Attach the waxed tying thread and wind using flat thread around the hook to the point on the hook shank shown in the photograph.

Photograph 2 Dub the thread using the mixed body dubbing and wind the dubbed thread back along the hook shank for a distance two thirds of the way back towards the hook eye. Form a shaped tapering body as you do so, thin at the rear and getting wider as you approach the front end of the body.

Photograph 3 Form a loop from the Flexifloss and tie in the loose ends over the thorax section of the hook shank and tie in, directly on the top of the hook shank, ensuring that the main length of the floss extends over the hook eye. Wind the thread, tying in the floss, to just short of the hook eye. When tying in the Flexifloss increase the tension on the floss, thereby stretching it, as you wind the thread along the shank.

Photograph 4 Cut off any Flexifloss extending at the body end. Now turn the Flexifloss back along the top of the hook shank and, with the floss under tension, wind the thread back to the body using very tight turns of thread, again tying in the floss as you go. Tying in the floss using this method ensures that it is locked in place and unable to be pulled away from the hook shank. The Flexifloss forms the post around which the hackle will be wound.

Photograph 5 Prepare the hackle and tie in by the stalk on to the hook shank, directly at the base of the Flexifloss post. Take the Flexifloss post loop and attach it to the hook of a gallows tool. The Flexifloss must be taut.

Photograph 6 Now make three or four winds of hackle around the Flexifloss post. The first wind should be the highest wind up the post, the following winds of hackle should be made below the first. Tie in the hackle on to the hook shank and cut off the excess hackle.

Photograph 7 Dub the tying thread with the thorax dubbing, which should be the same colour as the body dubbing with a little brown mixed in and wind over the thorax area forming a shaped thorax, wider in the middle than at either end. Form a small head directly behind the eye of the hook and complete a whip finish. Remove the tying thread.

Photograph 8 Untie the Flexifloss from the gallows tool. Now take the slice of foam cylinder and cut one end, using scissors, making that end slightly concave. Using a dubbing needle make a hole running through the centre of the slice of foam cylinder. This hole should be centred at both ends of the cylinder, again as per the inserted diagram. Feed a wire bobbin threader through the hole in the foam from the flat end of the cylinder. Now place the Flexifloss into the wire loop of the threader. Pull the Flexifloss through the foam cylinder using the bobbin threader. Double check that the slightly concave end of the foam is the end facing the hackle.

Photograph 9 Now pull the Flexifloss very tight and tie a single overhand knot as close to the foam as you possibly can. Pull the knot tight. Now relax the tension on the Flexifloss. Relaxing the tension will have the result of the Flexifloss pulling the foam down on to the hackle. Ensure that the extending edges of the slightly concave shape of the foam extend to either side of the hook and not along the length of the hook. The hackle will be pushed downward by the foam, resetting the fibres so that they are angled slightly downwards.

Photograph 10 My experience when tying using this technique is that the knot does not pull through the hole. To ensure that this remains the case, cut off the Flexifloss directly above the knot and place a single drop of Zap-a-Gap glue on to the knot and the top of the foam. This will secure the foam completely.

Photograph 11 The completed fly.

That completes the example of the Flex and Foam method. The use of foam and Flexifloss together offers many possibilities and the above example is just one. The beauty of the method is that the foam can be added to a fly pattern wherever it may be required, without actually changing the basic fly pattern to any great extent. In the case of the Yellow May Dun pattern described the foam not only adds that extra buoyancy, but also makes the fly pattern far easier to see when it is on the water. It also resets the hackle fibres so that rather than being horizontal as is normal in a parachute hackle, they angle downwards, which is something that will please many fly fishers. It is also possible to turn the foam ninety degrees and so to realign where the cut in the foam was made, doing so allows the hackle fibres to reset higher.

Failed Emergers

Any transition in an insect's life cycle is a time of some risk and can result in casualties. Not all eggs will hatch and of those that do, not all will survive the trauma of the event. Not all larvae will progress to become pupae and not all pupae and nymphs will successfully emerge as adult flies. Each transition has risks. I think that it is probably similar to human birth, if left completely to nature the incidence of mortality is high.

Emerging flies will not always achieve the goal of flight. There are those that fall victims as food for other creatures and there are those that fail to break through the surface tension of the water. Some break through that tension but fail to escape the pupa or nymph shuck. Yet others break through the surface tension of the water and successfully escape the shuck, but remain gripped by the water as if some magnetic force holds them within its grasp. For whatever the reason this failure to emerge successfully is, the fact remains that these flies will inevitably end up as food for fish or other creatures.

I call such flies 'failed emergers' others call them cripples or stuck-in- the-shucks. Whatever the name used, imitating them is a useful approach, especially after the hatch has trailed off and fish can be seen cruising around picking off the odd morsel from the water's surface. I find the period immediately after a hatch of flies to be a good time to concentrate that little bit extra on the fishing, the hatch may have ended but it seems to take a little time before the fish actually realize it. Another good time for fishing such fly patterns is early in the morning. On many of the waters I have fished over the years, I have seen large trout cruising nonchalantly in the shallows picking up the leftovers from the night before. This is best seen early in the morning just after sunrise, any time later than that will see these trout safely ensconced in their daytime abodes and usually well out of sight of anyone with a rod in their hand. I can remember a number of years ago fishing a large loch for a week in summer conditions. The fish we caught could be counted on the fingers of one hand and none of them were the specimens we knew lived in this particular water. Try as hard as we could, our catch was nothing but the odd small trout caught under a blue sky and a strong sun. By chance, returning from an early dawn stroll on the banks of the loch, I walked by a small bay or inlet heavily covered in reeds but with some clear water. This bay appeared for all intents and purposes to be separate from the main loch, however, if you tried to walk around, it became obvious that it was connected. The particular morning in question was the first that I had walked by this water so early in the morning and I was astonished to observe trout, the size of which we had only dreamt of all week. These fish were cruising around in just a few inches of water picking off the shucks, failed emergers and spinners from the night before and the smallest would have stretched the tape to 18 in (45 cm) and the largest half that size again. Good-sized fish were caught that week, all on spent spinners and failed emerger patterns. None of them came from the main loch, they were all caught in small bays and inlets in no more than 12 in (30 cm) of water, between five o'clock and six thirty in the morning. The remaining part of each day was spent as previously, casting into a shimmering haze and sleeping on the banks.

I like to keep the tying of failed emergers very simple and certainly never overdressed. The overall impression of the fly pattern should be a bit messy, a no winner of best dressed fly prizes. The following fly pattern is intended to imitate the wonderful blue winged olive stuck in the surface of the water, shuck bound and going nowhere.

Tying the Blue Winged Olive Failed Emerger

Materials Required

Hook	Klinkhamar style e.g. Partridge Klinkhamar hook.
Body	Brown and olive Antron dubbing mixed together.
Thorax	Very rough dubbing mixed with olive polypropylene dubbing. The rough dubbing is formed from the leftovers from just about anything – deer hair, hackle fibres, other types of dubbing and hair. These should be mixed

thoroughly with the polypropylene dubbing by rubbing together with the fingers and by grinding together with the thumb in the palm of the hand. Just behind the head of the pattern a few winds of the body dubbing can be made.

Underthorax Pre-formed polystyrene underbody, tapered at both ends.

Thread Own choice 8/0.

Photograph 1 Fix the hook into the jaws of the vice and test the hook for soundness. Attach the waxed thread and wind using flat thread around the bend of the hook. Dub the tying thread with the body dubbing and form a tapered body.

Photograph 2 Offer the pre-formed underbody to the thorax section of the hook and tie in using fairly random and open turns of tying thread. Ensure each end of the underbody is secured. The thorax underbody should extend just short of the hook eye and should be of a more stocky shape than normal. Return the tying thread to where the body meets the thorax.

Photograph 3 Form a dubbing loop with the tying thread and fix the loop in a dubbing spinner. Wind the tying thread to just short of the hook eye. Now wax the thread that forms the dubbing loop with tacky wax and carefully insert the mixed rough dubbing into the dubbing loop ensuring that the dubbing material is evenly spread. Spin the dubbing spinner, first slowly by hand and then give it a good spin letting the spinner complete the job on its own. The result should be a rough dubbing brush.

Photograph 4 Put a drop or two of Zap-a-Gap over the thorax foam underbody and immediately start winding the dubbed loop around the thorax. Tie in just short of the hook eye and cut off the excess dubbing loop. The resulting thorax should be a mess of materials.

Photograph 5 Dub the tying thread with a little body dubbing and make a few turns in front of the thorax. Remove any excess dubbing from the thread and form a small head, completing the fly pattern with a whip finish. Cut off the tying thread. That completes the tying of the Blue Winged Olive Failed Emerger.

This fly can be used during and after a hatch of emergers. The same pattern tied in various sizes will cover many different types of fly. It is always worth while checking out eddies and softer water downstream of a hatch of flies after the hatch has finished, or around the edges of a lake especially on the side where the wind is blowing. Trout will often mop up the flotsam and jetsam of a hatch in these areas and will feed enthusiastically on the failed emergers and empty shucks, although it is doubtful that the discarded shucks would have very much nutritional value. As mentioned earlier in this section the fly, fished early in the morning, can be very successful targeting the trout feeding on the remains of the hatches from the night before.

In the gallery of flies at the end of the book there is a selection of fly patterns including some tied using the methods and techniques described in this section.

2. FLOATING DOWN THE RIVER

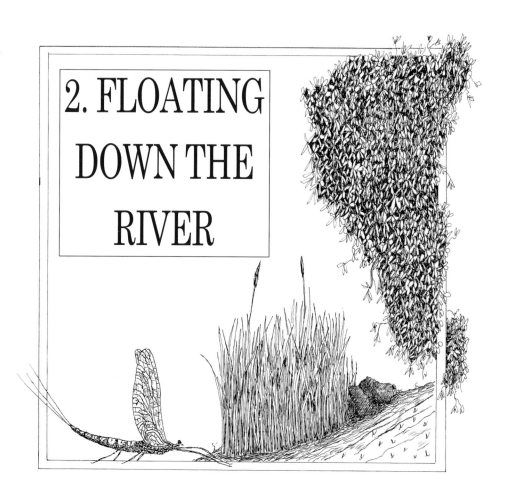

Part I

That's not bloody fly fishing, I don't know what it is, but it's not bloody fly fishing. There was silence for a moment, then 'I thought you said you caught it on the fly?' Luckily for me I was an eavesdropper, looking and listening from a safe distance and the tirade was, I am happy to say, not directed at me. Geordie had often laid his passion and belief firmly in the face of an unsuspecting and probably innocent wee fisher. Today was no different, there stood Geordie, tall and lanky, dressed in the old anorak I always saw him in, three days growth on his chin and pointing his pipe at the poor recipient of his onslaught. Earlier in the morning that poor man had, most probably, left his home, high in heart and believing he was set to enjoy the pleasures of the water, possibly shared with the bonhomie of fellow fishers. He met Geordie!

It's not that Geordie was malicious or even very bad tempered, although on occasion it was difficult to be certain that he wasn't the mean and cantankerous fellow he could so effectively portray. He was in fact the very best of company, whether on the water or off and a fine fishing companion, for those times when a companion is required or desired. It's just that Geordie thought fly fishing, real fly fishing that is, comprised presenting the fish with the dry fly and the true dry fly only. This principle was his guiding light and nothing and nobody would ever have changed his point of view. It was unfortunate that he felt it necessary to inflict his belief on many who came his way, like some evangelical prophet sent from realms beyond to keep us mere mortals on the path of fly fishing righteousness.

To my credit I believe I may have been responsible in having persuaded him, over the years, to accept that the emerging fly can be imitated legitimately within the parameters of his unyielding code. Indeed there have been times when he would tie an emerger pattern on his tippet with real enthusiasm, enthusiasm almost equal to that of when he tied on his precious real dry flies, but that was as far as it went. If the fly pattern was to be fished underwater or did not imitate a specified natural fly upon the water, then as far as Geordie was concerned it was definitely not fly fishing. He would have the grace to accept that it was fishing of some form or another, but not in a million years would he have considered it to be fly fishing.

There had been a few occasions when I'd felt brave, or perhaps foolish, enough to attempt to persuade him that the nymph imitation is a legitimate approach to fly fishing, however, I might just as well have been trying to talk a river into reversing its flow upstream. 'Don't talk nonsense lad, that's just another lure, it might catch you fish, but its not fly fishing, not real fly fishing!' As far as Geordie was concerned, 'if the fly pattern you use ain't an imitation of a real fly with wings, it shouldn't be tied upon your tippet'. 'Anyone can catch those trout spinning, those flies you use are just small spinners that don't even spin', would be his reaction on looking into your highly prized, nymph pattern box.

I would often remind him that the fly patterns he used when he was pursuing his beloved Atlantic salmon did not float and that they also did not imitate any natural fly, he always replied without hesitation and with complete and total conviction 'Aye you're right there lad, but it doesn't matter then, that's salmon fishing, not fly fishing!' It appeared, at least according to Geordie, that salmon fishing was a completely different sport to trout fishing and you just could not compare the two, no matter how hard you tried. I have often considered this argument over the years and at times I had thought it to be a convenient way for Geordie to justify his opinions. Thinking about it, however, in this case he is possibly right and there was much truth in his comments.

Geordie would always finish any conversation

about salmon fishing by making the same statement and it didn't matter how many times he had said it before to you. I can still see him as if it was just last night, unshaven and sitting on the riverbank, leaning against the trunk of a tree. His pipe would be lit and the tobacco smoke floating down the river and tainting the air with its mellow scent. Geordie would look up the river and then slowly down the river. Then he would cough and in a voice that suggested a great secret was about to be divulged, quietly say 'Do you know lad, trout are smart, very smart and salmon well they're stupid, very stupid. But they're not as stupid as those of us who fish for them.' The twinkle in his eye when he said this would leave you in no doubt that he considered himself well and truly within this category.

Fly fishing, at least as far as Geordie was concerned, began and ended with fishing the adult upwinged fly, more especially and almost exclusively the dun at that short period of time between emergence and flight. At a push an emerger pattern was acceptable and a spent spinner imitation could also, on occasion, find approval, but on the whole imitating the dun fly was the only legitimate way he considered to do the business. He was not in the least bit shy about expressing this opinion and he had no hesitation in letting others know what he believed, in a very clear and most pointed manner. If he was shown a caught fish and the fly pattern used to catch it, it was wise just to pray that the fly pattern fitted in with his conviction. If not, it would set him off on his soapbox and like a wind-up clock, he wouldn't stop until his spring had unwound. He would rattle the ears of the poor fisher who was foolish enough to show him anything but a dry fly pattern and, if a fish had been killed, the accusation of wanton murder was not beyond him. In fact even if the fish had been caught on the dry fly, but the fly pattern used did not imitate the actual flies on the water at that particular time, Geordie would consider that fish didn't count and had been duped and cheated out of the water. If that were the case you would instantly become the preferred target for the sharp side of his tongue, albeit that tongue would, more often than not, be sharpened in cheek.

I had got to know Geordie principally because, whenever I had met him on the water, I had taken the time to speak with him. When others backed away and made a detour just to avoid having to pass close to him, for some reason or another I always looked forward to meeting him. In fact when I fished the waters I knew he fished, the day would be incomplete and somehow less satisfying if I failed to cross his path. I think it was simply because I liked him.

When we had first met I had given him a few of my own fly patterns. From that day I seemed to have been accepted into his world. Geordie's world was a little like an exclusive club, there weren't too many members and being a member did not make you immune to a beating from his opinions, but it was a worthy club to be a member of. I had met a few other fishers who held the same opinion of Geordie as I did and they were also members, and without exception I liked them all.

Whenever I came up with a new fly pattern or devised a technique, which I thought would help make a pattern fish in a certain way, Geordie always received a few samples. Some he loved, and some he immediately thought ridiculous and as always he would tell me why, never sparing the sensitive side of my nature. He would christen the patterns he loved, always prefixing his chosen name with 'Ian's'. They would become 'Ian's Olive' or 'Ian's Mayfly' and would sit in his fly box amongst 'Jim's Blue Winged Olive', 'Tam's Fly' and the many other patterns he had acquired over the years.

Just like Geordie, for many years I never used anything but the dry fly. In my case that was because it was all I knew. I was ignorant of all and everything to do with fly fishing, I owned a few flies, all dry and kindly gifted to me by a friend, who had as little of an idea as I had what they were and what you were meant to do with them. I think my friend had acquired them as an extra in a fishing rod and reel kit he had bought from Woolworth's and the fly patterns were surplus to his requirements. To me they were items of fascination and wonder, made all the more so by my complete lack of information and knowledge of how they were made, what they were called or how they were to be fished. I know now that they were all dry fly patterns, but at the time I never even gave it a thought. Those fly patterns were meant to float on the surface and that, to me, became fly fishing, casting a fly on to the surface of the water in the hope that some fish would be considerate enough to make a young lad's day extra special. There was no one to tell me about any other types of fly patterns and it made sense, flies would land on the water, but they were really creatures of the air, so fishing the dry fly seemed the right and only thing to do. Years later it was a revelation to me when I discovered all the different ways that a fly pattern could be designed and fished, wet flies, nymphs, lures and streamers all conspiring to distract me from fishing the dry fly. It was a temptation I was very willing to indulge in.

These days when fishing for trout I fish the type of fly pattern I think to be the most appropriate for that moment. Sometimes the dry fly, at times the wet, sometimes a nymph at other times a lure. However, I always get the greatest thrill from fishing a dry fly, or, at the very least, a fly pattern designed to float in the surface of the water. There is an added element that is missing when fishing the sunk fly and that element is the visual. With the dry or emerger pattern you get to see the fish rise and take, rather than just feel it. It is this added bonus that makes fishing the floating fly so exhilarating. There is a direct visual link between the fisher and the fish at that most incredible and miraculous of moments, the moment when the fish actually rises up and takes the fly into its mouth.

After over forty years of fishing I still find it difficult to accept that a fish will take a fly that I present. When I arrive at any water the thought that a fish may actually be attracted to my offering to the degree that it is inspired to take a bite, all seems a little far fetched. That is until it actually happens. Then I'm all right for the rest of the day, convinced that not one single fish could possibly resist the irresistible tied to my tippet. But each day is new and begins with that feeling of incredulity and sense of the impossible, that is, until some co-operative fish proves otherwise. I am happy to say that there are times when they do and that these times are fairly regular, but this regularity in no way diminishes the wonder I

feel when I see the fly disappear in a swirl or ring of water. That moment of connection with a fish is a truly magical and heart stopping moment, being able to see the fish take the fly into its mouth emphasizes this even more so, more than when just the pull of a taking fish is felt.

The dun, more than any other insect that can be imitated with a floating fly pattern, is the fly that truly epitomizes and inspires fishing the true dry fly. There is an apparent delicacy and beauty to the dun, which to my eyes, cannot be found in other flies like the sedge or even the midge. Please don't get me wrong, I love fishing with sedge, midge and many other natural fly imitation patterns. But, for me, the essence of fishing the true dry fly is to be found when imitating the dun as it floats downstream, standing high on the water before the insect takes to air for the very first time. In this I stand with Geordie.

The time allocated to fish the dun is short. How long does it take for a fly to emerge and be ready to take to the wing? For some just a blink of an eye. For others a minute or two at the most. If every insect in a rise were to emerge and take to the air at exactly the same moment, I wouldn't have the time to tie a fly pattern on to my tippet and cast it on the water. I would still be looking into my fly box trying to decide what pattern to use, or, at best, still tying the knot on to my final choice. Luckily for us fly fishers, nature has been precise but not overly precise and while it may take just a moment for a single fly to take to the wing, the hundreds and sometimes thousands of insects emerging in a single rise take some time to do so. It is this that allows us to successfully fish a rise of emerging insect with our attempts to imitate the dun using a dry fly pattern.

It was observations like this that Geordie and I would spend our time discussing. Unlike with most folk, you could truly say what you believed or thought, when you had Geordie's ear. He knew what you were talking about and could elaborate on your private thoughts with his own. This made those moments spent together by the water precious, moments to be treasured.

Geordie is dead. He died one winter night a few years ago, sitting by his fireside. The sad thing is nobody found out about it for over a week. But then again Geordie wouldn't have minded. On a few occasions I have thought that I have seen him in the distance on the riverbank, but when I reach the place he is no longer there. So I take the time to sit and watch the river flow by, much like when Geordie was alive. I would swear on all the oaths available to man that, as the sound of the flowing water fills my ears and the gentle touch of the breeze cools my face, that a scent of pipe tobacco taints the air and a mist appears floating down the river like smoke. If I close my eyes Geordie is once again by my side, sitting with his back against a tree and I am content with life and all the good things it has to offer

As twiilight falls…fish rise

Part II

Traditionally the dry fly, at least for the greater extent, has been tied using the usual method of winding the hackle around the hook shank. There are other methods of providing a wound hackle on a fly and the Parachute and Paraloop are two that come immediately to mind, both, however, formed by winding around a separate post rather than the hook shank. The major difference between the traditional wound hackle and the Parachute and Paraloop hackle is that the traditional method lifts the front section of the hook shank high off the surface of the water. The general tendency of the Parachute and Paraloop is to hold the hook shank and therefore the body of the fly in the surface of the water. This being the case I find that the Parachute and Paraloop methods of providing a hackle are on the whole more suited to emerger, spent spinner and cripple imitations and the traditional wound hackle to the dry fly and true dry fly patterns.

Let me clarify what I mean when I say the true dry fly. Any fly that floats can be classified as a dry fly, but many are designed to sit within the surface of the water. In fact often part of the fly will be above the surface of the water and part will be below the surface. Flies designed this way may well be described as dry flies but they are not in my opinion true dry flies, I hesitate to call them damp flies but I am sure you get my meaning. For me the true dry fly is a fly designed to float high upon the surface of the water with only the point and spear of the hook actually penetrating the meniscus. The true dry fly is held up on the surface of the water by the hackle or hackles and perhaps the tail of the fly. The true dry fly pattern sits high and proud, riding upon the water, just like the recently emerged dun flies floating downstream supported on spindly legs and with newly unfolded wings held upwards.

After a large emergence of duns, flotillas of flies can usually be seen drifting downstream with the current. It is chance and chance alone that will see if they take to the air, one step closer to fulfilling their goal, or end up in the stomach of a fish rising up from below or in the beak of a swallow or other bird diving down from above.

Whilst the traditional wound hackle is extremely effective at holding the weight of the hook up above the surface of the water, I have never been particularly keen on the footprint it creates in the meniscus. Before I go any further let me explain what I mean by footprint. When I use the word footprint I am referring to the total impression created on the water by the fly pattern. My own opinion is that the traditionally wound hackle emphasizes the centre of the fly pattern, directly below the hook shank. The preferred emphasis of the footprint would be at both sides of the fly pattern so as to imitate the legs supporting the natural dun fly upon the water more accurately. As such the traditional wound hackle is far from ideal for creating a reasonably good imitation of the dun standing upon the surface of the water.

Personally I prefer a hackle that presents a clear space directly under the fly and with the hackle supporting the fly at either side of the body. The illustration opposite shows clearly what I am trying to explain.

The problem is how to achieve this space on the underside of the hackle. In the North of England the traditional method was to simply prune the fibres away with scissors. I am sure this method has been well used throughout the world, as it is easy to effect, provides a very attractive footprint in the water and will at times inspire even picky trout to rise when the full hackled fly pattern fails to gain any response at all. It has to be said that this method of pruning the hackle fibres is extremely effective and any hackled fly can be, at least in my opinion, enhanced by a little judicial clipping to the underside of the hackle. I have, however, never been overly happy with snipping away at my

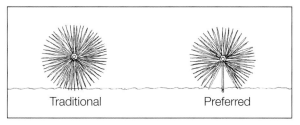

The traditional hackle on the left has the hackle around the whole of the hook shank. My preferred hackle is on the right and has the fibres removed directly below the hook shank.

own prize hackles, considering it a slightly inelegant way of achieving a result and elegance of technique and method is important when tying flies.

Snipping away at the fibres on the underside of the hackle allows the fly to more accurately imitate the dun prior to it taking flight and the position of the fly pattern, when on the water, can be controlled by the number of hackle fibres removed. But as I said it is not an elegant technique and, from a purely practical viewpoint, it removes the very fibres that allow the fly pattern to float high upon the water. Because of this I have for years desired a different method to achieve this result, a method that does not include taking scissors to the hackle fibres.

It was this that I was looking for when I stumbled upon the Paraloop method and while the Paraloop method will provide such a profile to a certain degree, it is limited in its flexibility.

The Paraloop provides little control over how much of the hackle extends below the hook shank and as such is far better suited to providing the hackle on low riding fly patterns or those actually sitting within the surface of the water, like emergers and spent winged imitations.

To solve this problem I came up with a very simple method that allows complete flexibility of the degree of angle the lower section of the hackle can be set to. The method is based on something fly tyers regularly apply to flies but normally to the top of the fly when adding a wing case. But in the case of changing the profile of the hackle it is applied to the underside of the fly. For this reason I have named the technique the 'Under-Thorax'. I have no idea if it is an original application, I have certainly never seen it before. If it is not original then it really does require to be better known as I now find it indispensable, applying it to most of my true dry flies.

The technique is so simple it is almost embarrassing, but I am forced to admit it is a real humdinger and one that allows complete control and flexibility in the separation of the hackle fibres on the underside of the fly pattern.

The Under-Thorax Technique

To demonstrate this technique I have chosen to use a version of a popular and very effective traditional fly pattern, the Greenwell's Glory. This fly pattern is a truly international fly, being

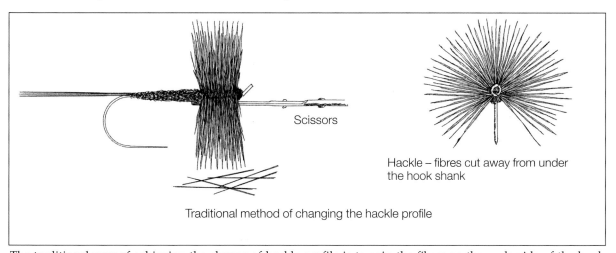

Scissors

Hackle – fibres cut away from under the hook shank

Traditional method of changing the hackle profile

The traditional way of achieving the change of hackle profile is to snip the fibres on the underside of the hook shank.

highly prized wherever and whenever the olive dun or similarly coloured flies show themselves. It was originally developed and tied for fishing on the River Tweed by the tyer James Wright in the mid-eighteen hundreds for Canon William Greenwell, hence the name Greenwell's Glory. I suspect, however, that it was a pattern or a close variation of a pattern regularly used on the River Tweed prior to it being patronized by the good Canon. It is a timeless fly that is as effective today as it ever was and any angler would be at a disadvantage if they were not to have a few examples of it in their fly box.

When tying this particular version of the Greenwell's I have taken the liberty of deviating from applying the materials normally used. I hope that this does not offend any tyers who are sensitive to such change and to acknowledge this I will call the fly a variant. The changes are for practical reasons only and, as far as I am concerned, they improve the overall performance of the fly. The first of these changes is that the wire rib is changed to one of thread. I do not like metal wire ribs on dry flies, seeing no practical reason for them whatsoever and the additional weight does nothing to improve the performance of the fly on the water, but rather reduces its ability to float effectively over a sustained period of fishing. A general rule would be to add no additional metal to a true dry fly, such flies should float high and be delicately perched upon the water surface not end up half sunk. My saving grace in dispensing with the wire rib is that on the original fly pattern there was no rib at all. So in effect the modern accepted version of the Canon's fly is a variant in its own right

As an alternative to the wire rib, thread serves the purpose well and waxed tying thread is perfect. I prefer to treat that which I use with silicon prior to tying and keep a supply of treated threads available for whenever they are required. I can assure any reader that replacing the metal rib with one made from thread makes not a jot of difference to the trout and they will take the thread ribbed pattern with gusto.

Another change I have made, which I do not include in the wet or emerger versions of this fly pattern, is the inclusion of a tail. The following pattern is being tied as a true dry fly and as such

some form of buoyancy must be included at the rear of the fly to ensure it fishes as is intended. The original fly pattern and some of the modern accepted versions of the original do not include a tail, although many tyers add one. Think about it and, if you have the time or inclination, test it out for yourself. The Greenwell's Glory, in its normal accepted form without a tail, will imitate the emerging dun more accurately than the fully emerged dun. The lack of a tail and the inclusion of the wire rib, both contribute to the rear of the fly being immersed within the surface of the water, which is not a good imitation of the fully hatched dun, but an excellent imitation of the emerging dun. It is for this reason that I have included a tail, so that the fully emerged dun can be effectively imitated. I have heard it said that the inclusion of the wire rib improves the effectiveness of the fly pattern and I would not dispute this point. The additional weight pulls the rear of the pattern down into the surface of the water and, as previously explained, imitates the emerging insect rather than the dun floating high upon the surface of the water. If fish are taking the insect as it emerges, then this imitation will more than likely be the most successful, but I would maintain that it is not a true dry fly and therefore does not imitate the fully emerged dun.

Under-thorax technique.

Tying the Greenwell's Glory variant using the Under-Thorax Method

Materials

Hook	Light wire dry fly hook. Partridge Captain Hamilton size 12 or 14.	**Hackle**	Furnace cock.
		Under-thorax	Light olive, ideally slightly darker than the body floss, GSP or half a dozen or so strands of polypropylene floss, separated from the main bulk of floss and spun together.
Tail	Coq de Leon tailing fibres mottled (Pardo).		
Body	Waxed primrose silk or light olive polypropylene floss.		
Rib	Gold or similar coloured thread.	**Thread**	Personal choice.

Photograph 1 Place the hook into the jaws of the vice and test for soundness. Wind the waxed tread using flat thread to the start of the hook bend and tie in the tail on to the top of the hook shank, use the pinch and loop/loose loop method of tying in materials. Wind the thread back along the hook shank to tie in the tailing fibres, only wind towards the hook eye, do not wind back towards the hook bend. Cut off the excess tail fibres. Keep the tail long, ideally at least one and a half times the length of the hook (eye to bend).

Photograph 2 Now offer the thread rib to the tying thread by looping the rib over the tying thread (see diagram overleaf), this is what I call the 'loop over thread' method. Run the rib loop up the tying thread and tie in on the underside of the hook shank by winding the tying thread back to the hook bend. (Useful Tip: After three or four winds of tying thread have been made to tie in the rib, gently pull the rib to remove any excess material prior to continuing to the hook bend.) Return the tying thread to a position two thirds of the way along the hook shank.

Photograph 3 Attach the body floss to the underside of the hook shank using the same method described to attach the thread rib ('loop over thread' method), only this time have the short end of the floss facing the hook bend. Make three or four turns of tightly wound tying thread to attach the body floss.

The 'Loop over the Thread Method'

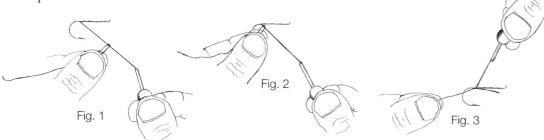

Fig. 1

Fig. 2

Fig. 3

Fig. 1 Pull the thread tight, lay the material to be applied over the top of the thread forming a loop around the thread.

Fig. 2 Pull the loop along the thread up to the hook shank, fixing the material on the hook shank.

Fig. 3 Fix the material with a couple of turns of thread and then gently pull the material back towards the hook bend to remove any excess.

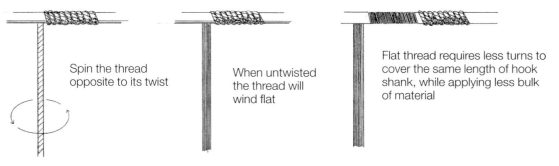

Spin the thread opposite to its twist

When untwisted the thread will wind flat

Flat thread requires less turns to cover the same length of hook shank, while applying less bulk of material

Photograph 4 This is the time to form the body. Firstly the floss must be wound flat, so remove any twist within the floss to allow you to do so. Now wind the floss back along the hook shank tying in the other end of the floss as you do so, continue to the start of the hook bend. Now continuing to wind the floss flat, form the shaped body. (By winding the floss flat, less floss is wound on to the hook shank at any one point, this gives far more flexibility in forming a shaped body.) When the body has been completed, tie in the floss on the underside of the hook shank using no more than three turns of thread, do not cut off the excess material at this point.

Photograph 5 Wind the thread rib around the body and tie in on the underside of the hook shank. Now complete the tying in of the body floss and rib and cut off the excess. Return the tying thread to the start of the body.

Photograph 6 Take a 2 in (5 cm) piece of the material to be used for the under-thorax (either GSP or the spilt floss), ideally this should be slightly darker than that used for the body. With the short end facing the hook eye tie in directly on the underside of the hook shank. If this material is pulled gently after three or four turns of thread there should be no excess material, however, if there is any excess material, remove it. Return the thread to the start of the body

Photograph 7 Prepare the hackle by removing any soft fibres from the base of the stalk and tie on the hook directly where the body ends. The hackle should be facing over the hook bend and the good side facing you. Tie in by winding the thread towards the hook eye and cut off any excess hackle stalk. Remember to leave enough space behind the hook eye to tie in the additional materials and create a small head.

Photograph 8 Wind the hackle towards the hook eye using touching turns. Tie in leaving plenty of room for the head. Now cut off the excess hackle.

Photograph 9 Take the under-thorax material, attached to the hook prior to tying in the hackle, and bring it forward towards the hook eye and directly underneath the hook shank. Feed it through the hackle making sure that no hackle fibres are caught under it. Keeping the under-thorax material taut, tie in behind the hook eye, using very tight turns of thread.

Photograph 10 Cut off the excess under-thorax material, form a small head and complete with a whip finish. That puts the finishing touches to the tying of the Greenwell's Glory variant incorporating an under-thorax.

Photograph 11 View of the finished fly pattern from the front.

Having finished the tying of the fly let's look at what this simple adjustment has achieved. Except for the addition of the under-thorax floss the fly pattern has been tied relatively conventionally, but the inclusion of the under-thorax has transformed the shape of the hackle below the hook shank, without removing any of the hackle fibres. As can be seen from the final photograph, the shape of the hackle has been altered to achieve the result that pruning the hackle would do. The big difference is that the hackle is intact and the number of fibres, which hold the fly on the water surface, have not been reduced. This simple method has achieved what we set out to do, that is to control the shape of the hackle.

Using the under-thorax method allows almost complete control over the degree that the hackle fibres are repositioned. This control is achieved in an equally simple way, by varying the thickness of the floss, or other suitable material, used. In a nutshell the thinner, or less bulky, the material used for the under-thorax, the lesser degree that the hackle fibres are repositioned. The thicker, or more bulky, the material used the greater degree the hackle fibres are repositioned.

The photograph illustrates this clearly and starting from the left moving to the right, the first fly shows the result of using a thin material as an under-thorax and as can be seen the repositioning of the hackle fibres is minimal. The next fly uses a slightly wider more bulky material for the under-thorax and the repositioning of the hackle fibres has been increased. The under-thorax material has been increased in bulk for each fly up to the final one on the far right. The material used for the under-thorax on this fly has increased in width/bulk to the point that it is possible to reposition the hackle fibres to the horizontal, into a spent wing position. So you can see the under-thorax method allows almost complete control regarding the positioning of the hackle fibres and it doesn't take too much imagination to see how useful the method could be when tying any number of different fly patterns.

The method described above is ideal for tying fly patterns that imitate the dun, but the following adaptation is, I believe, possibly a more effective use of the method to create an imitation of the dun riding high on the surface of the water. I call this adaptation the 'Double-Hackle-Under-Thorax' and it is designed specifically to keep the main body of the fly off the surface of the water and give the impression and footprint of the dun before it takes to the air for the first time after emergence. The pattern is in many ways an adaptation of the Fore and Aft fly patterns although it needs to be said these played no part in its development. The purpose of the smaller rear hackle is to lift the hook bend up so that it is partly out of the water and at the same time, by using the under-thorax method, give the impression of the rear legs on the surface of the water. The truth of the matter is that in the case of flies tied using both these methods the under-thorax in effect becomes an underbody and an under-thorax. This is a nice style of fly pattern and I like it very much. It is effective tied on many sizes of hook and imitating the large mayflies to the small olives. It is a fly pattern that I would have no hesitation in tying on to my tippet when the dun is on the surface of the water, even though my natural tendency is usually to opt for an emerging fly pattern.

The following tying is very easy and simple and is just an adaptation on a theme following the tying of the Greenwell's Glory. The fly pattern chosen to demonstrate the method is a Large Dark Olive. Most upwinged flies can be imitated using this combination of methods.

Tying The Large Dark Olive using the Double Hackle and Under-Thorax Techniques

Materials

Hook　　Dry Fly Partridge Captain Hamilton.

Hackle　　Two cock hackles are used. The first is the rear hackle and should be of a size suited to a hook at least two sizes smaller than the hook being used, the colour of this hackle should be light blue dun. The second is for the forward hackle and should be of the normal size for the hook being used. This hackle should be a furnace hackle.

Body　　Dark Olive polypropylene dubbing.

Tail　　Small bunch of Coq de Leon tailing fibres (I prefer mottled – Pardo).

Under-Thorax　　Medium olive GSP or half a dozen or so polypropylene floss strands spun together as described in the previous pattern.

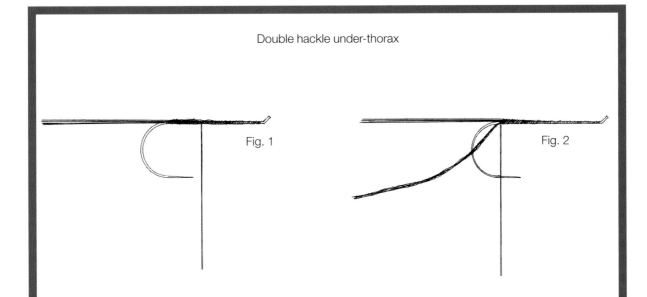

Double hackle under-thorax

Fig. 1

Fig. 2

Fig. 1 Fix the hook into the jaws of the vice and test the hook for soundness. Attach the waxed thread and wind the thread to the hook bend, using flat thread. Tie in the small bunch of Coq de Leon fibres. Make the tail long, forget about the 'as long as the hook ' rule, go at least half the length again. The illustration does not do justice to the length of the tail, but limited space enforced me to curtail it. Complete tying in the tail with the thread coming to rest away from the hook bend along the hook shank.

Fig. 2 Offer the under-thorax material to the underside of the hook and tie in by winding the thread back towards the hook bend. Use the 'loop over the thread' method, illustrated previously to initially attach the floss, Doing so will give complete control of material positioning. (Tip: After making the first few turns of thread, the material can be gently pulled backwards, while maintaining the tension of the tying thread, this will remove any excess material, then continue the thread to the hook bend.)

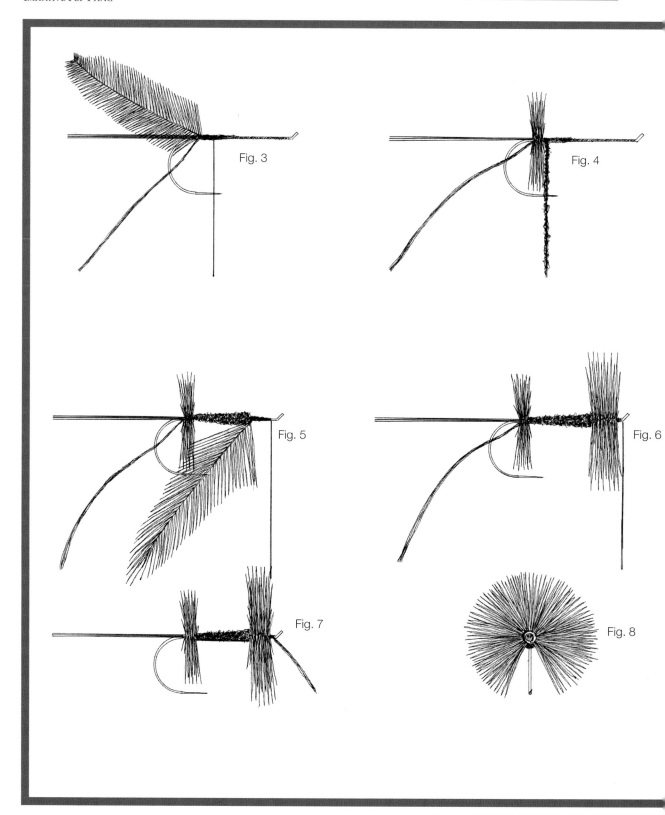

Fig. 3

Fig. 4

Fig. 5

Fig. 6

Fig. 7

Fig. 8

Fig. 3 Prepare and offer the smaller of the two hackles, the light blue dun, to the hook. This should be tied in as close as possible to where the tail starts. Tie in the hackle with the good side facing towards you and the main body of the hackle pointing over the rear of the hook. The hackle fibres should be of a length that ensures they stay within the gape of the hook.

Fig. 4 Now wind on the hackle, stopping before it reaches the position on the hook shank directly above the point of the hook. Tie in the hackle and cut off any excess. Now dub the thread with the polypropylene body dubbing.

Fig. 5 Wind the dubbed thread to between two thirds and three quarters of the way along the hook shank and form a shaped body, thicker at the front end than the rear. Prepare the larger hackle, the furnace hackle, by removing any soft fibres at the base of the stalk and tie in, with the good side facing you, directly at the point where the body starts.

Fig. 6 Wind on the hackle, tying in behind the hook eye using a few tight turns of thread. It is essential to leave enough space behind the hook eye to tie in the under thorax and form a small head. Cut off the excess hackle.

Fig. 7 Pull the under-thorax material from the rear of the fly through to the front of the fly, keeping it directly in line with the underside of the hook, also taking great care not to trap any hackle fibres as you do so. (It is better to work the under-thorax material through the hackle fibres to minimize the danger of trapping any fibres.) Now pull the under-thorax material taut and tie in directly behind the hook eye.

Fig. 8 Cut off the excess under-thorax material, form a small head with the tying thread and complete with a whip finish.

There is an addition that can be added when using these techniques combined. It is totally optional, but it does prevent the under-thorax floss from ever being pulled away from behind the hook eye. The addition of a thread rib can both strengthen the fly and give the impression of a segmented body, which, even if the trout are unable to perceive it, adds to its attraction for those of us who fish. The rib is added after the first hackle has been completed and tied in, prior to the body being formed. The following photographic sequence demonstrates this clearly.

The same fly as before, the large Dark Olive, is being used to demonstrate the inclusion of a rib. Obviously the same sequence of techniques can be applied to any number of flies.

A small stream where often the Dark Olive will prove successful.

The Large Dark Olive including a Rib

The tying of this pattern will start at the point that the rib is attached, as it is exactly the same as the previous tying, up to that point. Do not forget to attach the under-thorax material immediately after the tail.

Additional Materials
Rib   A 6 in (15 cm) piece of cream coloured tying thread, preferably silicon treated.

Photograph 1 After completing the fly pattern, up to and including the winding on and tying in of the light blue dun rear hackle (remember to include the under-thorax material), attach the rib thread to the hook shank, using the 'loop over the thread' method. Tie the rib thread in tightly using flat thread, not directly on the underside of the hook shank, but slightly off centre, over towards the far side of the hook shank. Now wind the tying thread to the halfway position on the hook shank and then back to the rear hackle. Cut off any excess rib thread, although if the excess floss was pulled back after the first few turns of tying thread there should be no excess.

Photograph 2 Dub the tying thread and wind on to form a shaped body as in the previous tying.

Photograph 3 When the body is completed tie on the second hackle, the furnace hackle, wind on, tie in and cut off the excess hackle, as described in the previous tying.

Photograph 4 Pull the under-thorax material into position, taking care not to catch any hackle fibres and tie it in behind the hook eye with five or six very tight turns of thread. **Do not** cut off the excess material at this stage.

Photograph 5 Now wind the rib thread tightly around the body and the under-thorax, making sure as you do so that the under-thorax material stays firmly in place directly on the underside of the hook shank. When the rib thread reaches the forward hackle, carefully continue the windings through the hackle itself. If care is taken this will not displace or trap any hackle fibres. Tie in behind the hook eye. Complete the tying in of the rib and under-thorax. Check to make sure the under-thorax material is tight before finally tying in and cutting off both the excess rib thread and the GSP or floss strands used to form the under-thorax. Now form a small head and complete with a whip finish.

Photograph 6 The completed fly.

Using this method of including a rib significantly strengthens the fly pattern and, while I am not a great lover of ribs on dry flies, this is an occasion when it can seriously enhance the durability. The use of a contrasting colour of thread to the main body colour does give a segmented appearance. The importance of this segmentation is, to the greater extent, lost on me, but I must admit it improves the overall look of the fly, which is probably reason enough to include it.

Applying Wings to Under-Thorax Fly Patterns

No matter if a single or double hackle is applied to a fly pattern, if a wing is desired then it can be applied in most cases as normal. The wings on such fly patterns, due to them imitating the dun, will be upright wings. As such hackle tips, feather slips and hair can be used to imitate the wing, pretty much as with most traditional dry flies. The following outlines the sequence of applying such wings:

Hackle Tip Wings

Hackle tip wings are attached to the hook at the start of the tying and before anything else but the thread has been applied. The wings are left pointing over the hook eye until the forward hackle has been attached, at which time they are set into their final position.

Photograph 1 The initial tying in of the wings, before anything else has been applied to the hook. The hackle tip wings are left pointing out over the hook eye.

Photograph 2 The hackle tip wings are tied into position prior to the forward hackle being wound on. The hackle is wound along the hook shank behind and in front of the wings.

Feather Slip Wings

No matter whether the feather tip wing is positioned to face over the hook eye or with tips pointing backwards over the body of the fly, they should be tied in at the commencement of tying, prior to anything else being added and left pointing over the hook eye. Adjustments can be made when fixing into the right position.

The procedure is the same as that for the hackle tip wings, with fixing into the final position taking place prior to winding on the forward hackle.

Photograph 1 The initial tying in of the wings, before anything else has been applied to the hook. The feather slip wings are left pointing out over the hook eye.

Photograph 2 The feather slip wings are tied into position prior to the forward hackle being wound on. The hackle is wound along the hook shank behind and just one or two turns in front of the wings.

Photograph 3 The finished fly with feather slip wings attached. Please note the wing has been exaggerated in size slightly to emphasize the technique.

Hair wings

As with both the hackle tip and the feather slip wings, hair wings should be applied to the hook prior to anything else and left pointing out over the hook eye. Again the wing/wings can be brought into position just prior to winding on the forward hackle. It is at this time that the wing can be split into two if required, or left as a single upright wing.

Photograph 1 The initial tying in of the wings, before anything else has been applied to the hook. The hair wing is left pointing out over the hook eye.

Photograph 2 The hair wing is tied into position prior to the forward hackle being wound on. It is at this time that the wing is split in two if required, by using figure of eight turns of tying thread. The hackle is wound along the hook shank behind and in front of the wing/wings.

Photograph 3 The finished fly with hair wing attached. (The size of the wing has been exaggerated.)

(Tip: When tying in hair wings, particularly hard hair like squirrel or polar bear, it is advisable to initially wind the thread flat around the hair, making sure the thread is well waxed. This is opposite to the normal recommendations made, where the thread is spun tight. After the wing has been tied in using waxed flat thread, the thread is spun very tight and biting turns of thread made over the previous wound flat thread. By initially winding the thread flat the area of thread actually in contact with the hair increases, this grips the hair. Using the thread wound tight over the previously flat thread locks everything into place, making it highly unlikely that any hair fibres will ever come adrift.)

Foam Underbodies on Dry Flies

In the chapter 'Air's Apparent II', there is a section describing and illustrating the formation of preformed underbodies using the polystyrene foam from disposable tea and coffee cups. In that particular section, the use of these polystyrene underbodies is to assist in the floating of emerger fly patterns, to hold them in the surface of the water. I briefly mentioned their use when applied to traditional dry flies and in this part of the book I will be looking at how I use foam underbodies for dry fly and true dry fly patterns and what are the advantages for doing so.

Foam in its many forms has a number of qualities that make its use desirable when designing and tying dry fly patterns. Some of these qualities are in addition to the obvious one that the material floats extremely well. Most of the time foam is added to a fly for its floating properties only, doing so seriously neglects the other, sometimes more important, qualities that foam has to offer the fly tyer.

One important quality that foam has to offer, which is not easily found using other materials, is one of bulk and weight. Put simply, foam can be used to add bulk to a fly pattern without significantly increasing its weight. Another quality to bear in mind when designing fly patterns is that bulk can be applied without increasing the absorption of water into the very core of the fly. These two additional qualities, besides the obvious one of floating, generally make foam in its

various forms a much underused and underrated material. The trick is to know when to use it, how to use it and what sort of foam is the most suitable for the task in hand. The possibilities of the use of foam in fly tying circles is only just being realized and I would expect its use to increase considerably in the future. (I make this statement well aware of the current usage of foam by many well-known and talented fly tyers. Foam has much to offer and we are only just beginning to scratch the surface on how it can be utilized.)

To understand how the use of foam can work advantageously when designing and tying dry or true dry flies, it is advisable to look at the anatomy of such fly patterns. Taking the time to understand their make up and how and why they perform in a certain way, will help when tying fly patterns that are designed to act in a particular manner when they are on the surface of the water. I find it is useful, up to a certain point, to follow the well worn paths laid down by generations of other fly tyers for there is much to learn and it is doubtful if any single lifetime could absorb it all. However, breaking away from that which is accepted often opens up possibilities and an understanding that can prove both practical and highly useful. Put simply, tradition is no reason why fly patterns should be tied in a particular way and that way only. As a fly fisher and fly tyer I find it very much more useful to understand what makes a fly pattern work in the way it is required to work when on the water. The design and construction of a fly pattern is dependent on how it will fulfil the task in hand, rather than following those methods generally accepted to be the way a fly pattern is tied.

I start by looking at the hook first, as this is the skeleton around which the fly is built, defining its size, shape and ability to float and I then work through to the whip finish. Each material is chosen carefully to ensure that the final result will be a success, not only as a catcher of fish, but in so far as the fly will act as intended when on the water. There is little merit in designing a fly pattern that doesn't do what it is supposed to do. The surface emerger pattern that sinks after a few casts, the slow sinking buzzer pattern that

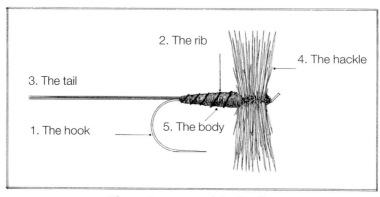

The various parts of the dry fly.

refuses to leave the top of the water and the true dry fly pattern that for all intents and purposes imitates a semi sunk emerger. None of these fulfil their original intention. Admittedly all of the above examples will catch fish, but then again so will just about any kind of fly pattern. The point is they fail to catch fish in the way they were devised. They may, more or less, imitate the natural fly, but more importantly, they do not imitate the natural fly at the specific point in its life cycle as intended and, as far as I am concerned, that is an important element of fly fishing for trout.

My attitude or view may appear to some readers to be slightly if not highly pedantic, but I make no apologies for viewing fly fishing for trout as a complete experience, an experience that is inextricably linked to the natural fly life upon which the fish feed. Imitating that fly life at those special moments when the natural fly becomes easy prey is, as far as I am concerned, the very essence of the total experience of fly fishing.

If you think about it, after the nymph or larvae, the time frame, for each stage of a fly's life cycle imitated by the angler, is amazingly short. If it wasn't for the fact that flies on the whole undergo their natural cycles en masse or at least in some numbers, it would be very difficult to decide which fly pattern to use. Taking the time to watch natural flies emerging, I have seen the process completed within the blink of an eye or take several minutes and sometimes the struggle ends in failure. Without the great numbers of emerging flies the whole process would be over in a very short period of time. Another example would be that of the fully emerged dun perched high on the surface of the water and being carried down the river or floating on some loch, lake or pond, but for how long? A few minutes at most, they take to the air as soon as they are able. It is that, in any single stage of the life cycle, more than one fly is involved and it is the overall time scale of all the individual insects involved that allows the successful imitation of each part of the life cycle. When attempting to imitate such precise and exacting moments it is an added pleasure to ensure the fly pattern used is equally precise and exacting. I accept that not all species of natural flies emerge in great numbers, but those that do play an important part in any fly fisher's life, important enough for me to imitate them as best I can. Don't get me wrong though, I don't like fly patterns that are over realistic, they lack the illusion of life. Fly patterns that give the impression of the real thing are, in my opinion, far better.

If we look at a typical traditional dry fly the following observations and conclusions can be made. Please forgive me if they appear obvious but I would like to take a little time to paint a full picture, without leaving out any detail.

1. The hook adds the greatest amount of weight.
2. If a metal rib (wire or tinsel) is used it will add more weight for its bulk than most other materials used.
3. The tail, especially if it is long, will assist in holding the rear of the fly in the surface of the water without adding any significant weight.
4. The hackle is the main flotant covering a large

area and adding very little weight. It also allows the fly to drop more softly through the air to land gently on the surface of the water, letting the fly pattern sit high.

5. The body usually contributes the largest bulk on the fly and as such tends to be the heaviest section of the fly after the hook. The body also acts like a sponge absorbing water into the very core of the fly pattern.

I have looked carefully at fly patterns and believe that the above sums up the traditional dry fly quite accurately. The question is how can these qualities be enhanced or counteracted as required? I use the following methods to ensure that a true dry fly fulfils its role.

1. The hook should be chosen carefully. Hooks vary considerably in their weight and strength and it is important that a strong light wire hook is used when tying true dry flies.

2. Any wire or tinsel rib should be left out of the fly pattern. If, however, a rib is required or preferred for the purpose of durability or overall look, then a thread or similar material should be used. Tightly spun GSP is excellent for this purpose, as it is very strong and will not absorb any water or add weight to the fly.

3. Use tails that are long and springy and not overly bulky.

4. Use high quality hackles that are springy and minimal in web. Treat the hackles with silicon spray overnight prior to using.

5. It is the body that poses the biggest problem, due to its bulk and absorption of water. For true dry flies try including a pre-formed polystyrene underbody. These underbodies add little weight to a fly, while increasing the bulk to form the body shape, a single layer of dubbing will suffice to cover the underbody. The foam underbody also eliminates water absorption into the very core of the fly, making the fly extremely easy to dry with a couple of false casts, the false casts not only drying out the hackle but also the dubbed body. The use of polystyrene as opposed to many other forms of foam is important, due to its comparative rigidity, which allows a floss or a dubbed thread to be wound over it successfully, without compromising the floatability of the foam.

How to apply a polystyrene pre-formed underbody to a true dry fly

The technique for applying a polystyrene pre-formed underbody to a dry fly is quite simple and utilizes the methods described in detail in the section on pre-formed underbodies found in the chapter 'Airs Apparent II'. The main reason polystyrene is used is that it is hard but can still be manipulated to a certain extent. It is necessary for the underbody to be hard to allow a dubbed thread, or floss to be wound around it successfully. The main difference to the underbodies described in the previous section, where they are used for emerger patterns, and in this section, is that only one end of the underbody is shaped by tapering. This can clearly be seen in the illustration overleaf, where in Fig. 1 the body length is cut from the formed polystyrene trough. In Fig. 2 one end of the body length is carefully tapered to produce the final product as shown in Fig. 3.

When using these pre-formed polystyrene underbodies on dry fly and true dry fly patterns, I like to add the underbody after the tail (and rib if included) has been tied in. Obviously, when the underbody is added will depend on the sequence being used to tie the particular fly, but usually after the tail (and rib if included) has been added. I also prefer to add the underbody to the hook shank with the trough up, fitting over the underside of the hook shank. This places the main bulk of the foam on the underside of the hook shank and not on top of the shank as described previously when tying emerger patterns.

As already explained in this section, the inclusion of a foam underbody is not necessary to add total buoyancy to a fly pattern. In many cases, if the fly pattern is to fish as it has been designed, the body itself will not actually be on the water and as such its buoyancy is not particularly an issue. In the case of true dry flies the inclusion of a foam underbody is important so as to add bulk to form the body shape without adding any significant weight, and it also minimizes the possibility of any water absorption into the very core of the fly pattern.

To demonstrate the use of the polystyrene

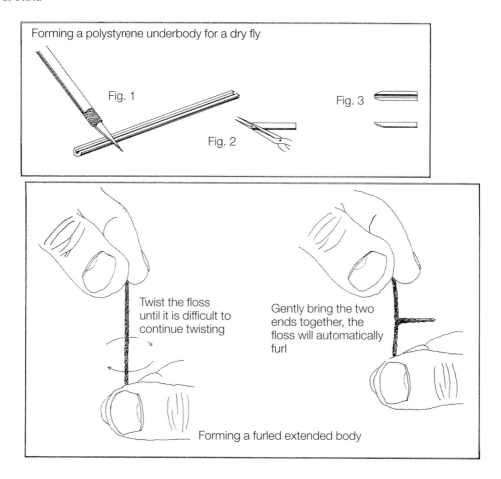

Forming a polystyrene underbody for a dry fly

Fig. 1

Fig. 2

Fig. 3

Twist the floss until it is difficult to continue twisting

Gently bring the two ends together, the floss will automatically furl

Forming a furled extended body

pre-formed underbodies when tying true dry flies I have chosen that most exciting of natural flies, the true mayfly (*Ephemera Danica* or *Vulgata*). Whenever I see the mayflies on the water I get excited. There is something special about these large upwinged flies and I also find them quite beautiful as they dance above the water in the summer light. With the mayfly on the water the fishing is pretty much assured to be good, in fact very good and at times exceptional. The mayfly has the ability to make normally wary trout cast all caution to the stream and there is always the chance that the bigger fish, which tend to stay out of the way of my fly patterns, might take a chance and sample that being offered. As I said with the mayfly on the water I get excited, in fact I get too excited, taking twice as long to set up my tackle and tie on my chosen fly pattern, my fingers and thumbs appearing to be working at a different rate to my mind. If the

truth is told when the mayfly are around I become a little kid, the same child that years ago first tied a fly upon the end of his cast and attempted to place it out upon the water. Mayfly time is a time of enthusiasm, a time when all pretence and pose is lost in the fullness of the fishing. Mayfly time is a good time.

The mayfly is a big fly and to give the impression of this I often use an extended body. The use of an extended body allows a big fly to be tied without having to resort to a very large hook. The following fly pattern used to demonstrate the inclusion of a pre-formed underbody also incorporates the double hackle and the under-thorax. The extended body is interesting in that it extends at the position normally used to tie in the tail. It is possible to add tails to such an extended body, but I do not include them in this particular tying.

Tying the Mayfly with Pre-formed polystyrene underbody

Materials

Hook	Up or down eyed dry fly. Partridge Captain Hamilton size 10 or 12.	**Body**	Cream polypropylene floss.
		Underbody	Pre-formed polystyrene body.
		Extended Body	Cream polypropylene floss.
Hackle	Forward hackle normal size for hook either coloured honey dun or light ginger cock. Rear hackle two sizes smaller than normal for hook size and coloured light blue dun.	**Rib**	Dark brown thread.
		Under-Thorax	Cream GSP or half a dozen or so polypropylene floss strands spun together as previously explained.

Photograph 1 Fix the hook into the jaws of the vice and test for soundness. Attach and wind the well waxed thread, using the thread wound flat, to the start of the hook bend. Take 3 in (7 cm) of the cream polypropylene body floss and twist it allowing the floss to furl back upon itself – (see diagram). When the extended body has been completed, offer it to the hook allowing ³/₈ in (10 mm) to extend beyond the start of the hook bend and tie in at the hook bend.

Photograph 2 Cut off the excess extended body floss and winding the tying thread flat return it to the bend of the hook.

Photograph 3 Tie in the under-thorax material directly onto the underside of the hook shank, using the loop over the thread method, remove any excess material by gently pulling the under-thorax backward after the first few turns of thread, complete the tying in of the under-thorax material. Then again return the thread to the start of the hook bend, still using the thread wound flat.

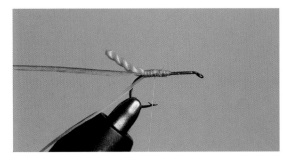

Photograph 4 Prepare and attach the rear hackle, the light blue dun, making sure that the good side is facing you. Cut off the excess hackle stalk.

Photograph 5 Wind on the hackle stopping before the hackle reaches the position on the hook shank that is directly above the point of the hook. Tie in the hackle and cut off the excess. Return the thread so that it butts up to the hackle.

Photograph 6 Attach the thread rib to the underside of the hook shank using the 'loop to thread' method. Do not tie this in directly on the underside but rather slightly offset, over to the far side of the underside of the shank. Make only two turns of thread to tie in the rib. Now offer the body floss directly to the underside of the hook shank and complete the tying in of both the body floss and the thread rib. Return the thread back to the hackle, remembering to use flat wound thread for all the tying.

Photograph 7 Set the polystyrene underbody into place by placing the trough (groove) of the underbody over the underside of the hook shank, butting up as close as possible to the rear hackle. Tie in by winding the thread tightly at each end of the underbody and with wide criss-cross, medium tight windings over the main body. Leave the tying thread at the hook eye end of the body.

Photograph 8 Wind the body floss over the under-body and tie in onto the underside of the hook shank, cut off the excess floss.

Photograph 9 Prepare and attach the forward hackle, the honey dun or light ginger, and wind on to the hook shank, leave enough space clear behind the hook eye to tie in the final materials and form a small head.

Photograph 10 Pull the under-thorax material forward directly on the underside of the hook shank. Bring the material up to the underside of the shank and carefully through both the rear and forward hackles, without catching up any hackle fibres as you do so. Tie in behind the hook eye with three or four very tight turns of thread. Do not cut off the excess under-thorax material at this stage.

Photograph 11 Wind the thread rib around the body and the under-thorax, taking care not to pull the under-thorax over to one side. Wind the rib carefully through the forward hackle taking care that no hackle fibres are trapped under the thread rib. Now tie off the rib behind the hook eye. Complete the tying in of the under-thorax and the thread rib, making sure as you do so that the under-thorax material is taut. Cut off the excess materials, form a small head and complete with a whip finish.

Photograph 12 The completed fly.

That completes the tying of the mayfly incorporating a polystyrene underbody. As mentioned previously, in the case of this fly pattern, the underbody is not used directly as a floating aid, but as a method of reducing the weight of the materials applied to the fly and reducing the tendency for the body to absorb water.

It will be clear to most readers that the use of the techniques described in this chapter can be easily utilized by any number of different fly patterns. There is one factor, which is, however, often ignored when fishing dry flies and that is the delivery, the actual presentation of the fly. The presentation of the fly is the most important factor when fishing the dry fly and especially when fishing the true dry fly, if the fly pattern is to be fished as it has been designed. If the presentation of the fly is clumsy, then no amount of careful tying will allow it to be fished as intended, with the fly more than likely sitting low in the water, rather than perched delicately on the surface. I'm not suggesting that flies presented clumsily will not catch fish, far from it. The truth is, they will catch fish but not in the way intended and as far as I am concerned this is one of the main principles of fly-fishing for trout,

imitating a fly at a specific time in its life cycle. A badly presented fly will more likely than not be partially sunk and as such cannot be said to be imitating the dun perched on the water. Partially sunken flies imitate emergers, spent spinners or crippled flies and not the dun. When fishing the true dry fly the cast must be made to allow the fly pattern to drop gently down upon the surface of the water under its own weight. The hackle not only allows the fly pattern to float, but also slows down the dropping of the fly through the air on to the water. Any unnecessary force and momentum from the cast will have the opposite effect to that required. This is most important and follows my belief that the best fly pattern is the fly pattern that is presented best.

At the end of this book in the Fly Gallery there is a selection of patterns that are all popular and proven fly patterns to which the techniques covered in this chapter have been applied. It would be correct to say that each of these particular patterns is a variant of the original rather than a new tying, as they have each been based on the accepted tying. The materials and the tying sequence used for each pattern have been included, as have each of the tying techniques.

3. LEGENDS
OF THE FALLS

The spinners return

Part I

As a fly fisherman I love the upwinged flies. Their rise and fall, the upward rise of the dun and the downfall of the spinner, highlights their importance in fly fishing terms. To be by the water fishing at that auspicious moment when there occurs a fall of spinners, is the stuff from which legends are made. Legends of the home and fireside type, a few pints of beer around the bar sort of legends. Legends that reverberate through your memory and maybe those of your friends and fishing buddies, to be sung of like some old Nordic saga whenever anglers meet and chew the fat of past experiences. – 'Do you remember that evening on the Tweed three years ago, just as the sun was going down over the hills'. 'Hey what about that fall of blue winged olives near the mill that time' – everyone who was there remembers and will momentarily be transported back to that certain evening and the thrill and wonder of one particular fall of spent spinners. A fall of spinners can be impressive and there is no doubt it is one of the hints of wonder that nature offers us mere mortals to the glory of life, albeit in one of its more modest forms.

A fall of spinners is an occasion packed and filled to the brim with significance. It is a sign that these flies have completed their mating rituals for yet another year. The eggs now deposited amongst the tumbling waters of some upland stream, below the sedate flow of a lowland river or upon the wind rippled-waters of a diamond clear or peat stained lake or loch. This single hatch of flies has lived out their own life cycle of egg, nymph, dun and spinner. Returning back to the element from which they hatched, lived and emerged, to be lost to the water, wings unable to function, as vital life seeps quickly away like sand in a upturned egg timer.

A fall of spinners is one of those times when a little knowledge enhances the beauty of the situation, to see and to know what is happening allows a far greater appreciation of the importance, significance and splendour of such events. Some events in nature require no knowledge to reach and touch that part of us that awakens under their influence. Take a sunset, a storm or simply a family of otters playing, these instantly reach deep within, no names, words or explanations are required. Without any knowledge of what is happening a fall of spinners could be passed without being seen. A rise of upwinged flies may perhaps be completely missed or, more to the point, unappreciated – 'Hell what's happening, why are all these bloody flies crawling over me?' – but a fall of spinners would go unnoticed, passing by invisible to the eye, another miracle of life hidden and lost. It is the eyes-open communion with the true, natural world around us that is perhaps one of fishing's greatest gifts.

A fall of spinners, however, will rarely go unnoticed by the trout, the emerging dun may not always inspire action, but on reflection I don't think I have ever seen even a small fall of spent flies pass by and peter out without a response from the fish. Looking at things from a trout's point of view, the dead or dying spinner is easy pickings, a sure and certain buffet, without the effort of a chase or possible chance of missing any fly selected. Here no fly is struggling to break the hold of the water and take to the air as quickly as newly unfolded wings will allow, life is gone or going, their time is up.

Not too far from where I live there flows a river where the presence of the upwinged fly in its many guises can be relied upon most days during the warmer months, especially from May onwards to July and sometimes even to the end of the season. During this time, if the conditions are right or almost right, fairly large hatches of flies take place on most days, you just have to make sure you are in the right place at the right time. It is always possible to have successful fishing using the emerging or adult fly pattern. But for the biggest trout it is better to try your luck later in the day, as the light starts to fade with the sun touching the top of the hills forming the valley through which the river flows. It is at this time that the larger fish start to show themselves, coming out from the deeper water to cruise the shallows. It is here that the dead or dying spinners are caught on the still or eddying water by the rocks and debris at the water's edge. If you didn't know better you would swear some of these fish were salmon or big sea trout, when they turn on some morsel of fly and each swirl is accompanied by an oath and the increased heartbeat of the watching angler. These fish nonchalantly mop up the dead and dying flies at a leisurely pace, taking their time and saving their energies like old sparring professionals. Sometimes they swim into water so shallow that their backs and dorsal fins constantly break the surface as they search every nook and cranny for the evening ration. Now is the time to carefully allow a spent spinner imitation to land on the water, preferably in the path of a cruising fish.

Fishing like this, I have found it best not to move the fly in any way at all, give it the freedom it requires to become a part of the scene taking place before you and simply let the fish find it for themselves. Keeping control of the line is essential, these may be big fish but they can take and reject the offered fly pattern instantly, leaving the fly requiring first aid before you can say 'I've a take' to yourself. This is not the usual form of river fishing and there are times when most of your line and leader will be lying on the bank, with only the last couple of feet on the water. There is no need for mending the line as this water is relatively still or slow, besides the fact that you would probably be mending line on to and into the bankside vegetation. Seeking out these areas of calmer water is what does the trick and is the secret to this type of fishing. Such water collects spent spinners throughout a fall, holding them secure and ready for the arrival of those fish that know where to look for such easy pickings.

Like most fishing there is an element of chance when fishing a fall of spinners, it's a little like a lottery with your fly as the lucky single ticket to be picked out of the hat amongst the many others. Unlike most lotteries, however, you do have some control, and your ticket can be manoeuvred carefully towards the choosing hand. Watching a fish rising regularly it is possible to predict, at least up to a certain extent, the route it may take. Sometimes a fish will act like water based vacuum cleaners mopping up flies in a continuous operation, at times following a straight line, at times up and down the water, but rarely in a totally random and unpredictable manner. Placing your fly, using an intelligent guess, gives the best chance of a take. This is exciting stuff and many a fly pattern has been whipped away from the open mouth of a co-operating fish before the take is complete. The problem is you can very often see the fish approaching and then rising slowly to your own fly pattern. The tension builds up as the fish gets closer and closer to where your fly patiently awaits its arrival. As the mouth opens the fly is struck away, tension and anticipation triumphing as the fish disappears with a single swirl. These days in this situation my heart still beats as it did when I was a small boy and a take from a fish was imminent. The difference now is that I am more relaxed, breathing gently and allowing the fish to complete its approach and take the fly pattern properly, before lifting the rod to tighten the line and confirm all is well with God in his heaven and also with me down here below.

Chance plays no greater part than when the flies on the water are caenis, the tiny so called 'anglers' curse'. I have never been able to workout why these flies were given that nickname as they have brought me much success and far from a curse I see them as a blessing. Admittedly they are small and usually your tiny fly is lost amongst many hundreds of others. The angler, however, has the advantage of being able to place a fly where a fish is most likely to find it, either in the current being covered by a rising fish, or in the path of a cruiser. Either way the odds have been reduced to a reasonable betting level, which I think is all we anglers can or should ever hope for. The odds are such that sometimes we win and at other times we lose, which sounds fair enough to me. When the caenis spinners fall, their bodies can cover the water. In fact they have covered everything beforehand as they leave the dun shucks covering all your clothing, it is not long after this that the spinners will fall, being ready for it can put you at a distinct advantage. As soon as I see the duns changing to spinners I reach for my fly box and tie on one of the caenis spent spinner imitation patterns I use. Soon the fish start to rise and getting your fly on the water early can give you a good chance before the main mass of flies descend.

A few years ago when out with my friend George the fishery owner we met with such a rise and fall. Now George's fishery has a sign saying 'Forget the Dog, Beware of the Owner'. The dog in question at the time was a large German Shepherd with teeth polished to perfection but never was a warning sign more accurate. When it came to fishing George was and is as amiable a companion as can be found. There is one restriction to this amiability, don't be too jovial early in the morning when he's just got out of bed, a few coffees and cigarettes are required to kick start the better side of his nature. The rise in question came late in the morning, with no breeze and the sun breaking out on occasions from behind the clouds. The first I noticed it was when I saw George's coat was dotted with flies and then saw my own was similarly covered. Within a short period of time the flies had mated and were returning to the water to deposit the eggs and the first spent flies became apparent mainly due to a good rise of feeding fish beginning. Now these fish were in mopping up mode, skimming the surface of the water with mouths open or gently sipping down individual flies in a manner hardly perceived. After a couple of casts and one nice trout I tapped my fly into the path of a sipping fish, the fly was taken without any fuss. The fish may have been surprised at being hooked, but it was nothing compared to my surprise, as a fish of well over 30 in (76 cm) of prime spotted silver muscle leaped 3 ft (1 m) out of the water. It always astonishes me that such large fish can be so gentle when taking the fly. The tippet was 3 lb double strength and the fly a size 22. You can do little more than stay in contact with the fish in such a situation, carefully trying to guide it away from any known snags and resigning yourself to the fact that the next twenty minutes or more will be spent walking up and down

the banks. I got about halfway through that allotted time when the fish dived deep, it rose again about thirty yards (27 m) away. Now the real problem became clear, the fish had swum under a long length of nylon monofilament, probably lost by a spin fisherman. Both ends of this nylon appeared to be solidly attached, needless to say when the fish swam back over the nylon and then again dived down and away my line was knotted. Soon I was bidding a sad goodbye to the largest fish I had ever hooked on a caenis pattern. By the time all this had run its course the fall had ended. I am yet to catch a fish of such a size on a caenis pattern or similar sized fly, but I know it is possible and I look forward to the day when another opportunity presents itself. The thing is you never know when that may be, possibly my next cast. George didn't give me much sympathy either and his comment that I lost the fish because I was a rubbish fisherman seemed particularly harsh, considering the circumstances and that he was my friend, but then again that's George for you.

At the other end of the size spectrum come the true mayflies, juicy delicacies fit to inspire any dour trout to take the time and make the effort to come up from the depths to sample. The true mayflies are big flies and there is no chance of a rise or fall going unnoticed by fish, bird or fisherman. It is said that anybody can catch a trout when the mayfly are on the water, on the basis that anyone could catch a fish no matter what fly is on the water, it is necessary to conclude that this statement is true. It must be said, however, that when the fish are feeding on the mayfly it is difficult not to find success, the enthusiasm shown by the feeding fish can at times be described as frenzied and all caution can be thrown to the current. This is the time when even those bigger fish, the ones that normally stay well out of the anglers' way, succumb to the allure of the fly, feeding with an enthusiasm equal to that of their smaller brethren. The mayfly is the reason and the catalyst for the famous 'duffers' fortnight' on the Southern English chalkstreams, a time when tradition maintains that even an idiot can catch a trout on the fly. Personally I have found such feasting to be few and far between, but that may have more to do with the waters in which I fish than anything else. On the rivers and streams I usually fish there are regular hatches of mayflies in June on through into July, they are not, unfortunately, huge hatches. Saying that the fish still respond willingly to their charms and there is no better way to fish the mayfly than using the spent fly. The flies are big and the fish take them with crashing rises, gentle sips or by sucking them down. I sat one summer's evening by an old disused mill pool on a small river in the Lothians. The mayfly were laying their eggs and falling regularly upon the surface of the water. As the current carried the dying flies through the pool, loud sucking noises could be heard. On closer examination I found these sucking sounds were accompanied by mini vortexes in the surface water of the pool. Initially I suspected there might be some drainpipe crossing the river causing the effect, the sound was so loud and the sucking so dynamic. The water was quite coloured and impossible to see into making it difficult to be sure what was causing this effect. It soon became clear that each vortex was centred on a spent fly and they were caused by fish, big fish sucking the mayflies down. I was not used to seeing fish of such a size in this particular river and I was determined to see if one could be caught. A large spent mayfly pattern proved this was possible as it was sucked down on its first drift down the pool.

The flies I use during a fall of spinners include classic patterns like Lunn's Particular tied Paraloop style with the wings set in the horizontal position. Setting the wings in this way and using the Paraloop hackle is, in my experience and opinion, more effective than when the traditional hackle is used. In fact just about any size, colour and shape of fly can be tied using hackle tip wings and the Paraloop hackle, these sit low in the water the wings imitating the spent wing more accurately than when tied using a traditional hackle. My favourite spent caenis pattern

was one I picked up from a magazine about ten years ago. White micro thread and one length of fine white polypropylene floss make it one of the simplest and most effective patterns I have used. Poly wings are tied to lie flat on the water, tied using what I call the 'crumpled furled hackle', spent Paraloops and 'ninety degreers', which are flies tied with one wing up and one wing horizontal. My major requirement for all these flies is that they float within the water surface rather than under or on top and float well even after prolonged serious abuse. Personally I cannot be bothered with flies that need constant attention to perform as they are intended to. I also like fly patterns that can be used after a fish has taken the fly. A quick wash in the water to remove the slime and squeezed between tissue or the cotton of my shirt and finally a couple of flicks of the rod being sufficient for it to be in a fit state to get on with its job. There's nothing worse than a lazy fly slacking off from its work after a single take.

To be on the water when a large hatch of duns occurs, no matter if they are tiny caenis, blue winged olives, mayflies or any of the many other species is a magical moment. It reminds me of when I was a young child and the rare occasions our winters were highlighted by a fall of snow. I would stand with my elbows on the window-sill wishing for the grey skies to give up their load of frozen crystals. The part of England where I lived experienced little snow, but when it did my friends and I were filled with excitement, our world becoming a new place, a place where many more things seemed to be possible. Being amongst a rise of duns has a similar effect on me today as the flies cover my jacket, hands, rod and face, slowly casting off their coats to reveal the full vivid beauty of their form. It is also a time of expectation, soon the same flies will return to the water to lay their eggs heralding the spent fly, and perhaps another chapter adding to the legends of the falls.

Part II

I like to think of fly fishing for trout, as being inextricably linked to those vital moments when the natural flies undergo one of the major changes in their life cycle. Those natural flies that begin their life cycle in water and are of interest and of importance to the fly fisher lead a busy and hectic life style. Once the shuck of the nymph or pupa has been cast aside and the adult flies leave the water, within which they have spent the greater portion of their lives, there is little time to complete the life cycle successfully. For the caddis flies and the midges, once they are free of the water, they are immediately in the position to proceed in the search of finding, or attracting a mate. The upwinged flies, however, still have to make that final, all-important transition from the dun to the spinner, before getting down to the serious business of sex and the resulting continuance of the species. Every stage of the life cycle is not only busy, but also fraught with danger and the process will inevitably result in the death of the fly, with luck after the successful completion of mating and laying the eggs. Along the way many flies will fall as food to other creatures without having had the chance of contributing to the gene pool and a speedy death is a fate that is inevitable for even those that finally achieve victory in the mating dance.

There can be no turning back from, or slowing down of this natural process, it is for all intent and purposes a rollercoaster ride. Once the life cycle has been completed, that particular act of the show has come to an end and it is time for the intermission, while we anglers wait for the next thrilling instalment. There is no repeat performance for the spinners and there is never a rehearsal, it is the real thing. The fly emerges from out of the water as the dun, it finds some shelter and awaits the transformation to the spinner. Then the job in hand, the only thing that matters, is to find a mate, complete the sex bit and then lay the eggs. That is it, win or lose the allotted time is

up. I am eternally grateful to many of the upwinged flies, in that they have the decency, generosity and consideration to fall dying upon the water. In doing so they offer me the opportunity to imitate their final moments by applying a few materials to a hook and thereby attempt to persuade a trout that my attempting at imitation of the natural fly is actually the real thing.

The evening and late afternoon are sometimes the most reliable times if the conditions and the unknown factors are right, to expect to see the falls of spent spinners on the water. This is not to say that these are the only times that falls of spinners occur. Even fishing streams with which I am well acquainted, a fall of spinners can catch me unawares, coming unexpectedly seemingly from nowhere. Morning, noon and afternoon can also see falls of spinners on the water. So I find it best to stay open to the possibility of such falls, whenever I am on the water, especially in spring and summer.

There is no question in my own mind that some of the most productive spent spinner fishing can successfully be enjoyed outside of the immediate event of a fall. For instance early in the morning is a good time to cover the shallows of a loch, lake or pond and on a river or stream, eddies, backwaters and soft water by the banks. The fall of spent spinners will have taken place the previous evening or night, but trout will often take the opportunity to mop up the leftovers, shucks and all, in the early morning. This pattern of feeding appears to me to be fairly standard and I have experienced it on just about all the different types of water I fish, everywhere that I fish. The common factor is that to experience and enjoy this particular type of fishing you have to get up early, at the crack of dawn, if you want the very best on offer. I find that when fishing the leftovers I have to be extra careful to ensure that I do not spook any fish. If I do spook a fish it is pretty much guaranteed that I will have to move on and try another spot. As any fish on that section of the water will have stopped feeding and will have moved into safety and it will be some time before they will venture out again. It is the splash of a startled fish and the resulting bow waves that indicate I should have taken more care in my approach.

Setting out early in the morning to fish the left-overs, the fly pattern I intend to use will normally be tied on to my tippet well before I arrive at the water, the pattern having been chosen on the previous evening or night. Getting up early when it is still dark is never that easy for me, especially if I have been fishing late into the night before. Being on the water the previous evening will, however, tell me just what fly pattern to use in the early morning. It is simple, whatever spinners fell the previous evening are the same ones that I try to imitate early in the morning. Besides which, when spent spinner fishing, the choice is fairly easy to make, as many of the different flies appear to look pretty much the same. Keeping the rod set up and ready to go from the night before is the best approach I know. It saves me from having to think too hard in the darkness or half light and to have to make a decision on what fly pattern I should use, especially when it takes just about all my effort to put one foot in front of the other.

Unless the true mayflies (*Ephemera Danica* or *Vulgata*), the yellow may spinners or caenis have been present the previous evening, I will generally use a fly with a blue dun wing and a red brown body. With the few exceptions that are mentioned above, plus a couple of others, this approach seems to cover just about every spinner that I would expect to see on the water. It is in changing the size of the fly pattern that the true art of selection lies. Some of the fly patterns I use will be tied with two tails and some with three, it just depends what was on the water during the previous evening. Some, however, will be tied with a bunch of hackle fibres or hair as a tail and I have never been sure quite how that works from the point of view of the trout, but work it does. As mentioned, one of the exceptions to this is when the real mayflies are on the water. If these big flies have been present during the previous evening, a chunky, light coloured body is the dish of the

morning. Trout love the mayflies and they will spend their time enthusiastically mopping the spinners up, from the surface of the water, long after the actual event of the fall. Even in the early morning the trout will still be on the look out for those dead flies that were missed the previous evening, before settling down for the day.

I find that I ignore spent spinner patterns at my peril when fishing for trout. Fish are attracted to spinners big time and fishing the spinner can be just about as exciting as fishing gets, which is pretty exciting and guaranteed to get the old juices flowing. It is visual fishing, requiring a careful presentation and approach and, when the fish are taking the spent fly, the sport can be fast and furious. These are the times when I want the right fly pattern tied to my tippet at the right time. A fall of spinners may only last a couple of minutes or seem to go on forever, but no matter how long the actual fall lasts, it will more than likely be one of the highlights of the fishing for that day. Often I find just making sure my fly is on the water is more than enough to ensure wonderful fishing, at such times it hardly matters what fly pattern is being used. At other times the fish will be more selective and unless the imitation used sends out the right signals, all casting and careful placing of the fly pattern will be in vain. After the actual fall has ended it is the time to go searching, looking out for the parts of the water that have the tendency to hold the dead or dying flies.

The first method of tying I would like to demonstrate in this section was originally inspired by the tying from the previous section 'Floating Down the River II'. It incorporates an adaptation of the under-thorax method. As explained in the previous section the under-thorax method allows almost complete flexibility when repositioning the hackle fibres. This is achieved by varying the width of the material used to form the under-thorax. I have named this adaptation the 'under- and over-thorax', which pretty much describes exactly what the technique achieves and gives more than a clue to how it is completed.

All fly tying techniques can be applied in more than one way and the under- and over-thorax is no exception. Sitting here by my tying bench, I can think of at least half a dozen ways in which this particular method could be applied and there will undoubtedly be many more. In the following demonstration sequence, the technique involves the under- and over-thorax method being applied at the start of the tying sequence and with the ongoing tying proceeding back along the hook shank, finally to be completed with a whip finish behind the hackle. I like tying fly patterns that do not include a head and I like to complete the whip finish on a fly pattern at various parts of a pattern's anatomy. Completing the whip finish at the end of the body and between the body and the hackle, are two of my preferred places to complete a tying. I see no reason why a fly pattern need always end with a head being formed. Obviously on some patterns that is essential, but certainly not on all fly patterns. The following is a case in point and throughout this book there will be other examples of the fly pattern being completed with a whip finish at some other point besides the head.

The fly pattern I have chosen to demonstrate the over- and under-thorax is the claret spinner. Like most spinners the natural fly has a generally red brown body but with a definite impression of claret colouring. I regularly see this fly on some of the small streams I fish on, but I cannot recall having ever seen it on lakes or lochs. I am, however, reliably informed that it is actually more common on lakes and ponds than rivers and streams. My not having seen this fly on still water would appear to be a case of wrong time, wrong place. Then again I tend to fish rivers and streams mostly, so it is probably not surprising that the claret spinner has alluded me on still waters.

The claret spinner, like most spinners, is a handsome and elegant creature that can be imitated by using a fairly large fly pattern. In the areas where I fish I normally expect to see them around July.

Tying the Claret Spinner using the Over- and Under-Thorax

Materials

Hook	Size 14 – Dry fly partridge Captain Hamilton or similar.
Hackle	Light blue dun cock.
Body	Mixed claret and light brown polypropylene dubbing.
Rib	Dark brown thread waxed.
Tail	Three micro fibbets.
Over- and under-thorax	Light brown polypropylene floss.
Thread	Of personal choice 8/0.

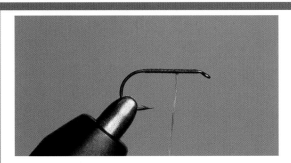

Photograph 1 Insert the hook into the vice and test for soundness. Attach the well waxed thread and wind along the hook shank, using flat turns of thread, to the start of the hook bend. Then return the thread to two thirds of the way back along the hook shank towards the hook eye. (It is vital to use flat thread when laying a foundation like this as it adds next to no bulk on to the fly pattern, laying such a foundation greatly strengthens the completed fly.)

Photograph 2 Tie in the light blue dun hackle at the point where the thread has come to rest (two thirds of the way along the hook shank from the start of the hook bend). Ensure that the good side of the hackle is facing you and that it is pointing over the rear of the hook. Cut off the excess hackle stalk and return the thread to the point where the hackle is first tied in.

Photograph 3 Take a 4 in (10 cm) length of the 'over- and under-thorax' floss and feed the centre of the floss over the hook eye and along the shank to where the hackle has been tied in and where the thread has come to rest. The floss should be directly above and below the hook shank.

Photograph 4 Using the first finger and thumb squeeze the floss onto the top and underside of the hook shank, with the loose ends extending over the hook eye. Now tie in the floss by winding the thread towards the hook eye, tying in the floss directly on to the underside and top of the hook shank as you go. Tie in right up to the hook eye, do not leave any space for a head. Leave the thread directly behind the hook eye.

Photograph 5 Wind on the hackle to behind the hook eye and tie in at that position, on the underside of the hook shank. Half a dozen tight turns of thread will be sufficient to secure the hackle.

Photograph 6 Now cut off the excess hackle stalk. Make a couple more turns of thread to ensure all is secured.

Photograph 7 Carefully wind the tying thread through the hackle, taking great care not to trap any hackle fibres as you do so. This will bring the thread directly to the other side of the hackle.

Photograph 8 Now using the thumb and first finger of both hands, compress the hackle at either side of the hook shank, by squeezing the hackle. Make sure that approximately the same numbers of hackle fibres are placed at either side of the hook shank. (See insert diagram.) Pull the 'over- and under' floss directly over and under the hackle and tie in behind the hackle. Take care not to trap any hackle fibres as you do so. If you find doing both the top and underside at the same time difficult, then complete the 'over' floss first and tie in using just two or three turns of thread, then follow with the 'under' floss. When both are in position tie them both in fully.

Photograph 9 Cut off the excess floss and take the three micro fibbets used for the tail. Start tying these in on the top of the hook shank, at the point where the floss has been cut off. Wind the thread to the start of the hook bend. Make sure the fibbets stay on the topside of the shank. Now it is time to separate the three tails so they imitate those on the natural insect. To do this I like to use the 'loop of thread under the hook bend' method. To complete this technique, see the diagram. After the loop of thread has been pulled up separating the tails, tie it in on the top of the hook shank. Do not return the thread to the hook bend.

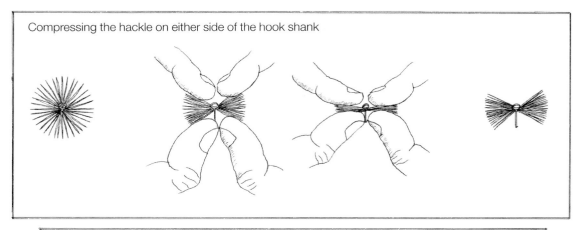

Compressing the hackle on either side of the hook shank

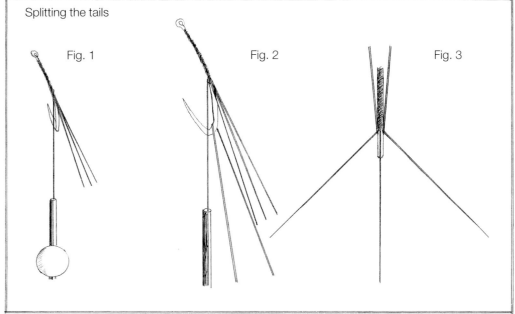

Splitting the tails

Fig. 1

Fig. 2

Fig. 3

Fig. 1 Tie in tails on top of hook shank   Fig. 2 Take thin thread under the hook bend.

Fig. 3 Pull thread up between tails and tie in.

Photograph 10 Wind the thread up to the hackle.

Photograph 11 Now offer the thread rib to the tying thread using the 'loop over the thread' method, moving it up the tying thread and tying in on the underside of the hook shank. Complete the tying in of the rib by winding the tying thread back to the start of the hook bend. If required cut off any excess material.

Photograph 12 Dub the tying thread using the mixed claret and light brown polypropylene dubbing. Now wind along the hook shank forming a shaped body extending all the way to the hackle. Wind on the thread rib and tie in between the hackle and the body. Cut off the excess rib material.

Photograph 13 Finish the fly pattern by making a very tight whip finish in between the end of the body and the hackle. Cut off the tying thread and the fly pattern is complete.

Photograph 14 The completed fly.

This method of producing the spent wing on a fly pattern is very simple and extremely effective. By using polypropylene floss the water absorption in the thorax area of the fly pattern is minimized. This allows the fly to be usable for longer than a pattern that allows the materials to absorb water.

Using Pre-Formed Detached Hackles When Tying Spent Spinners

The pre-formed detached hackles (the Perfect Furled and the Crumpled Furled Hackles) described in the chapter 'Air's Apparent' are ideal when tying spent winged flies. Like the emerging flies, the spent winged fly pattern is best presented to the trout low on, or in the surface of the water. This accurately imitates the natural fly as it dies or is actually dead. The traditional wound hackle lifts the front of a fly pattern off the water, a position that can be used to imitate the emerging fly or the spinner as it lands on the water during the process of laying the eggs. An example of this would be the Greendrake, the spinner of the mayfly, which can frequently land on the water during the process of laying the eggs. But it does not imitate accurately the natural spent spinner in its last moments of life. Both the Perfect Furled and the Crumpled Furled hackles can be used when tying spent winged patterns.

The next fly described and used to demonstrate the inclusion of a detached hackle when tying spent winged spinners, is the Spent Gnat, the real mayfly (*Ephemera Danica* or *Vulgata*) spinner. More particularly the female, which dies immediately after the eggs have been laid. The female is far bigger than the male. There are, I believe, only three species of true mayfly in the UK and of these *Ephemera Danica* is the most commonly found. The natural fly is to be found in most streams and rivers, where the water flow is fairly fast and at times in lakes and ponds, which is something I cannot remember ever having seen, but would love to sometime. A rise of mayflies on some of the small still waters I fish would be a sight worth seeing. The female of the species is quite a lot larger than the male and can have a body length of up to 2 cm and I suspect that some I have seen have exceeded that in length, although I wasn't measuring flies at such times. For me one of the most extraordinary features of the mayfly is the length of the tail, these can exceed twice the length of the body. It is amazing that during the transition from the dun to the spinner the length of the tail is increased considerably.

I like to tie the tails on my own mayfly spinner patterns long, not only do they imitate the natural fly more accurately, but they look better and appeal to my personal sense of aesthetics. I am also convinced that over the years the fly patterns I have used that incorporate a long tail, have given me more consistent success when actually fishing, than those fly patterns I have used with the more conventional length of tail.

The body of the natural fly is a creamy colour, there are times when I think this is best described as ivory, but on the whole I would say cream. The colour seems to vary slightly on different waters, but from the point of view of imitation, cream is sufficient. There is translucence to the body, which is hard to describe, but it gives the body a slight sheen.

Due to the size of the natural fly, imitation patterns are often tied on relatively large hooks, up to a size 8 not being unusual and I have even seen patterns tied on size 6 hooks. I am afraid I shy away from wielding such weapons when fishing for trout with a dry fly, preferring to tie my own patterns on hooks sized 10 at the very largest and usually size 12 and 14. Imitating the mayfly lends itself to the use of an extended body, allowing a larger fly pattern to be tied yet using a smaller hook, many of my own patterns incorporate an extended body.

The following pattern does not use an extended body and as such a size 10 or 12 hook is required to provide the necessary size of fly pattern required to imitate the size of the natural fly. The wings are of a bluish tinge in the natural fly.

Tying the Mayfly Spent Spinner using a Detached Pre-formed Hackle

Materials Required

Hook	Dry fly up or down eye partridge Captain Hamilton size 10 or 12.
Hackle	Light blue dun pre-formed detached Perfect Furled hackle.
Body	Cream polypropylene floss.
Tail	Micro-fibbetts.
Wing	Polypropylene floss blue dun or light grey.
Thorax	Light brown polypropylene dubbing.
Rib	Provided by the tying thread.
Thread	Of personal choice but suggest brown or yellow waxed using cobblers' wax.

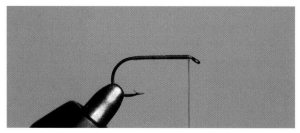

Photograph 1 Place the hook in the jaws of the vice and test for soundness. Attach the waxed tying thread and wind using flat tight wound thread to the start of the hook bend. Then wind the thread back to directly behind the eye of the hook. This lays a firm foundation for the other materials.

Photograph 2 Take the pre-formed detached Perfect Furled hackle and tie in directly behind the eye of the hook, with the main body of the hackle extending over the hook eye.

Photograph 3 Take the tying thread to the centre of the thorax position on the hook shank and tie in the wing floss cross-wise to the hook shank using figure of eight turns of thread. Cut the wing floss to the right length at this time to ensure that the floss does not get in the way of applying the other materials. Return the thread to behind the hook eye at the point where the hackle has been first tied in.

Photograph 4 Dub the thread with the thorax dubbing and wind over the thorax area, using figure of eight turns around the floss wings. Build up a shaped thorax, it should be wider in the centre, where the wing is tied in, than at either end of the thorax.

Photograph 5 Pull the detached hackle over the top of the thorax and tie in directly behind the thorax. If you brush the hackle fibres, using a dubbing brush, away from the part of the hackle to be tied in, it will minimize the number of hackle fibres caught up when tying in the hackle. Expect to tie in a few hackle fibres so don't be over concerned if a few fibres are tied in, as it will not make any difference to the final pattern.

Photograph 6 Cut off the remaining detached hackle and place the hackle to the side ready for tying the next fly. Use a spare pair of hackle pliers to lock the loose end of the detached hackle (as shown on page 33). Complete the tying in of the end of the detached hackle and wind on the thread to the start of the hook bend. Take three long micro-fibbetts and tie in on to the top of the hook shank. Return the thread to the start of the hook bend and split the tails using the 'thread under the hook bend' method (as described on page 95). When completed return the thread back to the hackle.

Photograph 7 Attach the cream body floss using the 'loop over the thread' method, the short end of the floss should be facing over the length of the hook shank. Tie in the body floss using just three or four turns of thread. Now unwind any twist in the body floss to allow it to be wound flat and wind to the hook bend tying in the other end of the floss as you go. Now wind the floss back to the hackle, forming a tapered shaped body. Tie in the body floss right up behind the hackle and cut off the excess body floss.

This next procedure is very important. Place two locking loops of thread directly between the hackle and the body, these locking turns must be very tight. Locking turns can be either half hitches or two turns of whipping as per a whip finish.

Photograph 8 Wax the 1 in (25 mm) of the tying thread extending from the fly body, using dark cobbler's wax. Wind the waxed tying thread back along the body towards the tail, forming the rib. At the point where the body ends and the tails start, make three turns of thread and complete with a whip finish. Then cut off the tying thread. A touch of varnish or glue at the point the whip finish is made will bond the thread if you lack confidence in the whip finish holding. Cut the wings to the right length.

Photograph 9 The completed fly.

That completes the tying of the Mayfly Spent Spinner using the Perfect Furled Hackle. It is what I consider quite a neat tying and I personally really like the use of the tying thread as a rib and tying off at bend of the hook, it makes for an interesting tying sequence. As mentioned in the tying sequence, you can, if you like, apply a tiny drop of waterproof glue or a touch of varnish to the final whipping. Both give an impression of translucence at the start of the tail and more importantly completely lock the whip finish. I often don't bother to do this on my own fly patterns and very rarely, if ever, do I have a fly pattern come apart at the seams and joints.

The following is one of the simplest tyings I have ever used for a fly pattern, other than perhaps certain midge larvae patterns. It is a 'must have' pattern for my fly box during certain times of the year especially mid summer, it is a pattern I feel confident to use when the caenis are on the water. The pattern is one that I came across a number of years ago and I have been using it with some notable successes since that time. It is not an original tying and I was either shown it by another tyer or saw it described in a magazine. No matter where I came across it, the tying is simple and very effective and I have enjoyed tying and fishing with it for many years. This pattern has been responsible for all my largest fish when fishing the caenis and, without doubt, the greatest number of fish I have caught whilst using a fly pattern designed to imitate the caenis spinner. These days it is odds on that, during a rise and fall of the caenis fly, this will be the pattern I have tied on my leader.

In the case of the caenis the transition from the nymph to the dun, from the dun to the spinner and from the spinner to laying the eggs and dying, can all take place within just a few minutes. In fact this is one of the only times that I can think of where the spinner can have returned to the water to lay the eggs and die, while the dun is still rising up from the water. It is for this reason that I refer to the caenis on the water as a 'rise and fall' as both events can occur simultaneously. The first thing that indicates that a caenis rise is on the go, is seeing a few dun changing to the spinner on my hands and clothing. Within a few minutes the air and just about everything else can be filled and covered with the hatched flies. These hatches can be very localized almost to the point where you can pin point the few square yards of water from which the duns are emerging.

Finding myself amidst a rise and fall of caenis flies, during a day fishing, is like winning a prize in a lottery, a lottery that I had forgotten I had a ticket for. It is a special treat and will undoubtedly be one of the memorable highlights of any day's fishing. A highlight that will last for just a brief length of time, but during that time the opportunity to take fish increases considerably, especially if the day has been short on action. Fishing during a rise and fall of caenis is fantastic fun, but ensuring that I have the right patterns in the fly box is essential. If I do not have the right fly with me, all the fun can be missed.

When fishing such a rise, the time is spent covering rising fish and attempting to intercept those fish cruising the surface of the water with complete abandon, sipping in the spent flies as they go. The greatest problem lies in persuading the fish to take your fly pattern as opposed to the thousands of natural flies that can cover the water. It is for this reason that the caenis has been nicknamed the 'Anglers' Curse' or the 'White Curse'. Personally, as mentioned in part one of this chapter, I would prefer to call them the 'Anglers' Blessing' or the 'White Blessing', as I have enjoyed such good sport when fishing during a rise and fall. The following pattern is now the only one I use when the caenis are on the water, I simply don't bother with any other imitation as I have seen none that I believe are better and that have proved so effective.

Tying the Simple Caenis

Materials Required

Hook	Dry fly up-eye, size 18 to 24. Partridge Captain Hamilton or similar.
Body	Fine white polypropylene floss.
Wing	As the body formed from same length of floss.
Thread	White very fine depending on size of hook used 8/0 to 17/0.

Tying the simple caenis

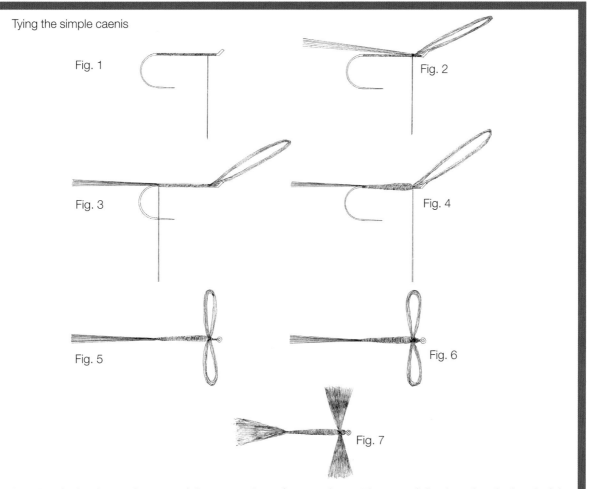

Fig. 1
Fig. 2
Fig. 3
Fig. 4
Fig. 5
Fig. 6
Fig. 7

Fig. 1 Fix the hook into the jaws of the vice and test for soundness. Then wind the thread to the bend of the hook using flat thread. Continuing to wind the thread flat, take the thread back along the hook shank to a position just behind the hook eye, where the head will be formed.

Fig. 2 Form a loop with the fine white polypropylene floss and tie in behind the hook eye, with the loose end of the loop extending back over the hook shank and beyond the hook bend.

Fig. 3 Wind the tying thread, using flat thread, down the hook shank to the start of the hook bend, tying in the floss on to the top of the hook shank as you go.

Fig. 4 Wind the thread back along the hook shank and form a slightly tapered body.

Fig. 5 Take the centre of the loop end of the floss (the hook eye end) and bring it backwards to where the body starts, making sure that there are equal lengths of floss either side of the hook shank. Now using figure of eight turns of tying thread, tie in the floss loop so that it is positioned crossways to the hook shank. This will form the wing.

Fig. 6 Form a small head behind the hook eye with the tying thread. Complete a whip finish and cut off the tying thread.

Fig. 7 The final touch is to prune the wings and tail to length. On my own tyings I tend to cut away a few of the tail fibres to make the tail less bulky, but that is just a matter of personal preference and is optional.

As I mentioned before this is a very simple tying, but do not let this simplicity fool you, it is without doubt the most effective caenis pattern that I have ever used, on both stream, rivers and still waters. Fished tied to a fine tippet and placed in the path of a feeding trout or allowed to be carried by the current into the path of a regular riser, the pattern takes, at least for me, many more than its fair share of fish. I have received a few comments over the years that the pattern does not sport a darker patch on the body or thorax, as per the natural insect. To be honest I couldn't care less, the pattern gives an excellent impression of the natural spent fly on the water and is taken readily by the trout, which seem to share my view regarding a dark patch.

Whenever a fall of spent flies takes place, the normally accepted way to deal with the situation is to use a fly pattern that imitates such flies on the surface of the water and in most cases this is the ideal and most effective way to present the fly pattern. There are times, however, when fishing in fast flowing and fairly turbulent water that the floating fly is not particularly ideal for more than one reason. Firstly, the turbulence can be such that very few fly patterns are capable of floating successfully, at least not in the way intended when they were designed. Even those made from foam and other buoyant materials succumb to the water's embrace. Secondly, it is very difficult to stay in touch with, or to see the fly pattern in such water conditions and as such hooking a fish is more a matter of luck than design, although it has to be said many fish oblige by hooking themselves.

This being the case, when fishing the spent fly in very heavy water, I prefer to use a fly pattern designed to be fished in such water, rather than a floating fly pattern. Let's face it, a spent fly caught up in such water will, more often than not, be engulfed and dragged downward. The fly pattern described in the following section is intended to imitate the natural spent fly caught up in heavy fast water. In such conditions I usually prefer to use a fly that is intended to sink and with a little more weight in its make up than a pattern that is designed to float. The heavier fly is easier to stay in contact with and from an imitation point of view the fly pattern very accu-

rately imitates the natural fly caught in the tumult of water. Fishing this type of fly pattern allows not only the faster water to be covered, but also the softer pocket water and probable fish holding lies outside of the main current. Takes by fish are generally of the fairly hard to the real rod bending variety. There is very little subtlety in such takes and the fish are usually hooked without striking, a simple lift of the rod being all that is required to set the hook.

The next fly pattern has been designed to imitate the spent spinner engulfed in fast water. Like most wet flies there is always the possibility that this pattern will be taken by the fish as some other insect than that intended, for example a nymph. If the pattern is fished during a fall of spinners, however, the chances are that it will be taken as just another dead spinner lost to the water. The hackle used is a hen hackle, long and soft in the hackle fibres. The use of this type of hackle is to give an impression of the tails, legs and wings of the natural fly flailing in the water. The pattern incorporates a small gold bead at the head. I am not always keen on using gold beads when fishing slower waters, but in the faster waters they can be excellent, both as an additional weight and as a possible attractor. The hackle is palmered, but not in the normal way. Instead I like to minimize the amount of hackle by making fewer turns of hackle around the body of the fly, maximum of three turns is all that

is required. This is an old technique, used in bygone years on the River Tweed, of hackling a fly and one that should, at least in my opinion, be used more often. I have not come across any modern flies other than my own tyings that incorporate a palmered hackle with such few turns and I liken them to almost elongated spider patterns.

An interesting side-point is the source of the word palmered, I am sure many readers will be acquainted with its origins, but for those readers who are not, please allow me to explain. In bygone days in England an alternative name for a pilgrim was a palmer. The word related to the wanderings of these holy aspirants. In the early days of fly tying a common fly pattern was based on a hairy caterpillar, which hairy caterpillar it represented I have no idea, but safe to say this was a popular imitation at least according to the available literature from the time. The hackle wound generously around the hook gave a good impression of the hairy caterpillar. Anyone who has seen big hairy caterpillars will acknowledge that they appear to wander wherever they fancy. The early tyers equated these wanderings of the caterpillar to that of a pilgrim or palmer, hence the words palmering and palmered. The imitating of a large caterpillar is not something I have found to be particularly useful and I suspect that the application of the hackle to a hook in the style of palmering came before the association with the caterpillar, with some early enterprising fly tyer looking around the insect world to see what creature most closely resembled the palmered fly.

Getting back to the following tying. The rib is there to add a little extra weight and as such a medium to heavy copper wire, depending on the size of the pattern is added. The rib has another important function besides adding weight to the pattern and that is to protect the palmered hackle from the teeth of a taking fish. Unlike most trout flies, however, in the case of this pattern the rib is wound around the body of the pattern prior to the hackle being wound. When the hackle is wound around the body it is wound directly behind the rib, with the intention that any teeth pulling along the body of the fly pattern will hit the metal rib and not the hackle stalk. The

technique of using a hackle and a rib in this way harks back to the tying of traditional salmon flies and is a very effective method by which the hackle can be protected.

The hackle is doubled. Doubling the hackle, at least in my opinion, can make the difference between a fly pattern tied well and a pattern of the run-of–the-mill variety. The doubling method shown to me a number of years ago by Ally Gowans of Ally's Shrimp fame and described in the chapter entitled 'Air's Apparent II'. It is the easiest and most efficient that I have ever used and these days I don't bother myself with any other doubling technique. A good tip when using this method is to double the hackle or hackles prior to tying the actual fly, having them ready and waiting for when you need them. The benefit of this is that, if you break a hackle when doubling, then you don't have to retie the whole fly pattern as is often the case when the hackle is tied in place on the actual fly pattern. Saying that, with a little practice there is little chance that the hackle will break, although if the technique is new to you, there is a distinct possibility of doing so.

Tying the Drowned Spent Spinner with Sparse Palmered Hackle

This particular pattern is non-specific in what fly it imitates rather it is a general spent spinner pattern. Changing the hook size and perhaps the colours of the materials and just about any spent spinner can be imitated. As previously explained the pattern is designed for use in fast turbulent water and it is particularly effective when picking out the pockets of softer holding water amidst a heavy flow.

Materials Required

Hook	Medium or heavy weight traditional wet fly hook.
Hackle	Medium blue dun hen or cock hackle with long feather fibres.
Body	Red and brown dubbing mixed.
Rib	Medium to heavy weight copper wire.
Head	Gold bead or, if preferred, a tungsten bead.
Thread	Of own choice 8/0.

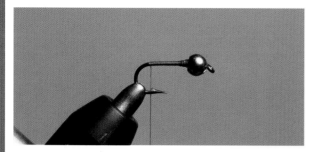

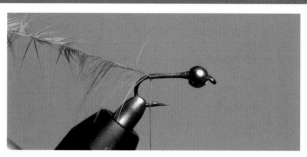

Photograph 1 Place the gold or tungsten bead on to the hook shank, by feeding it around the hook bend. If the size of the hole through the bead varies from one side to the other then feed the bead on to the shank leading with the smaller hole. Place the hook in the jaws of the vice and then test for soundness. Move the bead so that it is up against the hook eye and attach the waxed thread to the hook shank immediately behind the bead. Make just a few turns of thread behind the bead, but not enough to secure it in place, just enough turns of thread to discourage it from wandering too easily back along the hook shank. Now wind the tying thread using flat turns of thread to the start of the hook bend.

Photograph 2 Tie in the doubled hackle by the tip, at the start of the hook bend. If you wish you can attach the hackle and double it when tied to the hook (see page 21). Return the thread back to the start of the hook bend.

Photograph 3 Tie in the copper wire to use as the rib on to the underside of the hook shank, using the 'loop over the thread' method. Then return the thread to the start of the hook bend. Now dub the thread with the mixed red and brown body dubbing.

Photograph 4 Wind on the body dubbing to form a shaped body, thinner at the tail end than the gold bead end. The body should extend all the way to the gold or tungsten bead.

Photograph 5 Wind on the copper wire as a rib, taking care not to exceed three turns around the whole length of the body. Tie in the rib on the underside of the hook shank and directly behind the bead head. Break off the excess copper wire.

Photograph 6 Holding the stalk of the doubled hackle wind it carefully around the body, butting up the stalk directly behind the previously wound copper wire rib. The fibres of the hackle should be leaning slightly over to the rear of the hook. Wind the hackle up to the bead head and tie in on the underside of the hook shank. Cut off the excess hackle.

Photograph 7 Lightly dub a very small length of the tying thread with the body dubbing and wind on directly behind the bead head. Complete with a whip finish between the body and the bead head, the whip finish should be very tight so that the thread is lost between the body and bead.

Photograph 8 The completed fly.

Please note that the bead head should have been locked into place automatically as the materials were added. If for some reason it is still loose, then make a few extra turns of the dubbed thread prior to completing the whip finish. This will be more than sufficient to lock the bead into place.

I like tying fly patterns using the palmered hackle in this way and like most techniques it can be applied to any number of different patterns. It is also an alternative method for tying traditional spider patterns. Usually in a spider pattern a sparse hackle is wound directly behind where a small head will be formed. Using the method described above the hackle starts at the tail and one, two or three complete winds are made around the body, prior to tying the hackle in behind the hook eye. Personally I usually make one complete wind of the hackle directly behind where the head will be formed prior to tying in, but that is just something I like to do because it looks good, rather than having any particularly practical purpose.

The fly tyer's art more often than not attempts to produce fly patterns where everything is perfect, the wings either upright as on the dun imitations or perfectly at ninety degrees to the hook shank on spent winged patterns. In nature this is not always the case and the spent fly is anything but a perfect cross shape in the water. Bent, twisted or broken wings and lost tails are very common and so long as the size and basic shape of the fly pattern imitate the natural fly fairly accurately, these imperfect appendages can be added to great effect.

The following pattern takes this into consideration proving a simple tying with a twist. Such patterns can be fished long after the actual fall of spinners has taken place and still be most effective.

I call the following pattern the Vagabond as it is scruffy and not everything is in place as it should be. One wing sits as normal while the other is bent backwards, one tail is full length the other broken off, all in all it is a pretty poor example of the art of tying a fly pattern. It does, however, imitate fairly accurately many of the spent spinners after the force of the water has pummelled and battered them.

The actual tying is very sparse and as such a foam underbody and thorax has been incorporated to ensure the fly pattern will float successfully even in fairly fast water.

Tying the Vagabond

Materials Required

Hook Lightweight dry fly. Partridge Captain Hamilton or similar.

Body Rusty brown polypropylene dubbing.

Underbody Pre-formed polystyrene underbody extending to cover the thorax of the fly as well as the body.

Tail Two micro-fibbetts blue dun.

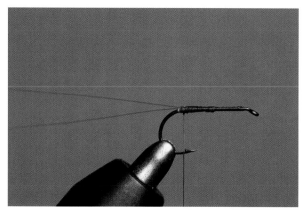

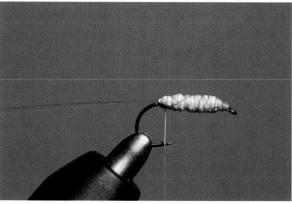

Photograph 1 Fix the hook in the jaws of the vice and again test for soundness. Attach and wind the waxed tying thread, using flat turns of thread, to the start of the hook bend. Tie in the two micro-fibbets on to the top of the hook shank and using the 'loop of thread under the hook bend' method split the two tails. Return the thread to the start of the hook bend.

Photograph 2 Take the pre-formed polystyrene underbody and slip it over the hook shank. The under body should extend from the point where the tails are tied in to very close to the hook eye, but ensuring enough space is left behind the eye to tie in all the required materials and form a small head. Wind the tying thread around the underbody using wide, almost random, turns. Make sure the underbody is tied in tightly at each end. Return the thread to the start of the hook bend.

Photograph 3 Dub the tying thread with the rusty brown polypropylene dubbing. The dubbing should be thorough, but not over bulky. Wind on the dubbed thread around the underbody in touching but not overlapping turns. The turns of dubbed thread can be made fairly tight around the underbody, as the polystyrene is capable of maintaining its shape, up to a certain extent, when under pressure. Do not crush the underbody. Wind the dubbed thread to a position just beyond a point two thirds of the way along the hook shank, this is the start of the thorax section. A couple of turns of tight thread can be made at this point, as they will help emphasize the difference between the thorax and the body. Now wind the dubbing free thread to the centre of the thorax section and tie in the cock hackle tip wings. To tie in the hackle tips on either side of the thorax, they first must be prepared. Then with the hackle tips facing back over the rear of the hook, wind the thread back to the dubbed body leaving plenty of striped hackle stalk free of the tying thread.

| **Wing** | Two cock hackle tips light blue dun. | **Thread** | Own choice 8/0. |
| **Thorax** | Brown polypropylene dubbing mixed with a little pearl Lite Brite. | | |

Photograph 4 Pull the hackle tips forward so they extend over the hook eye and wind the thread back to the centre of the thorax tying in the hackle stalks as you go. Tying in the hackle tips this way locks the hackle stalks and stops them from pulling out. This is not usually necessary but when tying over the polystyrene underbody, this method helps to secure the hackle tips when the thread cannot be wound very tight. Now wind the thread back to the start of the thorax.

Photograph 5 Dub the tying thread with the thorax dubbing having thoroughly mixed the polypropylene dubbing with a little pearl Lite Brite. Start to wind the dubbed thread over the thorax. The wings can be set in whatever position you want, but they should not be symmetrical. When the wings are set in position, continue the dubbed thread to behind the hook eye.

Photograph 6 Form a small head and complete the pattern with a whip finish, cut off the thread. Use a dubbing brush to pull out the dubbing fibres on both the upper and lower sides of the thorax and finally, snip the top off one of the micro-fibbet tails.

Photograph 7 The completed fly.

The River Tweed winding through the Scottish Borders. A great salmon, sea trout, brown trout and grayling river.

This pattern is really at its best in still or relatively slow moving water. It is a 'cast out and leave' pattern on still water, one used to cover cruising trout searching for food. On flowing water it is best when used where fish are picking up spent spinners downstream of where they have fallen on the water. It is a pattern that can sometimes get a result when nothing else seems to work. It also becomes more effective the more worn and tatty the pattern becomes, so don't worry if it starts to resemble something the dog tied on a bad day, ideally that's the look you want. It is certainly not a pattern to win any prizes for fly tying, but it will more than make up for that by the prizes taken on the water.

I hope that the methods used to create the fly patterns described in this section of the book will be of use to readers. The techniques are, for the greater part, the most important aspect of this book and I hope that they will be applied to many other tyings besides those described.

In the Fly Gallery there is a selection of patterns tied using the techniques described in this section.

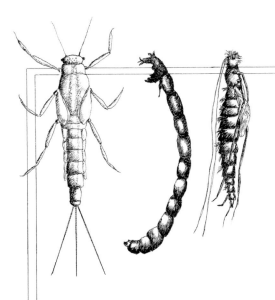

4. NYMPHS, LARVAE
AND PUPAE

Part I

In 1961 I became aware of a small pond close to my home. It was a tiny piece of water, but the surrounding bushes could be seen clearly from my bedroom window and had held a fascination for me since I was tall enough to peer over the window-sill, along the road and out over the fields. I was four years old and was now considered old enough to explore the slightly wider world a little further from my home. Accompanied by my friends Peter and David, who were both a little older than me, I climbed over the fence, which separated the end of the road on which our house stood and the newly mown field, bringing me face to face with the water those bushes surrounded. The walk from the fence to the pond was no more than a hundred yards, but for a four-year-old let off the leash, it was journey of near epic proportions. It would be no exaggeration to say that the journey's end was a paradise.

The small pond never really had a name it was only ever referred to as 'the pond' and whilst in later years I became aware of the many ponds and pits which dotted the local area, all of which had a name, the pond simply remained 'the pond'. What it lacked in name it made up for in mythology. According to local legend and gossip the pond was bottomless and many young boys had been lost within its weed locked waters. We didn't know of anyone who had been lost, so we never really thought about these warning stories and only ever repeated them to impress some new acquaintance with our bravery in playing upon its banks. I think, even at that early age, we were instinctively wise to the deviousness of the world and how such stories were told to keep curiosity at bay. Whoever came up with the ruse, however, did not understand small boys, for whom such tales are an additional attraction beyond those which are readily apparent. Another example of this would be the empty buildings near the top street in the main part of town. Local legend had these as being haunted. We had a lot of fun in those old rooms even though one of them contained a couple of old coffins, which to a young mind was at least a step towards or an indication of a possible haunting. Here also the tale was a major and additional attraction. In the case of the pond we pointed out that it couldn't be bottomless because if we took a long wooden pole we could easily touch the bottom. The story was then changed to the mud being bottomless and any young boy falling in would be sucked under as sure as night turns to day.

Over the following years my friends and I all fell in the pond at one time and in one way or another and while the mud smelt very strongly, it never strove to suck any of us down. The smell of that mud, when encountered elsewhere in later years, would and still does evoke such feelings of excitement and pleasure in me that I am transported back to those early days of discovery, play and adventure. No other fragrance or pleasing vapour could ever seek to equal the power of that rank scent, which clung for weeks to my boots and clothing. So we continued to play around the banks and upon the water, the attractions far exceeding any make believe fear. We built dens amongst the bushes, rafts to float on its waters and would step gingerly out along the branches that extended far over the pond. In the days when collecting birds' eggs was a legal and normal way of life for a country youngster, we raided nests built in the bushes and reeds to add to our growing collections of blown eggs. These were kept in cardboard boxes, with each egg wrapped up for protection in cotton wool and stored in the wooden garden sheds we all had in our back gardens.

The pond held no fish, this was something we were sure of, no fish that is except a multitude of sticklebacks. Sticklebacks, however, were not our idea of real fish, being common, easy to catch

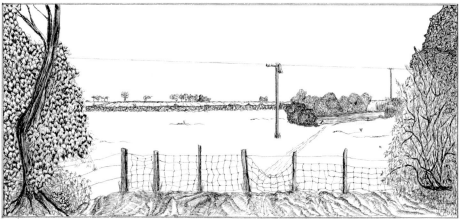
The pond

and above all small. The presence of the stickle-backs, however, indicated that fish could live in the water and we were soon to discover just how true this was.

At the far side of town there was a pond we often fished. Named the Bexton Carp Pit it held massive numbers of crucian carp. Bexton was an area of housing development and the plans included filling in the Carp Pit. There were no plans to net the fish and transfer them elsewhere, the pond was to be drained and bulldozed over to make way for another three bedroomed semi-detached house. To our way of thinking this seemed a crime, and it is unlikely that such a blatant destruction of fish life could take place today, without a substantial protest from fishers. In the nineteen sixties things were different and there was no official objection to the loss of the pond. Fathers and friends were all drafted in to help catch as many fish as possible and transfer them, using any available container that held water, to ponds we knew held few, if any, fish. The main pond for stocking was to be the pond in the field at the end of our road.

Before we could attempt any successful stocking of the pond it was necessary to remove much of the clogging and strangling weed, which choked it. It was in doing this that I first became closely familiar with many of the creatures living under the surface and amongst the weeds and mud.

We dragged the waters with homemade rakes made from lengths of wood through which eight inch nails were hammered, the whole thing weighted with lead and then tied to a rope. These rakes brought a wealth of pond life to my attention in a way that I had never experienced before. This was nature up close and personal, what would be described today as in your face. Each time the rakes were dragged back the gathered weed would reveal a thriving metropolis of creatures. As the weed was dislodged from the nails all manner of animals would make their presence known. Newts and frogs were my first interest, but slowly I became aware of the many different insects, red blood worms, kicking shrimps, cased caddis and others, which to me were an assortment of creepy crawlies. Some of them would make my spine shiver and I would panic if they happened to crawl on my hand and any further investigation of them was made using a stick and the 'poke it and see' method of inspection. Dragging the pond made me, for the first time in my few years, truly aware of the richness of life that even a comparatively small area of water could hold. Nymphs, larvae and pupa were all revealed to me, although it is true to say that at the time I had no idea of the intricacy and wonder of their life cycles, or indeed what many of these creatures were or what they would become. Keeping creatures in old jam jars allowed me to view how they lived, many caddis flies pupated and left the jars without me ever knowing, leaving me with a case made from leaves or sticks and a question about where they had gone. Some mornings there would be three nymphs in a jar and the following day only one. At the time I thought they had been eaten, but it is now clear that they emerged and took to flight leaving the shelter of the jam jars, completing their life cycle far beyond glass confines.

In later years when my fishing had turned mainly to that of using the fly I gradually became aware of how these water creatures related to the flies I now endeavoured to imitate when fishing. How those wiggling red worms would change into pupae, to emerge as winged midges. How the constructed tubes found on all the waters I fished, contained the larvae of the caddis fly. How the large, fierce looking insects seen crawling through the weed stems transformed into the damselfly and how the assortment of nymphs of different shapes and sizes provided the source of the mayflies, olives and the many other upwinged flies seen dancing above the water of a summer's evening. Fly fishing gave me the reason and the opportunity for all this to be revealed.

In my early years of fly fishing the only flies I had and used were dry flies, not through any misguided purism, but simply because I knew of nothing else. I knew no other fly fishers and so there was no one to tell me otherwise and my reading matter was severely limited. Wet flies, nymphs, larvae and pupa patterns played no part at all in my conception of fly fishing. It would be true to say that over half of my fishing life was spent in this way. For me fly fishing was literally that, fishing with a fly imitation on the surface, it never occurred to me that it could be anything else. It would also be true to say that my enjoyment was in no way limited by my ignorance, rather the opposite, the simplicity of it all lent an enjoyment I have found in few things. So called progress, it would appear, cannot be denied and those information-free days of bliss are long gone to be replaced by a greater depth of understanding. That is not to say the joy of fishing is in any way impaired, because it is not. The pleasure of fly fishing these days is tempered with knowledge and an understanding of what fly I am using and why.

One thing that confused me for sometime was the difference between a nymph and a larva. This confusion was increased when fly patterns with names like 'Hatching Midge Nymph' and 'Mayfly Larva' came to my notice. In the end the dust of confusion settled and the simple explanation became clear. Those flies, which complete two parts of their life cycle in aquatic forms, for example the midges and the caddisflies, on hatching from the egg become larvae, going on to transform into the pupa. Whilst those flies with a single part of their life cycle in an aquatic form, after hatching from the egg, become nymphs, examples of these are the mayflies and damselflies. Fly patterns given names like 'Hatching Midge Nymph' and 'Mayfly larva' are inaccurate descriptions of this natural process, only serving to confuse anyone willing and wishing to learn, with 'Hatching Midge Pupa' and 'Mayfly Nymph' being the more fitting appropriate names.

As a youngster the first water bugs to grab my attention were the cased caddis and I remain to this day equally fascinated by the beauty and intricacy displayed by the mini shelters created by some species of caddis larva. Twigs, stones, sand, leaf debris and many other materials are used for these constructions, each one unique and most different species leaving their individual signature in the materials used. Not all species of caddisflies build their own movable shelter, but the ones I could easily identify did, because of their numbers and the ease of observing, from the bankside, as the living cases moved amongst the weed, and along the silt and mud.

In later years I was able to identify roughly many of the other insects that I came across when fishing, each one providing me with a different fascination and appreciation. The mayflies could now be related to the nymph, as could the stonefly. The empty nymph shuck of the large stonefly could often be found along the banks of the rivers and streams I fished, usually isolated on the top of a rock or stone. The empty husks of damselflies that I found attached to reeds were not dried out and dead insects as I originally thought, but a visiting card that life goes on. The midge pupa that I first saw in the water butt at the side of my grandparent's house as a child, now became part of the cycle of larva, pupa and fly. It was only through fly fishing that the knowledge of these miniature beasts increased. A knowledge, it must be admitted, that was and is severely limited and never more than that of the interested amateur, but enough knowledge to allow me to recognize many of the different kinds of nymphs, larvae and pupae that come my way. This is an ideal situation, just enough information to allow me to fish in the many situations I find myself and to be able to design and tie flies to imitate the various stages of a particular fly's life cycle.

There has been a tendency in recent years for many tyers to imitate closely the natural insect in their tyings and some of these examples of the art of modelling are very nice. I am of the opinion that this accuracy of detail is no more clearly demonstrated than when tying nymphs, larvae and pupae. Some examples are so accurate that I find it difficult to distinguish between the imitation and the natural fly. When it comes to fishing though I very rarely use a fly tied this way, they somehow remind me of the joke insects made from moulded plastic that I would buy as a boy to frighten my friends and they inspire me with little or no confidence. That is not to say I never have fished with them, on the contrary, a few years ago many of my flies were tied in this way and my nymph box was an impressive display waiting to catch the eye of any angler who saw it. These realistic fly patterns had the exact number of legs and even the exact number of body segments that the natural insect had, short of adding mouth parts and applying the breath of life, there was little that could have been done to make them more realistic. Each leg was carefully bent and fixed to a precise position, I fully expected them to get up and run for the water after the hook was released from the vice. Did they catch fish? The answer to that is yes, but not as well and as often as the more impressionistic patterns used. I probably lost the last of those models on the Cong Canal, where it runs out of Lough Mask in Ireland five years ago, I have not been tempted to replace them.

When it comes to tying nymphs, larvae and pupae I like them tied rough and tough. Rough for movement and tough to withstand the abuse they will have to take. Although many of the patterns I use regularly bear no resemblance to any particular natural insect, there can be no discounting their effectiveness. When fishing fast water, the patterns I would normally use could only be described as big and ugly. Big in that they are usually bigger than the natural I am trying to imitate and ugly because the materials have no distinct shape, rather they give an overall impression of that being imitated when cast and placed in the hands of the water. I would also use that most simple but highly effective style of fly, the spider, tied in various guises. For use in less rapid water the fly patterns will tend more accurately to correspond with the size of the natural. They are designed less ugly or rough, but with the materials used still tied to allow an element of movement, with underbodies of water absorbent fur overdubbed with synthetic materials. The patterns used for still or relatively slow running water will accurately match the size of the natural fly being imitated and will be a slightly closer depiction of the real beast, but still allowing material movement and not verging towards the so called realistic. In still or slow moving water movement of the fly is provided, to the greater extent, by the angler, rather than the flow of the water, it is equally important that the materials used give even a little indication of movement and life. To this end I often incorporate a small amount of flash into the fly pattern, small is the indicator word used here. A touch of sparkle added to the body or thorax can make all the difference between a good fly and a really good one. Overdo the sparkle and the fly pattern becomes a whole different type of fly, a fly which at times can be very successful but also runs the risk of spooking the fish, which after a careful bit of stalking can be, to say the least, frustrating.

In the heavier water and to get the fly down quickly and efficiently it is often necessary to use flies with added weight. Although fast sinking tips and lines can help they are often not sufficient to allow the fly to fish at the depth required, especially in a strong current. When this is the case, patterns tied incorporating lead and metal beads come into their own. There is one problem when adding weight and that is that the bulk of the fly increases, which in fast water can be problematic as the current will play on the bulk, reducing the chances of the fly sinking quickly. To get around this when using lead I flatten the lead used to produce the underbody. This has two effects, both of which are advantageous, firstly the fly more accurately imitates the general shape of the natural insect and secondly the fly appears to sink faster and more efficiently especially in fast water. Unfortunately it is impossible to do this with a metal bead, but saying that I have found metal bead headed flies to be extremely successful, although sometimes the brighter varieties can make the fish very nervous when compared to more subtle tyings. An example of this was when I was fishing a comparatively large pool on a small stream where I can often be found, rod in hand, crawling in and out from amongst the bushes and trees like a well seasoned poacher. The only way to fish this pool is from above by hanging over the trunk of one of the many trees forming a near solid roof above the pool. From this position you can see the fish clearly and due to an eddy they tend, under normal conditions, to lie partially facing downstream, the eddy diverting the flow around and under the trunk of the tree. The method used to catch these fish is to slowly feed the rod out over the water, ideally using one of the branches of the tree as cover and feed the fly slowly down through the water. The rod must be no more than 6 ft (1.8 m) in length, otherwise it is impossible to miss the branches of the tree hanging from the other bank, this length also gives you control to allow your fly to catch the eddy and come within the range of the fish. Gold headed flies always scare these fish and even a small pattern carefully allowed to come close to the lie will result in the fish becoming extremely jumpy. A fur dubbed lead-underbody fly has no such effect and will either be ignored completely without any apparent nervous reaction or will happily result in a positive take. The current here is slow and the trout have as much time as they want to see the fly approach.

Whenever I arrive at the waterside like most fly fishers one of the first questions I ask is 'are any fish showing themselves?' If they are rising to the adult, the emerging fly or the surface clinging midge pupa, I will usually try to tempt the fish with versions of the dry or semi dry fly. That is not to say, even in the conditions where the fish are freely rising, that these fly patterns will always be the most effective, as this is not always the case. The reason I do this is because fishing

for trout with the dry or semi dry fly can be my most favourite form of trout fishing. I love fishing the dry fly and the emerging fly. To see a fish rising and to cover that fish with a carefully presented fly, resulting in a positive take is one of the most satisfying and life confirming moments available to us mortals. When it is done properly, with careful thought about the fly being used, why it is being used and the skill of a presentation honed over many years, the result is one of joy and fulfilment. Watching a skilled caster present a fly is entrancing, I can watch them for hours and rarely require or desire to take their place. I suspect I prefer being the caster myself although I have to say these days I seem, at times, quite content to just blend into the background and watch others.

Arriving at a water, even if there are no fish rising I will sometimes choose to fish the fly on or in the surface, trusting it to entice a fish up from the depths. Let's face it, every hatch of flies starts with one nymph or pupa making a break for the top of the water and often one fly can be all it takes to inspire action from watchful fish. There are times when fish concentrate on sub-surface food and refuse point-blank to consider anything else. There are also times when the water cannot be fished properly or effectively with a surface fly. These are a couple of the circumstances when the many different forms of the wet fly come into their own. There are more nymphs, larvae and pupae than there ever are adult flies. The fact is that every stage in insect development is completed by less than at the previous stage, simply due to them becoming victims of their own nutritional value. It stands to reason that trout eat more nymphs, larvae and pupae than ever they eat the adult or even the emerging fly. The truth is that the insects in their early forms are present in greater numbers and for a far longer time than the relative moments of emergence. Personally I view the transition of flies from the larva and pupa to the adult as the cherry on the cake or the extra dollop of ice cream albeit with a bit more protein. They are the times when the process of fish taking insects for food becomes eminently visible and access to the insect is at its easiest, whilst the nymph, larvae and pupae are the everyday, anytime mainstay of the table.

Part II

There was a time, not so long ago, when in certain fly fishing circles, tying a nymph or other wet fly on the end of your leader, in whatever shape or form, would have been tantamount to sacrilege and seriously frowned upon as not playing the game in the right way. Somehow the idea that fishing the dry fly was the only real way to fish, had worked its way into the consciousness of a relative few, but fairly influential individuals. Looking at it with the benfit of hindsight, a hundred years or so ago, when such ideas were first being cast around, the majority of anglers would not have cared what a few comparatively privileged individuals thought or believed. Most anglers, if they were ever aware of such concepts, would have ignored them and continued fishing the fly in the way they were accustomed and choose to do.

Even today there exists a small band who believe that fishing the dry fly exclusively entitles them to become a part of some imagined fly fishing elite. The last time I directly experienced such an attitude was when standing, with rod in hand, on a bridge over one of my local streams. It was a few years ago, maybe three or four, but I can remember the event clearly.

'The only way to take a trout in this stream is with the dry fly!' Was his opening line. 'Is that so?' being my curt but hopefully not unpleasant reply. 'Yes, only real way to catch trout you know' he continued. 'Um' being my total visible reaction. 'No other way but the dry fly when fishing a stream for trout' was his final remark as he went on his way, leaving me to ponder what, after a successful morning fishing using the nymph, was a slightly surreal moment.

Now to complete the picture, this brief meeting took place at the end of the fishing season on this particular water, and the end of the season sees very little if any fly life. The occasional almost confused upwinged fly, but no major rises and the odd terrestrial fly blown onto the surface of the water from the surrounding trees and bushes. As he walked away, I just continued looking down through the flowing water at the parr and small brown trout suspended in the current of the stream, waiting for a passing morsel to come their way.

I have fished that stream for nearly fifteen years and it would be safe to say that I had fished it more than anyone else over that period. Like all streams, rivers and lakes there are times to fish the dry fly and times to fish the sunk fly in its many forms including the nymph. To fish the dry fly only would ignore the nature of the fish and its feeding habits and would considerably reduce the chances of connecting with any fish. To fish the dry fly only, fails to recognize that which the fish are feeding on for much of the time.

Fishing the nymph, larva or pupa is as skilled and as legitimate as any other form of fly fishing. If the essence of fly fishing is recognizing the natural insects on which the fish are feeding on at any particular time and imitating those insects in an attempt to dupe the fish into grabbing the hook, then fishing a nymph, larva or pupa is an essential piece of the jigsaw puzzle, without which the puzzle would be incomplete.

There are many times when I am on the water and there is no hatch of flies whatsoever, no emergers and definitely no spent spinners. It is quite possible to entice a fish to rise to a floating fly pattern even when there are no natural flies apparent. To do so in the belief that the dry fly is superior ignores the skill required to fish in other ways and the actual insects that are providing the trout with their food.

I love dry fly fishing and will sometimes fish with the dry fly when there are no natural flies upon the water, I do so because I enjoy it. I also love fishing using the wet fly and nymph and will do so when there are natural flies rising and upon the water. The reason? Because I also enjoy doing so. Sometimes I may get a result, sometimes I won't, but in many ways it doesn't matter. Just so long as the pleasure of being on the water with a rod in hand is being appreciated and enjoyed, then that is all there is to be concerned about. There is really no room or necessity in the world of fly fishing for different factions, each believing themselves superior to all others, it says more about the individuals concerned than it will ever say about the gentle art. As fly fishers, respect, care and love are the only things we need concern ourselves with, they being the qualities that are truly superior.

On many of the waters I fish unless there is a large rise of flies or there has been a rise earlier in the day, the larger fish will tend to stay well clear of any dry fly that I may present. To entice these fish it is necessary to fish deeper and sometimes just off the bottom. There are many ways in which a fly can be fished deep, each method has its pluses and minuses and will wholly depend on how I want the fly pattern to be presented to the fish.

When fishing a relatively long line in the traditional method of casting across the stream and letting the current of the stream bring the flies round to the dangle ('the dangle' refers to the position when the line and the fly pattern or patterns are directly downstream of the anglers and is no longer being drawn towards the bank by the current), I prefer if there is sufficient depth of water to let the actual fly line do the sinking, to keep the fly patterns being used as light as possible. To fish this way requires the employment of fly lines with different rates of sinking, usually ranging from medium to very fast sinking. The choice of line to use will depend on the strength of the current, the depth of the water and at what height in the water the fly pattern is required to be fished.

When fishing in this way I like to use very lightweight fly patterns, such flies are much more mobile in the water compared to weighted fly patterns, they also hook up on the bottom less often. Every small change in the current will effect a lightweight fly pattern, whilst heavy weighted flies tend to be more sluggish and as a result appear to me to be less attractive.

Keeping in touch with the fly is essential when fishing this way, right from the moment the flies touch the water, to the time they are lifted out into the cast. To do this effectively I find it is necessary to retrieve the line as it is swung back across the water by the current and personally I like to use a variable 'figure of eight' retrieve.

Using this method of sunk fly fishing, whole sections of a river or stream can be covered efficiently. In effect a slice of the water is covered with each cast, taking one step downstream will cut another slice and so on and so forth. This is best described by the diagram, which illustrates how to use the longer line when fishing the nymph, larva or pupa.

This method is traditional in that it has been used for hundreds of years. The only difference

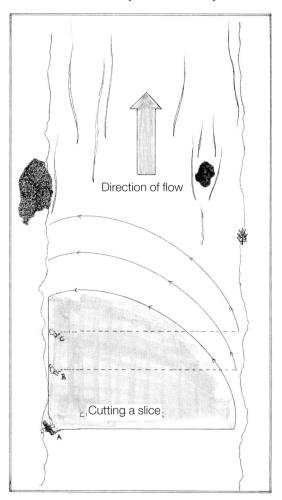

Direction of flow

Cutting a slice

Cutting slices out of the water when fishing the sunk fly.

is that now we have access to such a large range of sinking lines, as a result of which the depth the fly pattern is presented can be controlled reasonably accurately. A couple of different lines on spools kept in a pocket allow a change to be made quickly.

I incorporate loops on all of my fly lines, this allows me easily to make any changes required. I like to use braided loops and after many years of using them, I believe I now utilize the best method for attaching them to the fly line. I have seen many fish lost over the years, both by others

and myself, from using braided loops in the wrong way. Whether these losses were caused by the loop coming loose, the loop attachment sticking in the top ring or breakage of the actual loop, due to wear and tear, it is of no matter, the following method will reduce such problem to practically zero. The method involves whipping the loop to the line and produces a very smooth joint, which is ideal when playing big fish as it allows the joint to pass easily through the top eye of the rod. Unlike the plastic sleeves, which at times can catch on the rod tip ring and then suddenly release with a jerk, which is something I would choose not to have happen when playing a good fish.

It is important when using a braided loop that the actual loop is as close to the fly line as possible. I often see anglers using loops with 8 or 9 in (20 or 23 cm) of braided nylon between the loop and the fly line. This is unnecessary and in my opinion provides a questionable joint that becomes even more questionable the more often it is used. Because of this I **do not** make my own braided loops. This is an occasion when I have no hesitation in directly recommending a commercially available product. The braided loops produced by Roman Moser and available from many tackle shops, are the very best I have come across, without any close rival, being vastly superior to any other braided loops on the market. I use them on all my lines. Mr Moser has

How to attach a braided loop.

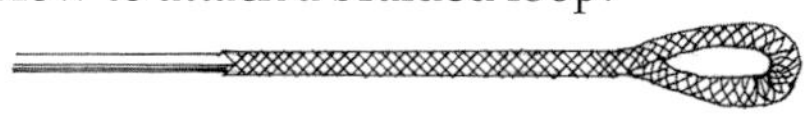

Fig. 1 Feed the braid over the end of the fly line.

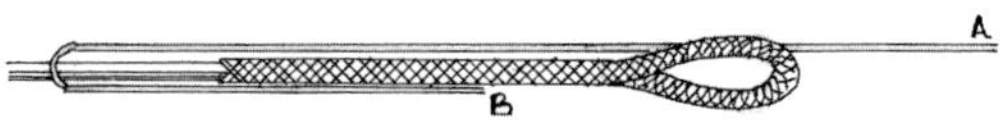

Fig. 2 Take a length of very strong thread, kevlar or GSP is ideal, and form a loop as shown.

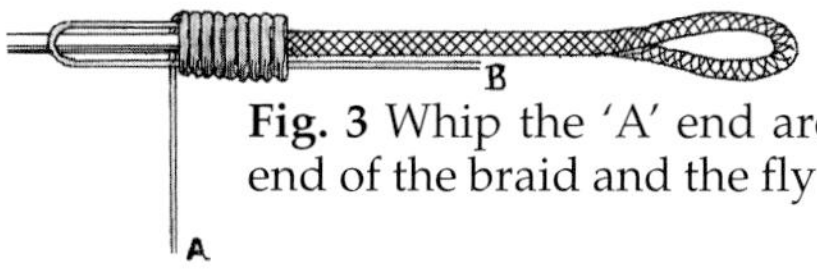

Fig. 3 Whip the 'A' end around the end of the braid and the fly line.

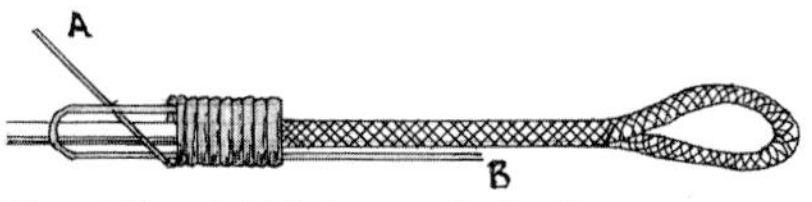

Fig. 4 Feed 'A' through the loop.

Fig. 5 Pull 'B' so as to pull the loop into the windings of the whipping.

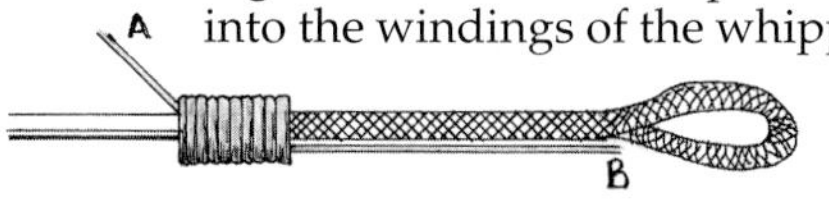

Fig. 6 Cut off the loose ends and lock with superglue.

Roman Moser braided loops.

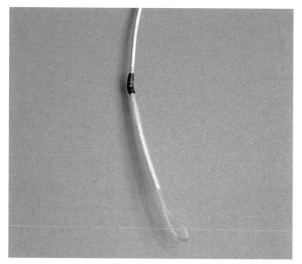

Roman Moser Braided Loop attached to the fly line by whipping.

and the current ensures that the fly is dragged down through the water to the required depth. Fly patterns can be designed to assist in this process and they can be made lightweight to be completely buoyant.

When tying my own nymph, larva or pupa patterns that require an element of buoyancy, I achieve it by adding a foam underbody to the fly pattern. The underbodies described in 'Floating Down the River' (page 46) and used for tying dry flies are ideal for this purpose. The following fly pattern has been designed to imitate the nymph of the large dark olive (*Baetis rhodani*). This is a common and fairly large nymph, extending up to 12 or 13 mm in length if the tail is included. As such the natural fly can be imitated on a fairly large hook. Contrary to when tying most nymph patterns, the hook should be a lightweight hook and I prefer to use a dry fly hook rather than a normal nymph hook. The reason for this is that I want the fly to be as buoyant as possible and most nymph hooks are a little too heavy for my liking when tying this type of fly pattern. This can on occasion cause a slight problem. Sometimes the take from a fish on these fly patterns can be very hard indeed and I have found that if I strike with too much enthusiasm the hook can bend and the fish be lost. Gently lifting into a taking fish is all that is required.

managed to provide a braided loop where the two ends of the braid extend over the fly line. This has the effect of strengthening the overall joint and, importantly, allows the fly line to butt up right up to the actual loop. I like this very much, I throw away the plastic sleeves Mr Moser provides and stick to whipping the joint as previously described. Between whipping the joint and the Roman Moser braided loop, I have the best loop on my fly line that I have ever used and I have no hesitation in recommending its use. By the way I have no connections with Mr Moser other than admiring his product!

As an aside, it is sometimes useful to attach a loop to monofilament, without having a knot. I find that the two methods described in the diagram fulfil this admirably. The resulting joint, if completed properly, is stronger than the nylon, at least in tests I have undertaken. Under stress the monofilament will break before the joint gives way.

Getting back to fishing the nymph or larva on a sinking line: when using a fast sinking line to place the fly pattern or patterns as close as possible to the bottom of a river or stream, I like to use patterns that are fairly, if not completely, buoyant. Using buoyant fly patterns minimizes any hook-ups on the bottom and more importantly the fly pattern is more mobile. The fly line is used to set the depth that the fly will be in the water

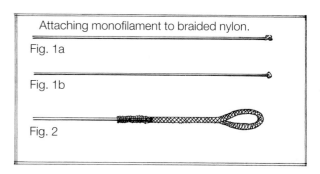

Fig.1a A knot is tied in the monofilament and the loose end cut off.

Fig. 1b The end of the monofilament is melted into a small ball.

Fig. 2 The braided loop is placed over the monofilament and whipped on with thread. The knot or melted ball butts up to the whipping. Seal the whipping with superglue.

Tying the buoyant Large Dark Olive Nymph

Materials

Hook	Partridge Klinkhamar hook size 8 or equivalent.
Body	Fine polypropylene dubbing medium brown.
Rib	Dark brown thread.
Underbody	Preformed polystyrene underbody tapered at the tail end,
Tail	Three pheasant tail feather fibres.
Thorax	Polypropylene dubbing light brown plus a little pearl Lite Bright.
Legs	Partridge feather.
Thorax cover	Flexible foam sheet dark brown.
Thread	Personal choice 8/0.

Photograph 1 Fix the hook in the jaws of the vice and test for soundness. Wind the waxed thread around the hook as in the photograph and tie in the three pheasant tail feather fibres, extend the tails for approximately five millimetres beyond the bend of the hook. These tails can be formed into a 'V' shape for the outer tails and the middle one set in the centre if required, but I don't usually bother as in the water they tend to cling together anyway. Now return the thread to the start of the hook bend.

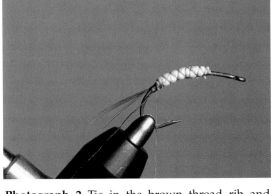

Photograph 2 Tie in the brown thread rib and return the thread again to the start of the hook bend. Now place a preformed polystyrene underbody along the hook shank, this under body should extend just into what will become the thorax section of the fly pattern and the opposite end butts up to where the tail has been tied in. Tie the underbody in by using criss-cross turns of thread, these turns can be fairly random but make sure each end of the underbody is secured firmly by the thread. Return the thread to the tail end of the underbody.

Photograph 3 Dub the tying thread with the body dubbing, I like to wax the thread prior to doing this. Now wind the dubbed tying thread over the polystyrene underbody, for a distance equal to that of the length of the tails. The dubbing must cover this section of the underbody completely, but using only one layer of dubbed tying thread. Remove the excess dubbing from the tying thread. Now wind on the thread rib and tie in on the underside of the hook. This rib can be wound through to well into the thorax and secured with just a couple of turns of tying thread. Cut off any thread rib that extends into the head area of the fly pattern.

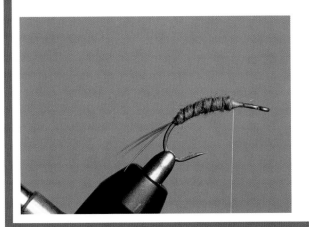

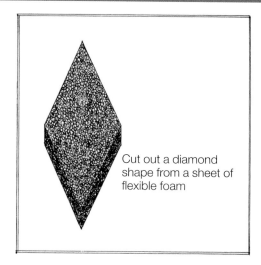

Cut out a diamond shape from a sheet of flexible foam

Photograph 4 Cut a diamond shape from the foam sheet used for the thorax cover (see insert diagram) and tie in one end directly on the upper side of the thorax area at the point where the body dubbing ends. Return the thread to where the thorax cover is first tied in.

Photograph 5 Take the tip of the partridge feather used for the legs and tie in the tip, making sure the good side is facing upwards and with the tip facing in the direction of the hook eye. Cut off the excess tip and return the thread to where it was first tied in.

Photograph 6 Dub the tying thread with the thorax dubbing and wind along the hook shank towards the eye, forming a shaped thorax that is wider in the middle than at either end. At its widest the thorax should be just slightly wider than the widest part of the body and it should be slightly thinner than the body at the point where body and thorax meet. Make sure after winding on the dubbing that there is enough space left behind the hook eye to tie in all the required materials and form a small head. Remove any excess dubbing material from the tying thread.

Photograph 7 Pull the partridge feather over the top of the thorax dubbing, ensuring that the central stalk is in line with the centre of the thorax, and tie in behind the hook eye. Cut off the excess feather. Before finally tying the partridge feather in behind the hook eye, ensure that there are at least five or six feather fibres extending to either side of the thorax. There should be the same number of feather fibres extending either side. Although there are only three legs on either side of the natural insect five or more feather fibres are, I think, better than just three or less.

Photograph 8 Pull the foam thorax cover over the top of the thorax area, ensuring that it is centred. Now tie it in behind the hook eye using very tight turns of thread, after the foam has been secured, stretch the excess and remove with a knife or scissors. Now form a small head with the tying thread and complete the fly with a whip finish.

Photograph 9 The completed fly.

That completes the buoyant large dark olive nymph to be used when fishing using a relatively long and fast sinking line. As will be clear to most readers, just about any nymph pattern could be tied and fished in this way, changing the size of hook, colour of materials and at times the shape, being all that is required.

I have found that it is often necessary, when using certain fishing techniques, to add weight directly to a nymph pattern, incorporating it within the tying. Obviously this added weight assists in making the pattern sink quickly. Even the early fly patterns designed specifically to imitate nymphs included additional weight in some form or another. Frank Sawyer's pheasant tail nymph incorporated copper wire, in that particular case the wire was more than just a method of adding weight, but actually formed the general shape of the nymph pattern. There are times when that bit of extra weight is required and lead wire, gold beads and tungsten beads are amongst the many ways that I have used over the years. Unless I need to have a pattern weighted extra heavily for fishing nymphs bug style, I tend to weight my nymphs using lead wire as an underbody. There is a slight problem when adding bulk to a fly that is intended to sink quickly and that is that the more bulk you add to the fly pattern, the more it is carried away by the current. The ideal heavyweight fly pattern would be heavy and slim, if only that were possible. What I like to do is add the weight to the fly pattern and make the pattern as streamlined as possible. Doing this helps to make it sink quickly getting down to where the fish are,

before being carried away in the current of the water.

The following method of flattening a wound lead underbody is a good compromise between adding weight and maintaining a streamlined shape to the fly pattern. The added benefit is that the procedure produces a superb nymph shape, a shape that by itself, without the addition of other materials can provide an excellent imitation of a nymph. The method is described in detail in the following sequence and as mentioned the result can be used as a nymph pattern in its own right, or as the shaped underbody to a more elaborate tying. I have had a lot of success using the basic flattened lead body as shown when fishing for both trout and grayling and would recommend the simple tying to anyone. For those tyers who prefer their fly patterns tied more decoratively, the basic flattened lead shape can be adjusted to suit any particular nymph shape you require and the extra materials added where needed. In this way any number of nymph patterns can be tied using the basic flattened lead method.

The hook used is a medium to heavyweight hook, although there have been occasions when I have found a lightweight hook to be ideal for a particular nymph I am attempting to imitate.

The pattern described in the illustrated sequence is a slight elaboration on the basic flattened lead underbody. The tying remains extremely simple, but the addition of the tails, the stripe of holographic tinsel and the varnish finish, makes the tying a fly pattern in its own right, rather than just a underbody.

A small river where care must be taken when fishing, so as not to disturb the fish. A good place to use the nymph.

Flattened Lead Method for Tying Nymph Patterns

Materials Required

Hook	Any suitable nymph hook, medium to heavyweight.	**Tail**	Three micro fibbets.
		Upper body and thorax	Length of holographic tinsel.
Body	Wound lead wire, bound with tying thread and waterproof superglue or Zap-a-Gap.	**Thread**	Own choice 8/0.

Beefing up micro-fibbetts. Sometimes a more solid tail is required than is supplied by micro-fibbetts. When this is the case I take the required number of fibbett fibres lay them together so that the tips are together and then run the nozzle of a tube containing superglue or Zap-a-Gap along the fibbetts. When dry I then varnish the glued fibbetts. This makes a much more substantial tail suitable for larger nymphs.

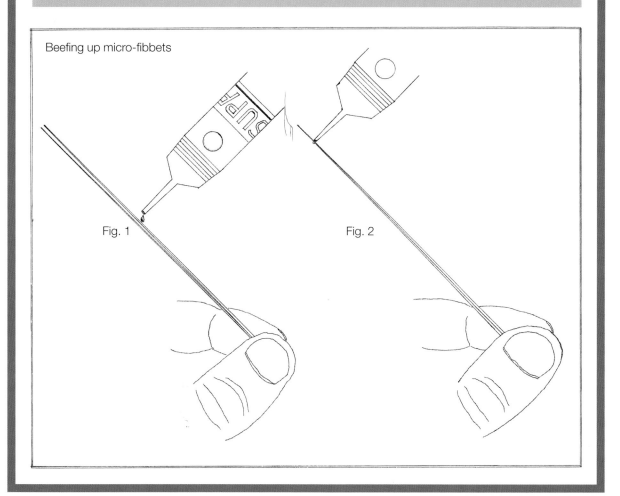

Beefing up micro-fibbets

Fig. 1

Fig. 2

Flattened Lead Method for nymphs

Fig. 1 Wind thread to hook bend and tie in tails.
Return thread to hook eye.

Fig. 2 Wind lead wire, leaving space behind hook
eye and in front of tail.

Fig. 3 Wind on second layer of lead wire over front
section of previous windings. Fix with superglue.

Fig. 4 Fully bind with thread.

Fig. 5 Crush front section of lead.

Fig 5a. Use pliers to press the
lead flat. Complete whip finish
and remove thread.

Fig. 5a

Fig. 3

Fig. 2

Fig. 4

Fig. 1

Fig. 5

Fig. 6 Colour top of lead with marker pen. Cover
in varnish.

Fig. 7 Lay strip of holographic tinsel along top of
nymph, pressing tinsel into wet varnish. Now
varnish.

Fig. 6

Fig. 7

Fig. 1 Fix the hook in the jaws of the vice and as ever test the hook for soundness. Now spin the thread tight and, as described, wind the thread to the start of the hook bend. Spinning the thread tight provides a rough base for the lead wire to be wound around, the rough base giving additional grip. Tie in the tails on to the top of the hook shank. Now split the tails using the thread loop under the hook bend method. As explained return the thread to behind the hook eye. Sometimes it is desirable to beef up the micro-fibbetts; this is best done as illustrated.

Fig. 2 Now wind the lead wire forming a single layer along the hook shank. Each turn of lead wire must be touching. As explained it is essential that a small space is left at the tail section and a larger space left between the wound lead and the hook eye, this is to allow the expansion of the lead wire when it is flattened. I find that if you leave the space you think you should and then add a little more, you will not go far wrong. When winding the lead wire, wind as tightly as possible, without running the risk of breaking the wire.

Fig. 3 Now wind a second layer of lead wire over the front section of the first layer of wound wire and as shown in the diagram apply waterproof superglue to the wound lead wire. The application of the lead wire will determine the final shape of the pattern. Some nymphs are wider at the thorax section and in that case a second layer of lead wire is added at the thorax section as in the illustration. To imitate a slim nymph a second layer of lead wire may not be required and to imitate a more bulky nymph the second layer of lead wire may cover most of the first layer, leaving a space at each end.

Fig. 4 As shown in the diagram, bind the lead with the tying thread using criss-cross turns of thread placed fairly randomly all over the wound lead wire. This should be performed immediately after the glue has been applied, so the glue bonds the tying thread to the lead wire.

Fig. 5 To flatten the wound lead wire I prefer to use a pair of long nosed pliers. This is best performed by first flattening from the near side and then from the far side, to ensure the flattening is even. Complete a whip finish and cut off the tying thread. This completes the basic nymph shape, which can be used either as an under body or as a nymph pattern in its own right.

Fig. 6 In the particular example illustrated, the basic body has been slightly elaborated by colouring the upper section of the pattern with a dark marker pen. The complete pattern is then varnished.

Fig. 7 Before the initial coat of varnish has dried, a strip of holographic tinsel is embedded into the wet varnish along the centre of the pattern as shown in the illustration. I find this is best achieved by using a dubbing needle to place the tinsel into the correct position and to force it into the wet varnish. Once the strip of tinsel is in place, varnish the whole pattern for a second time.

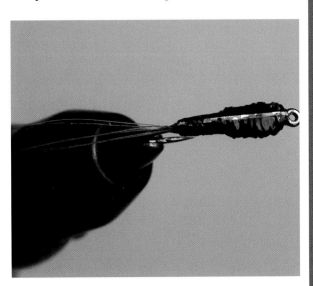

That completes the very basic flattened lead wire nymph, with a little elaboration. The pattern takes only a few minutes to tie, but I find the patterns tied using this simple technique are excellent and imitate the natural insect far better than many of the more complex and intricate patterns available. The particular pattern illustrated makes for an excellent *Baetis* imitation.

Using the Flattened Lead Wire Method for an underbody

I cannot say that making the flattened lead nymph more intricate and elaborate in anyway improves it as a fish catcher. There are times, however, that as a fly tyer I choose to develop the basic pattern and make it a little more complex, rather than sticking to the very basic pattern.

As previously explained the flattened lead underbody can be used as the foundation for more intricate nymph patterns. As an example of this I have used the stonefly nymph of the Yellow Sally. The Yellow Sally nymph is a very distinctive stonefly nymph, distinctive in that when compared to other stonefly nymphs, it is very light in colour. It is often of a distinctive yellow colour, hence the name, with a hint of green and with darker shades of brown on the head and thorax. The colours vary, however, from place to place and to imitate accurately the colours of a local Yellow Sally nymph it is a distinct advantage to have seen the local natural insect.

The natural nymph can reach a size of around ³/₄ in (2 cm) and whilst they are often smaller than this, I like to fish with a nymph pattern of this size. This nymph, like all stonefly nymphs, has two short but sturdy tails and is, I believe, best imitated using a long shank lure or nymph hook.

Tying the Yellow Sally Nymph using a flattened lead underbody

Materials Required

Hook	Long shank lure or nymph hook.
Tail	3 micro fibbetts glued together for both tails.
Body Rib	Dark brown or black 8/0 thread.
Thorax Rib	Gold wire fine
Body	Yellow and light brown antron floss blended together.
Underbody	Lead wire.
Thorax	Yellow dubbing plus pearl Lite Brite.
Thorax cover	Light brown stretchable body wrap.
Legs	Partridge hackle dyed yellow/olive.
Thread	Light colour (yellow) 8/0.

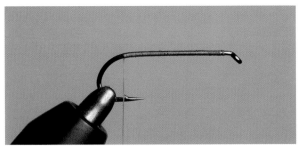

Photograph 1 Place the hook in the jaws of the vice and test the hook for soundness. Attach and wind the waxed thread, using flat thread, to the start of the hook bend.

Photograph 2 Prepare and tie in the two tails ensuring that they form a distinct fork. Return the thread to the start of the hook bend. Attach the thread body rib to the underside of the hook shank, using the loop over the tying thread method. Now spin the tying thread tight and wind the thread along the whole of the hook shank using wide turns of thread and then return the thread to the start of the hook bend, allowing the thread to unspin to normal. This procedure lays a rough foundation on the hook shank and will increase the grip between the lead underbody and the hook shank.

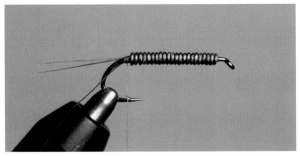

Photograph 3 Now wind a single layer of medium weight lead wire along the hook shank, using touching turns. The lead wire should be wound as tightly as possible, without risking breaking the wire. Leave a small space at the tail end of the hook shank and a larger space at the hook eye end: this is to allow for the expansion of the lead wire when flattened using pliers.

Photograph 4 When the lead wire has been wound, apply a little superglue or Zap-a-Gap to the wound lead wire and immediately start winding the thread in criss-cross, fairly random turns. When the lead wire is secured, return the thread to the start of the hook bend.

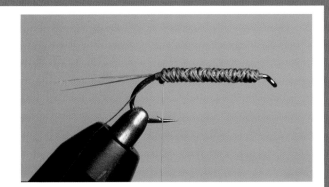

Photograph 5 Take a pair of pliers, I prefer to use the long nosed versions as they are more exacting and thinner at the point. Now very slightly squeeze the **rear** half of the wound lead wire, using the pliers from the side facing. Repeat this process by taking the pliers over to the far side of the hook. Squeezing the lead wire from the near side and the far side ensures that the flattening is even and does not have a slant formed by the angle of the pliers. The rear half should only be flattened slightly so do not be over enthusiastic when squeezing this section. Now apply the pliers to the front half of the wound lead wire, again squeezing from both sides. This time flatten the lead wire to the degree that it extends beyond the rear windings when viewed from above or below and thinner than the rear winds of lead wire when viewed from the side, basically flatten it more!

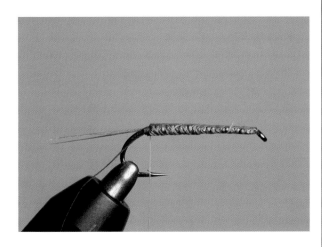

Photograph 6 Using the loop over the tying thread method attach the body floss to the underside of the underbody. Wind the tying thread to the halfway position on the hook shank, the start of where the lead has been flattened more. Now wind on the body floss to the halfway point on the hook shank, any twist in the floss should be removed by unspinning and the floss should be wound flat over the underbody, applying the minimum of bulk with each wind. Tie in the floss, using just a couple of turns of tying thread, on to the underside of the body at the halfway point on the hook shank. Do not tie in fully at this time and do not remove the excess floss material.

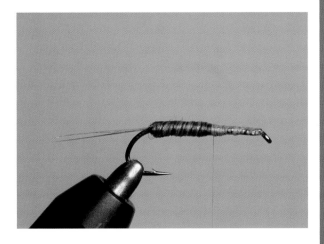

Now wind on the thread rib along the floss body, making seven or nine turns of rib, depending on the size of the hook. I like to use an odd number of turns when adding a rib, it seems to look better than when an even number of turns are made. The natural insect in this case has ten segments on the body, which requires nine turns of rib. Nine can, however, be excessive and spoil the overall look of the pattern, depending on the length of the hook shank and the thickness of thread rib being used. When this is the case I settle for seven turns of rib or even five, but never an even number of turns. Tie in the thread rib on the underside of the underbody and at the same time complete the tying in of the body floss, cut off the excess rib and body floss and return the tying thread to the halfway point.

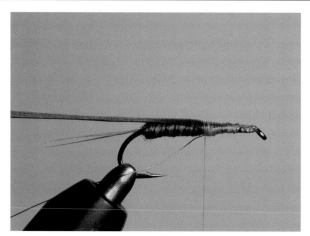

Photograph 7 Now tie in the gold wire thorax rib on the underside of the thorax section exactly at the point where the floss body ends, use the loop over the tying thread method. Only use three or four turns of thread to initially secure the gold wire rib. Take the stretch body wrap and cut the edges away at an angle at one end to produce a blunt point. This is for the thorax cover. Tie the blunt pointed end directly on to the top of the thorax, exactly at the point where the body floss ends. Complete the tying in of the thorax cover and the thread rib, then return the thread to the halfway point.

Photograph 8 Prepare the yellow/olive partridge hackle to be used for the legs by removing all the lower feather fibres to a point on the stalk where the stalk is very flexible and not over thick. Now tie the prepared hackle directly centred on to the top of the thorax section by the prepared tip, with the good side of the feather facing downwards and towards the hook bend. Cut off the excess hackle stalk and return the thread again to the halfway point.

Photograph 9 Now dub the tying thread with the thorax dubbing. Wind on the thorax dubbing ensuring that enough space is left behind the hook eye to tie in all the materials and to form a medium sized head. If the whole thorax section where to be split into quarters, the dubbing should extend to three-quarters of the way along the thorax section.

Photograph 10 Pull the hackle over the top of the thorax and tie in using just three turns of tying thread. Now pull and stretch the thorax cover over the top of the thorax and make a tight winding of the gold rib around the thorax and the thorax cover at a point one quarter of the way along the thorax. Make sure two or three hackle fibres are behind this first turn of gold wire rib on both sides of the thorax, each side should have equal hackle fibres and no hackle fibres should be trapped

Photograph 11 Now maintaining tension on the gold wire, loop the thorax cover material back over the thorax to the point where the body starts. Then loop it back over the thorax and make a winding of the gold wire rib around the thorax and the thorax cover at the halfway point along the thorax section, taking care not to trap any hackle fibres. Again make sure two or three hackle fibres are behind this second turn of gold wire rib on each side of the thorax.

Photograph 12 Repeat the process described in Photograph 10, only this time loop the thorax cover backwards so that it extends just beyond where the first turn of gold rib wire was made. Then loop it back over the thorax making a turn of gold wire rib around the thorax and over the thorax cover at the point three-quarters of the way along the thorax at the position where the dubbing ends. As previously, make sure that two or three hackle fibres are placed on either side of the thorax behind this turn of the wire rib.

Now tie in the gold wire rib using a few turns of tightly wound tying thread and cut off the excess wire rib. Return the thread to where the rib was first tied in.

Photograph 13 Again repeat the previous process by looping the thorax cover back over the thorax and just extending beyond the second turn of gold wire rib. Then loop the thorax cover back over the thorax and tie in using five turns of tying thread at the point where the wire rib was tied in (three-quarters of the way along the thorax). Once again ensure that two or three hackle fibres are placed at either side of the thorax behind where the thorax cover has been tied in.

Photograph 14 Without initially cutting off any excess material, start to form a head tying in the materials as you go. Cut off the excess thorax cover material and the centre stalk of the hackle, make sure that two or three hackle fibres are left extending out either side of the hook eye.

Photograph 15 Now wind the tying thread to just behind the hook eye, ensuring that the remaining hackle fibres are placed at either side of the hook eye as you wind the thread. Complete a generously sized head and end with a whip finish.

Photograph 16 Using contact adhesive bond the hen hackle fibres that extend at either side of the hook eye to form two antennae. If you wish, a brown permanent ink pen can be used to slightly darken the upper side of the head. That completes the tying of the Yellow Sally nymph incorporating a flattened lead underbody.

Photograph 17 The completed fly.

One of my favourite all time nymph patterns is a strange beast that owes its creation to messing around at my tying bench. It is difficult to be precise about what particular insect it actually imitates, but there is no doubt that it could be applied on behalf of many different insects. I put its success down to being of a shape which generally suggest to the fish that it is something tasty, being not unlike any number of nymphs. Its shape obviously triggers a response because it is one of my most successful patterns. I find it is at its best when tied large and yet again I can think of no obvious reason why this should be the case, but the results show that it just is. I guess that if I were pushed I would describe it as a general large stonefly or mayfly nymph pattern, although the colours used in the pattern do not accurately imitate any particular insect I am acquainted with.

The original pattern came about around eight years ago and by mistake rather than careful design, which is a lineage that many successful fly patterns can claim. I had been messing about for a number of nights trying out a basic weaving method for forming the body on various flies. While doing so I came to various conclusions regarding woven fly bodies, these conclusions are as follows:

- It is best if a shaped underbody is formed prior to weaving and that the underbody should usually not be overly bulky but kept fairly slim.
- That weaving a body is far easier if the materials used are well waxed to enhance their grip.
- That not only should the material being used for weaving be waxed, but the underbody of the fly pattern should also be generously waxed prior to proceeding with the weaving.
- That the best effect is achieved when using a light and a dark material for the weaving. The lighter material is used for the underside and the darker for the upperside. This contrast in colour enhances the look of the pattern tied. The weaving method is the only technique that I am currently aware of that allows this contrast to be applied to a pattern and is the best way in which the technique can be utilized.

With experience and a sensible choice of material it is not necessary to wax the materials.

But for anyone who has never woven a fly body, or anyone who has tried and given up because they have found it difficult, the above conclusions and suggestions will make tying such flies fairly straightforward.

After following the above conclusions and suggestions I found it very easy to produce woven bodies quickly and efficiently. Personally I think that the generous application of wax enhances the overall look of the resulting fly pattern. These simple guidelines have been passed on to many other tyers over the last few years and the feedback has always been enthusiastic and positive, with many tyers starting to weave bodies where previously they would not have bothered, thinking it to be too much hassle. When I look at many of the woven flies on the market, I wonder why anyone bothered to take the trouble to tie them using a weaving method. As far as I am concerned the only distinction weaving has, as previously mentioned, is that a different colour or shade of material can be placed on the upperside of a fly as compared to the underside. Unless this distinction is achieved, weaving is on the whole an unnecessary method of forming a body. Saying that, when the colour distinction is required there is no better way to achieve it than weaving.

The following photographic sequence and accompanying diagram describe how to weave a body easily and simply. The result is my accidental fly. I make no apologies for the colours used in the pattern, they have proved themselves to be most successful and I for one am not inclined to fix something if it doesn't need fixing. The colour combination is the most successful of this particular fly that I have used and I have tried many others.

Tying the Woven Bodied Nymph

Materials Required

Hook	Heavy long shank lure size 6.
Body	Black and yellow thick rayon floss.
Underbody	Wound tying thread.
Thorax	Cock grizzle hackle dyed hot orange.
Thorax cover	As per body.
Tail	Bunch of cock grizzle hackle fibres dyed hot orange.

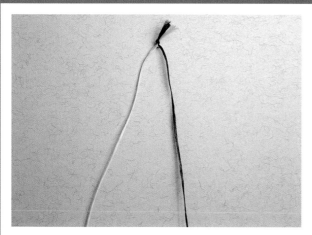

Photograph 1 The first thing required to do is to prepare the body material for weaving. This is done by taking an equal length of the black and yellow rayon floss and tying one end of each together using a non-slip knot. I find that using a longer length is better than using a shorter length and so recommend that the floss be 12 in (30 cm) long, this length can be used to tie a number of flies. Now take each length of floss and pull each through a block of cobbler's wax, or other hard wax. Ensure that each length of floss is thoroughly covered with wax.

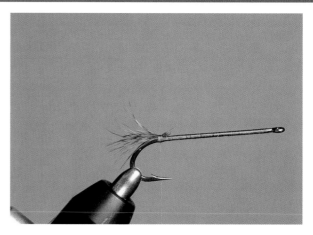

Photograph 2 Fix the hook in the jaws of the vice and test the hook for soundness. Attach the waxed thread and wind along the shank to the start of the hook bend. Take a generous bunch of cock grizzle hackle fibres dyed hot orange and tie in on the top of the hook shank to create the tail, use the loose loop/open loop method to tie in the tailing fibres. Return the tying thread back to the start of the hook bend. It is not necessary to cut off the excess hackle fibres as they can be incorporated into the underbody.

Photograph 3 Wind the tying thread towards the hook eye, but leaving plenty of space behind the eye. Now form a slightly shaped tapered body using the tying thread. Then spin the thread tight and with well-spaced turns of thread wind to the start of the hook bend and then back to the hook eye. These windings should be well spaced. Using tight spun thread makes for a rough base to tie in the other materials.

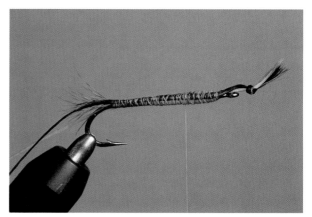

Photograph 4 Take the knotted floss and lay it along the hook shank, with the knotted end extending beyond the hook eye. The black floss should be nearest you and the yellow floss on the far side of the hook shank. Now tie in the floss along the hook shank, taking care to ensure that both colours of floss continue to lie straight along the hook shank as they are tied in. Leave space behind the hook eye and cut off the knotted end of the floss. Using the tying thread form a slim shaped underbody, tapering down to the tail end. When the underbody is complete take the tying thread to a position two thirds of the way along the hook shank.

Photograph 5 Take a piece of dark cobbler's wax or other hard wax and rub it along the shaped under-body ensuring that the underbody is completely covered in wax. Doing so will make it far easier to weave the two colours of floss together, as the materials will grip far better, reducing the chances of slipping and spoiling the final look of the fly. With practice you may choose not to be so generous with the wax as I suggest, but for anyone who has not woven a fly body before, or who has found doing so difficult, the use of wax will make a big difference. It is now time to start the weaving. The first thing to do is turn the vice so that the jaws are directly pointing towards you at a comfortable working height. Take the black floss from the left of the hook shank over the top of the hook to the right side of the hook shank. Then bring the yellow floss over the top of

the black floss on the right side of the shank and then directly down and under to left of the hook shank. This procedure is the basic pattern used for forming the woven body and can perhaps be seen more clearly in the diagram entitled 'Weaving a body'.

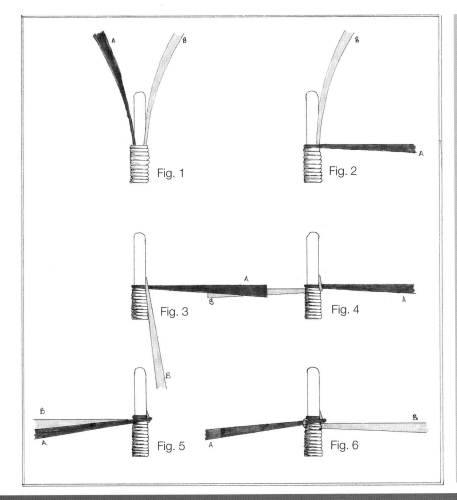

Weaving a body – one technique.

Fig. 1 The upper material and lower material are tied in on each side of the hook shank.

Fig. 2 Pull the upper material over to the right of the hook shank.

Fig. 3 Pull the lower material over the upper material.

Fig. 4 Then bring the lower material under the hook shank.

Fig. 5 Bring the upper material over the top and to the left of the hook shank.

Fig. 6 Now bring the lower material over the upper material and then under the hook shank.

This continues until the whole of the body is formed.

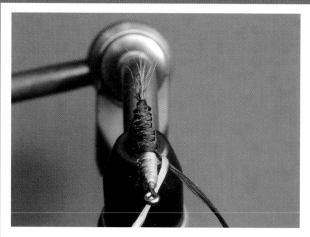

Photograph 6 Now bring the black floss directly over the top of the hook shank to the left side and again bring the yellow floss up over the black floss and down under the hook shank. Tension must be applied on both colours of floss as you do so to ensure that the point where the two colours of floss loop over, does not move, up or down, from the side of the hook shank. Repeat this procedure until the woven body reaches the position two thirds of the way along the hook shank, where the thread is hanging. The diagram on page 133 shows the weaving procedure perhaps more clearly than the photographs.

Photograph 7 This photograph shows the woven body from a side angle. The points where the two different coloured floss loop each other is clearly seen, the result is very buggy. It is important that these loops are all running in a straight line along the side of the hook shank. It is for this reason that I recommend, at least for beginners to the art of weaving a fly body and those tyers who find it a little difficult, that wax is used generously. The use of wax will help prevent the looped floss from being pulled around the hook shank and therefore spoiling the look of the finished nymph pattern.

Photograph 8 Pull both colours of floss directly up above the hook, one colour of floss should come up from the left side of the hook shank and the other colour extend from the right side of the hook shank. Tie a single overhand knot with the floss and pull it down tightly on to the top of the hook shank. The single hand knot will be sufficient to lock the waxed floss.

Photograph 9 Reattach the tying thread and wind the tying thread over the knotted floss, forcing the floss to lie back over the hook. Now prepare and tie in the grizzle cock hackle dyed hot orange. Cut off any excess hackle stalk. Take the thread to just behind the hook eye.

Photograph 10 Wind on the hackle and tie in behind the hook eye, making sure that a little space is left behind the eye to tie in the thorax cover. Cut off the excess hackle.

Photograph 11 Take the body floss and pull it over the top of the thorax hackle and tie in directly behind the hook eye using half a dozen tight turns of thread. The thorax cover will be yellow on one side and black on the other, giving a slightly harlequin look to the pattern. I quite like this but if you prefer, both colours of floss can be blended by pulling the fibres apart and mixing them prior to completing this procedure. Personally I like it just as it is, even though it does not accurately imitate any natural insect.

Photograph 12 Now carefully wind the tying thread back through the hackle and over the thorax cover, taking care not to trap any hackle fibres as you go. Take the thread back to where the thorax begins.

Photograph 13 Pull the floss back over the thorax and tie in at the position where the thorax begins, complete the tying in of the floss with a whip finish, cut off the tying thread. Now using sharp scissors cut off the floss leaving a small tag pointing back over the body. The final act is to give the thorax hackle a haircut. This is done by drawing the thumb and forefinger down with the thorax between and squeezing the hackle downwards. Scissors are then run along below the thumb and forefinger cutting off the projecting hackle fibres. The result is a very bristly hackle.

Photograph 14 The completed fly.

That completes one of my favourite and most successful large nymph patterns. This particular pattern has often saved me from having a blank day, tempting a fish from a pool or run of water when all my other attempts have failed. It is a pattern that catches a larger than average fish and for many years was the pattern that had caught me my largest wild brown trout. I was fishing the neck of a pool on one of my favourite small rivers and failing completely to tempt one of the many fish I knew lived in the depths. Nothing I could do seemed to get a response, the odd tap on the line, possibly a fish touching the leader, but nothing more. It was almost desperation that made me look through my fly box and pick out the monster that I had tied the previous year and by chance had placed in my fly box, rather than deposit it in the reject tray. After casting it into the main flow running into the pool the fly sunk quickly, the weight of the heavy lure hook pulling it down. To maximize the depth the fly would fish and to prevent it being pulled out of the deeper water by the drag of the line, it was necessary to throw a large loop of fly line downstream, directly in line with the main flow of the water. On the second attempt this worked and the line was pulled back heavily against the current. Lifting the rod I found myself attached to the largest brown trout that I had hooked to that date, 5 lb of river toned muscle. That was the first time I had used the pattern described above. Over the years I have continued to use it with great success and, for some reason or another, the fish I catch when using it are always on the large size, maybe the two toned thorax frightens anything smaller.

Some years ago I started experimenting with different fly patterns to imitate the midge larva and the midge pupa prior to the pupa entering the mode for the adult fly to emerge. Some of the attempts were comical, some ridiculous and some proved very successful. At times some were both comical and ridiculous and involved complex combinations of fly patterns to attain certain types of movement. Others reduced the chance of hooking a taking fish by a factor that made it unlikely I would ever land a fish using those particular patterns. The saving grace in all these endeavours was the fun and farce enjoyed by myself and those watching my attempt to fish these experimental fly patterns. In the end I came to the conclusion that there was much merit in keeping matters simple and that fly design, Heath Robinson style was a luxury I could happily do without.

There were a couple of ideas inspired by watching the natural pupa that did ring bells and that have since allowed me to imitate the natural insect more accurately than I had done previously. There is an important point I would like to make regarding these aspirations to accuracy of imitation and that is on the whole they do not improve my catch rate in any way at all, compared to when I did not incorporate such observations into my fly patterns, but then again they do not reduce it either. The success I have enjoyed when using midge pupa patterns has always been high and there is little doubt that, given suitable conditions, the midge as a larva or pupa forms a large part in the diet of a trout. The main reason for this is availability, that is to say that compared to all other insects that start their life cycle as aquatic insects, the midge is by far the most numerous. Admittedly in a fast flowing stream the midge may not be so important as in slower running water or still water, but it is my experience that the midge may be found just about anywhere that there is water.

Of all the natural flies imitated by the fly tyer, the midge has in the past been viewed as the least interesting, the least important and for certain the least glamorous. With the growth in still water trout fishing the importance of the midge has become clear and it is now an unprepared angler who ventures out on the water without a selection of midge pupa patterns in their fly box.

I like to tie my own midge pupa patterns using two different hooks. When imitating the pupa below the surface of the water, I prefer to use a continuous bend hook. When imitating the insect upon or just within the surface of the water, a standard lightweight dry fly hook, Klinkhamar or lightweight continuous bend hook are my preferred choices, just depending on how the fly is required to look.

Most midge pupa patterns designed to sit in or just below the surface of the water have the bulge of the thorax topside. In fact when I watch the natural insect in situ, for most of the time they sit with the thorax bulge downwards and the thin body section pointing upwards with the breathers in the water surface. I would say that the midge pupa spend far more time in this inverted position than in the position imitated by the many suspender buzzer/midge patterns.

It was because of this that I started to tie many of my own suspender buzzer patterns with the thorax bulge at the bend end of the hook, rather than the hook eye end. These fly patterns have proved extremely successful, but I am unsure if they are any more successful than the more usual style of tying. Saying that they do imitate the natural insect more accurately, at least for most of the time.

The following illustration describes how to tie such a midge pupa pattern. This fly pattern has been designed to float suspended in the surface of the water, but only for so long. After floating for some time it will start to sink slowly. A couple of false casts are enough to make the fly float again and the whole procedure of floating suspended in the surface and then slowly sinking, starts again. I find this fly pattern extremely useful and fish will take it both when suspended and when it is slowly sinking. As the fly pattern is not designed to float indefinitely, it is important that the presentation is made carefully and the pattern is allowed to land gently on to the surface of the water. If the pattern is cast too hard upon the surface it will not be suspended for very long and may even start sinking immediately.

The insect chosen to imitate in the illustration is the Black Midge Pupa. It seems that there is often an assumption that imitating the midge in whatever stage of the life cycle requires the use of a small hook. Nothing could be further from the truth, with many midge patterns requiring up to a size 10 hook to imitate accurately. In the case of the Black Midge Pupa a hook size of 14 or 16 is my preference. The tying is very simple but extremely effective.

Tying the Black Midge Pupa

Materials Required

Hook	Partridge Captain Hamilton up-eyed dry fly hook sized 14/16 or equivalent.
Body	Soft black dubbing with a small amount of pearl Lite Brite mixed in.
Rib and cheeks	Red Superfloss / Flexifloss.
Hackle	Dark blue dun cock a size smaller than normal for a hook.
Post	GSP or Kevlar.
Thread	Black of own choice 8/0.

Although not essential, I prefer to use a gallows tool when tying this fly pattern.

Securing the hackle

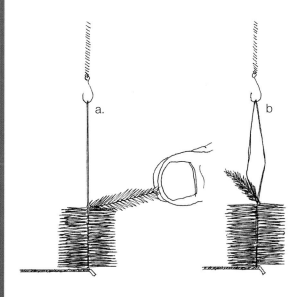

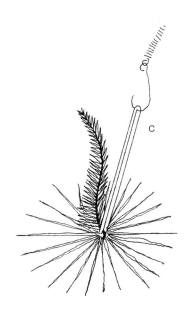

a. Wind the hackle up the post loop for the required number of turns
b. Open up the loop above the wound hackle and feed the end of the hackle between the opened loop
c. Close the loop to secure the end of the hackle

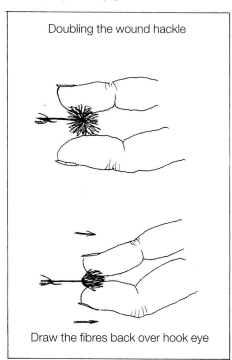

Doubling the wound hackle

Draw the fibres back over hook eye

The Black Midge Pupa

Fig. 1

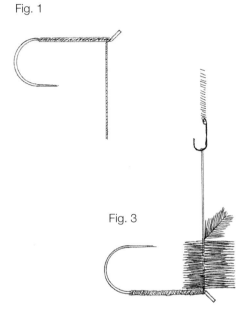

Fig. 2

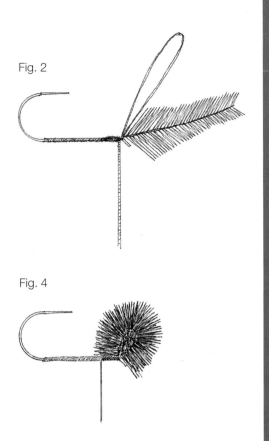

Fig. 3

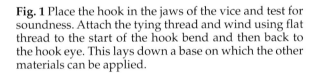

Fig. 4

Fig. 1 Place the hook in the jaws of the vice and test for soundness. Attach the tying thread and wind using flat thread to the start of the hook bend and then back to the hook eye. This lays down a base on which the other materials can be applied.

Fig. 2 Turn the hook upside down by rotating the jaws of the vice. (This is one of those times when a true rotary vice is an advantage, but don't worry if your vice is not true rotary, if this is the case then withdraw the hook from the jaws of the vice and reset it upside down.) Form a loop with a 5 in (13 cm) length of GSP or Kevlar and tie in directly behind the hook eye, directly on the underside of the hook shank. Then prepare and tie in the dark blue dun cock hackle directly at the base of the post. Cut off the excess hackle stalk and GSP. The hackle should be pointing out over the hook eye.

Fig. 3 Attach the GSP or Kevlar post loop to the hook of a gallows tool ensuring the post loop is held taut. Then wind the hackle up the post in fairly close even turns for a distance not exceeding ¾ in (2 cm). When the hackle has been wound for this distance, take a dubbing needle and part the two sides of the post loop above the wound hackle. When the two sides have been separated feed the end of the hackle tip through the post loop and pull all of the unwound hackle through the separated loop (see inserted diagram).

Now allow the post loop to close over the hackle. This procedure locks the hackle within the post loop preventing it from unwinding. That completes the hackle brush. Now slightly compress the hackle brush by using a dubbing needle placed through the post loop, above the hackle and press it downward. Also double the hackle brush by brushing the hackle fibres over away from the hook, using the thumb and first finger (see inserted diagram). Doubling resets the hackle fibres so that they are facing to one side of the hackle brush rather than all around the central post.

Fig. 4 Pull the doubled hackle brush over and down upon the hook shank directly behind where the post was originally tied in, ensuring that the doubled fibres stick out from the central post all around the looped hackle brush and do not twist into the inside of the looped hackle brush. Tie in the post and the protruding hackle on to the hook shank and cut off the excess hackle and post material.

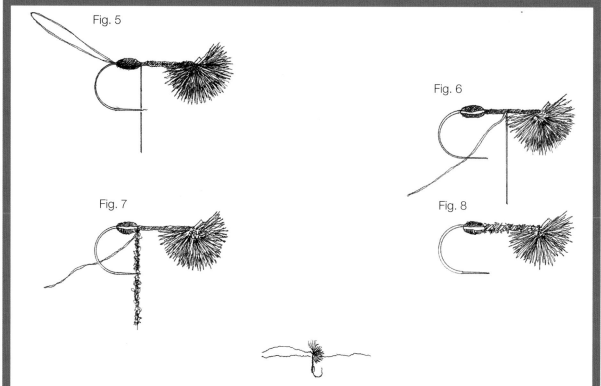

Fig. 5

Fig. 6

Fig. 7

Fig. 8

Fig. 5 Return the hook to the upright position by rotating the vice jaws or removing the hook and resetting. Wind the thread to the start of the hook bend. Take a 4 in (10 cm) length of the red Flexifloss for use as the rib and cheeks and form it into a loop tying in tightly at the start of the hook bend. It is important that one end of the Flexifloss extends out over the bend from the near side of the hook shank and that the other end extends out along the far side of the hook shank. Cut off any excess Flexifloss.

Now form a bulge of thread between the start of the hook bend and the point on the hook shank that is directly above the point of the hook. Forming this bulge is best performed by using the thread spun flat, as this will give a smoother finish to the wound thread bulge. Finish with the tying thread on the hook eye side of the thread bulge. This bulge imitates the thorax on the natural insect.

Fig. 6 Now pull the Flexifloss loop directly along the side of the bulge and tie in directly at the opposite end of the bulge. It is important that the Flexifloss is tied in so that it forms cheeks on either side of the thread bulge. Stretch the Flexifloss loop along the length of the hook shank and wind the thread, using tight turns of flat thread, along the

hook shank tying in the stretched floss as you go. Stop tying in the Flexifloss when you reach the halfway point along the hook shank. Now cut the Flexifloss only on the far side of the hook shank. Make sure that when you cut the Flexifloss it does not leave any excess, this is achieved by stretching it and then cutting. By doing this the small excess will contract under the last turn or two of thread.

Fig. 7 Holding the thread tight, pull the remaining end of the Flexifloss back over towards the thread bulge and again tie in by winding the thread using tight turns back to the base of the bulge. The loose Flexifloss will now be extending back over the thread bulge from a point at the start of the thread bulge. Lightly dub the thread with the body dubbing mixed with a little pearl Lite Brite

Fig. 8 Wind on the dubbed thread forming a slim but slightly tapered body, tapering down towards the hook eye, wind right up to the GSP or Kevlar post pulling the hackle over the hook eye to give better access. Now wind on the Flexifloss as a rib, making sure that the floss is stretched as you do so. Tie in the rib using a few tight turns of the dubbed thread, then looping the Flexifloss back and make another few turns of tight thread to lock the Flexifloss in place. Complete the fly with a whip finish protruding under the hackle.

A fish rising to the midge on a summer evening

That completes the tying of the Black Midge Pupa designed to imitate the natural insect prior to it going into the emerging mode. The use of the Paraloop hackle brush with only upward windings of hackle, rather than upward and then downward windings, reduces the number of hackle fibres to assist in making the pattern float, the reduction in the size of the hackle has a similar effect. The result of this hackle and the varnished body allow the pattern to float but only float for a short time, it will then start to slowly sink – first just under the surface and then slowly downward, which is what the pattern is designed to do.

Because of this the fly pattern must be cast as if it was a delicate dry fly and allowed to land on the water like thistledown. If the presentation is not performed in this way then the fly pattern will not float at all and start sinking immediately. Prior to using the pattern it is advisable to treat the hackle generously with a silicon compound. This is best done the day before you set off to the water, or better still immediately after the fly pattern has been tied. Allow time for the silicon compound to be absorbed and to dry on the hackle.

When fishing with this pattern, after the fly has started to sink, leave it for sometime and watch the leader where it enters the surface of the water, this is the bite indicator. Short of the odd twitch and keeping in touch with the fly pattern I would not be tempted to retrieve when using this fly pattern, the best results come when it is left well alone.

After each cast dry out the fly pattern by performing a couple of false casts before once again presenting it to the water.

When fishing with a midge pupa pattern in a non-floating version, I find it very difficult to use any other pattern besides the varnished or epoxy buzzer (a buzzer is another name for the midge pupa). In its simplest form the previous tying without the hackle would be an example. The procedure for tying them is very simple and straightforward. There are many different styles incorporated by tyers for tying these fly patterns and the following is the method I use. I have chosen to imitate a grey midge commonly referred to as the Grey Boy to demonstrate this particular tying.

Tying the Varnished Grey Boy Buzzer

Materials Required

Hook	Continuous bend hook. Kamasan B110 or B100 or similar.
Body and Thorax	Grey floss.
Rib	Single strand of pearl coloured Lite Brite, Flashabou or similar.
Cheeks	Orange floss.
Thread	Own choice 8/0.

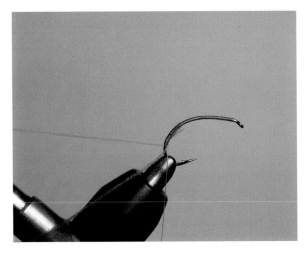

Photograph 1 Fix the hook in the jaws of the vice and test for soundness. Using the waxed thread spun flat, wind the tying thread right around the bend as shown in the photograph. Using 'the loop over the tying thread' method first tie in the rib and then attach the body floss.

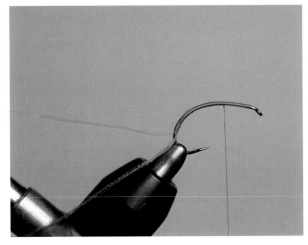

Photograph 2 Wind the tying thread, using flat thread, back along the hook shank to a position two thirds of the way to the hook eye. As you wind the thread complete the tying in of the rib and body floss. It should be unnecessary but if there are any excess materials cut them off well prior to the thread reaching this position.

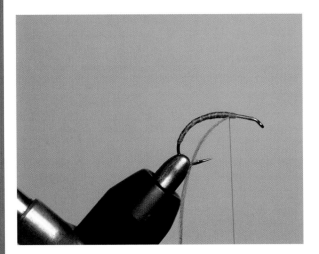

Photograph 3 Wind the body floss, using the floss spun flat, to a position two thirds of the way back along the hook shank towards the hook eye. Form a slightly tapering body with the body floss thin at one end and getting slightly thicker as it approaches the position two thirds of the way back along the hook shank. Tie in the body floss on the underside of the hook shank using just two turns of thread. Now wind on the rib and tie in at the same point as the body floss is tied in, complete tying in both materials and cut off the excess rib but leave the body floss.

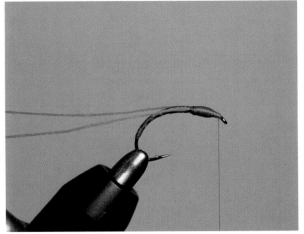

Photograph 4 Take a 6 in (15 cm) length of orange floss to be used as the cheeks and form into a loop. Tie in both loose ends, one on the far side of the hook shank, the other on the near side of the hook shank and take the tying thread to behind the eye of the hook. The length is just a suggestion and it is far more than is needed to tie one pattern, but it can be used over and over to produce many patterns. Now form a thorax bulge using the body floss (keep the floss spun flat), on completion of the thorax bulge tie in the body floss behind the hook eye and cut off the excess material.

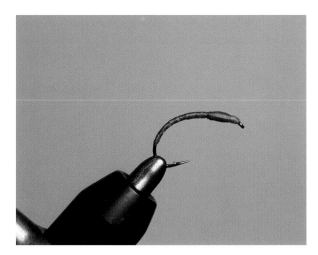

Photograph 5 Pull the cheek floss loop over the front of the hook, ensuring that, as you do so, the floss is in the position to form cheeks on either side of the thorax bulge. Tie in the cheek floss behind the hook eye and cut off the excess.

Photograph 6 Now form a small head and complete with a whip finish. It is time now to varnish the completed fly pattern using three or four coats of varnish. Let each coat dry before applying the next so that there is no wrinkling of the varnish. That completes the pattern.

Photograph 7 The completed fly.

My tendency is to complete the fly up to and including the whip finish and then stick it in some foam. After I have tied enough for my needs I varnish them all together, leaving them in the foam until the last coat of varnish has completely dried.

As a lad one of the more obvious aquatic insects to come my way, when dredging the pond, was the midge larva. These insects stood out against the weed because of their colour, most of them being a fairly strong red colour, although I have seen them coloured differently. This red colour is due to the presence of haemoglobin in the blood and this lets the blood store oxygen and so allows the insect to live in an oxygen depleted environment, such as the mud in the bottom of ponds and lakes. The red colour is the reason this larva is referred to as the bloodworm.

There can be little doubt that where the midge is in attendance, midge larvae provide a substantial part of the trout's diet. Again I have found that imitating this insect is best achieved by keeping it simple. So simple to the extent that I am not averse to using a continuous bend hook painted red along the shank. A slight elaboration on that most basic of fly patterns is to wind a white or light coloured tying thread flat along the hook shank of a continuous bend hook. Then tie in a thread to act as a rib, wind the thread back to the eye of the hook and then wind on the rib, tie in the rib and complete with a whip finish. The whole lot is then coloured using a bright red permanent ink pen. Such flies are as simple as anything that a fly tyer will sit down at the tying bench to complete.

There are slightly more elaborate patterns, such as fixing a piece cut from a thin red rubber band to a hook (Arthur Cove's Rubber Band Fly). Or furling red floss and attaching it to a hook. Such tyings require no explanation on how to tie them as common sense is enough to decipher the steps. The photograph shows various options, all of which have proved successful over the years in imitating the midge larva.

That ends this section on Nymphs, Larvae and Pupa. In the Fly Gallery at the end of this book there is a selection of patterns tied using the techniques described in this chapter.

A simple parachute style midge emerger.

A CDC suspender type buzzer tied so that the CDC sits at ninety degrees to the hook shank. This is achieved by winding thread between the hook eye and the position the CDC has been tied on the hook shank. Doing this will alter slightly the position the fly pattern will sit when in the water, making it sit more horizontally compared to when the CDC is tied in to extend over the hook eye and horizontally along the hook shank.

5. IT'S A SMALL STREAM AFFAIR

Part I

For me fishing small streams is a solitary affair. I have thought about this carefully and 'affair' is the correct word, implying an intimacy separate from the regularity of my life, such is small stream fishing. Although, on further reflection, describing it as a solitary affair is not wholly true. Preferring to fish alone is not for the sake of being alone, but rather to remove unnecessary distraction. I find fishing such waters is best when it becomes a personal communion, a communion between the stream and myself.

Rarely do I have anyone else join me when I set out to fish one of the many tributaries, or tributaries of tributaries, flowing amongst the hills that lie within easy travelling distance from my home. That is not to say I am always alone when fishing such waters, sometimes I even share a rod, but on the whole this is less than satisfactory. I end up acting as an unpaid guide, describing the water and pointing out likely lies, which I know will often hold a fish above average size.

Friends have, on a few occasions, persuaded me, against my better judgement, to let them tag along rod in hand. Hearing me sing the praises of fishing small streams, they want someone to hold their hand when giving it a try. This misses the point altogether, far better to find out for yourself by yourself, as I said it is a solitary affair.

Small stream fishing is usually free, only requiring permission from the owner. This is one of its attractions and results in two tangible benefits. The first is in the wallet, the second on the way the streams are managed. Basically they aren't, they are of no monetary value and so to the greater extent they are left untouched. Some of the trees may be cut back from time to time, but only if they trespass over an adjacent road, or the banks may be built up and strengthened where a bend in the stream begins to eat into grazing or other valuable land. But generally they are undisturbed. You will find no carefully tended banks here, no trees cut back to allow the sweep of a rod, no branches pruned to save the careless fly, no hut to shelter from the rain and no rustic benches carefully positioned to give the best view of the water. This is backwoods fishing, rough fishing, where the finesse is limited to the delivery of the fly. It is also distance fishing where the casts are short and I walk the distance. Five, six or even eight miles in a day is not unusual and don't forget the walk back. After a day on the water I return home feeling good, tired but good. It's satisfying, something along the lines of 'if you work hard you get paid', an ethic built within our genes or sub-conscious mind. And work you must if the best is to be experienced from a small stream, they demand time and effort and what they offer cannot be bought or stolen.

The fish in these waters are brown trout, I come across a lot of salmon parr, but the quarry is the brown trout. They are feisty, have a go trout, not usually big, but tough and when hooked they never give in, fighting all the way. These trout are pretty fish, ranging in colour from almost silver to deep yellow and brown, dotted with bright, seemingly fluorescent, red spots. In the high reaches where the stream begins and flows through peat, the water will be tinted a deep golden beer-brown. When these waters are deep, as in the pools, they appear dark and forbidding. Trout found in such sombre basins can be the colour of the wet peat itself, closer to black than brown.

Sometimes I hook, by chance or, more rarely, design, much larger fish than the normal and my largest trout to date from a small stream scaled a little over 3½ lb (1.6 kg). This was caught one glorious summer Saturday morning close to my home. Such prizes are few and far between and years can pass without winning one. Generally the fish are pan-sized. The name is appropriate as three or four cleaned fit neatly into a small pan, just add a knob of butter and fry over a stone lined fire. Throwing in a large pinch of salt and a generous covering of ground pepper as they sizzle away, will provide a feast to remember. The smell alone is enough to get excited about and can justify the effort of building the fire. Rancid butter does nothing for the dish, however, as I found out to my eternal disappointment a few years ago, it tastes awful and after a tough day fishing was a hard cross to bear.

The choice of fly when fishing a small stream is, in my experience, less important than when fishing larger streams and rivers. The fish are opportunistic and will respond to most flies if they are presented well. It's like the three 'Ps' guide for opening a new restaurant, the three most important factors being 'Position', 'Position', 'Position'. When fishing for small stream trout it's 'Presentation', 'Presentation', 'Presentation'. Accuracy is an important part of that presentation, although not for the usual reasons. It is important because small trout and salmon parr will snatch your fly in a flash, often as soon as it lands on the surface of the water. For that reason the target fish must be covered very closely, to ensure that it has a chance to rise before the fly is grabbed by a tiny slip of energy. It's amazing to see the size of fly a tiny trout or salmon parr will rise to. These little fish can successfully take a size eight hook, tied as a daddylonglegs and how their mouths manage to stretch so wide is a wonder to see.

The flies I use are all simple, mostly true dries and emerger patterns often tied Paraloop or Devaux style. Tied this way they float far better than traditional and parachute hackled flies. Black gnats, olives, sedges and stonefly nymphs for most of the time, a basic selection of terrestrial patterns and a medium sized daddylonglegs or two thrown in for the later part of the season. A few just-in-case weighted nymphs and spider patterns complete the package. Even when there is no rising fish a dry fly can be used to good effect and will often draw a good fish up from the depths. Matching any hatch is not essential, although doing so adds an additional dimension to the fishing, like being dealt the final card in a royal flush, it allows all the parts of the operation to click firmly into place.

A rise to the fly on a small stream is far from leisurely, it is a snatch, a smash-and-grab of a take. If they don't get there first, then some other fish will, depriving them of what's on offer, this makes each take quick, lightning quick. If I haven't fished such water for a few months, I'll be rusty and my hand co-ordination not all it's cracked up to be, as a result some takes will be missed. With a little practice the touch soon returns and I'll find myself connecting more often than not. In the faster waters running into or out of pools, or where the stream narrows, keeping in touch with the fly is really all that is required. Do that and the fish hook themselves in their enthusiasm.

A small stream runs by my home and every few steps taken along its banks presents a new fishing challenge, each requiring a unique solution, no twenty-yard stretch is the same. All told it only flows for around eight miles, getting narrower as you head upstream. It's a tributary of a tributary of the River Tweed, way down the pecking order in so far as fishing waters go. This suits me just fine, as I rarely see anyone else casting a line there. Living so close to the water lets me fish on a whim, at just a moment's notice, whether it is for a few minutes or a whole day. Seeing a good trout under the bridge, I can grab a rod and spend five minutes trying to tempt it, or waking up early, decide it's time to be on the water and three hours pass quickly fishing the upper reaches before breakfast.

At one time, or so the story goes, Saturday mornings would see fishers head out by train from Edinburgh on the old Border Line. Until its closure forty odd years ago, this line connected Edinburgh to Carlisle in the north west of England running right through the Scottish Borders. Some passengers would leave the train at Heriot Station, to fish the Heriot Water and those fishing the Galawater would alight at Stow. Those heading for the Tweed would continue on to Galashiels and make the walk to the river from the station. When the train left Edinburgh it would be full, after Galashiels almost empty, most passengers having left, creel on shoulder and rod held firmly in hand.

Although the brown trout season on the Tweed River system starts in April, in the high, upper reaches of the small feeder streams, the fishing doesn't begin for real until mid to late May or, in some years, well into June. Here the waters are cold and it takes exposure to the spring sun to awaken them. The first flies to show themselves in any number are the midges, black with light grey wings, the Blae and Black of Scottish flies. They start to show in numbers from the middle of April, but it is not until the sedge and olives emerge that the stream can be said to have come truly alive. My favourite time to fish is from the last few days of June to the end of the season on the final day of September. This makes the season short, being a little over three months long. That is not to say fish cannot be caught before June, I have landed many fish in April, but the full richness of the water can rarely be experienced before this time.

High moorland streams speak to the heart in a way untouched by other waters. Don't get me wrong I'm not saying they are better, just different. It is, however, fishing not suited to everyone. To hike a few miles over marram grass and bog, to cast a fly on a stream where the trout average 24 in (61 cm), but only when you place three or four of them head to tail. Set in a landscape where the only features are the shape of the hills, the sky and, well the shape of the hills, is not everybody's cup of tea. I love it. This is where the trout are measured in numbers not by size, although the lesser gods of chance sometimes deal a hand that breaks the usual run of the mill, supplying a fish of far greater dimensions. There is never any telling what lies in the depths of a peat stained moorland pool.

I have never fished a stream completely from one end to the other, but it is something I would like and intend to do some day. I'd start off where it meets its destiny, most probably another stream and from there, move on up, until I could cast no more, the water petering out to a trickle. I sometimes think if I did, then I would know that stream like a close friend, not just in parts but the whole thing. When sleep demanded my eyes to close, I would lie by the running waters, it would be the last sound I heard and the first when I woke. Ideally the stream should be unknown to me, so each turn, each pool would be like a new world opening up before my very eyes and the thrill of the new from the unknown making each moment one to savour. It would need to be long, at least two days long, so the initial novelty has time to wear off. Upstream I would fish the dry fly and returning down, the wet fly and nymph.

I suspect though, that I would no more know that stream after four days upon its banks, than I did before I started. True it will have teased and thrilled me, the siren play of its water drawing me closer, yet never allowing me to truly touch its heart. Only time permits such a bond, time measured in years not days. When I say I know such a water, what I should be saying is I am acquainted with it, I meet it on occasion, like some regular in a bar, someone who I share a drink with from time to time. I enjoy their company and slowly what they do and like will be revealed, most of their life, however, will still remain a mystery to me.

Fishing a small stream with no desire to keep any fish, other than perhaps a couple to eat by the side of the water from which they came, is the test of a true fisher. There is no one there to impress with knowledge, tackle or casting, no victory trophy to be shown, just you, the water and the fish. There's usually nothing much to tell, the experience may be profound but how many times can you tell the guys that without their eyes glazing over. Fishing small streams tends to make me quieter, elements of humility stalk me along the banks and, as I become older and perhaps a little wiser, I am less inclined to resist their advances.

Part II

One of the wonderful things about small stream fishing is that there is so much of it. There are few parts of any country where, within reasonable travelling distance, the opportunity does not exist for anglers to enjoy what small streams have to offer. The variety offered by such waters is more than enough to satisfy any true angler.

Fly Patterns for Small Streams

The fly patterns I use when fishing small streams are imitative patterns. Ideally, for the full experience of fly fishing, imitations of flies found on or in the water at the time you are fishing are the best to use. This may sound obvious, but how many times is a fly tied on a tippet just because it looks good in the fly box, rather than matched to the natural flies around at the time? The fly patterns come into three categories – dries, emergers and wet. The dry flies are those which imitate the adult fly, either newly emerged or spent and the terrestrial flies, those land based flies blown on to the water by the wind. The emerger patterns imitate the adult fly at the different stages of its struggling from the skin of the nymph or pupa. The wet fly, and I include nymphs in this category, imitates the earlier stages in the life cycles of flies – the larva, pupa and nymph. Saying all that, small stream trout are not very fussy and will usually have a go at most patterns offered to them, even those which resemble nothing like that available to them naturally, as I mentioned in Part I of this chapter, they are 'have a go' trout. Bearing that in mind, however, I get the best results from imitating those flies the fish are feeding on at any one time, particularly if I am looking to hook something bigger than the normal run of the mill fish.

I find the most important flies from a fly fish-ing point of view when fishing small streams are the midges, upwinged flies (mayflies), sedges, stoneflies and the terrestrials, which pretty much covers the whole gamut of natural flies imitated by the fly patterns I tie. Many of the smaller waters I fish have prolific hatches of all these flies at different times and each can be fished successfully at all stages of the life cycles. The one exception to this is when the stonefly is on the water. The stoneflies, ranging from tiny Needle Flies to large beasts imitated best on a size 8 or 10 hook, is best imitated, at least in my opinion, by the use of the nymph. This holds true even when there are plenty of flies in the air, the fish seeming to prefer it and I am not the one to argue with that.

The Midges

One of the earliest flies of the year to be seen on any small stream is the midge and the first of these that I see is usually the black midge. One of my favourite fly patterns used for imitating this fly in its emerging adult form is the Black Gnat, preferably tied Paraloop or Parachute style. Although originally designed to imitate the real Black Gnat, a completely different fly than the midge, its effectiveness as a black midge imitation cannot be denied and it slips into this role easily. The following tying sequence is described in detail in the accompanying illustration, 'Tying Paraloop Flies – The Black Gnat'. Tied using the Paraloop allows the fly to sit low in the water whilst maintaining a reasonable amount of hackle. The lack of hackle under the hook shank greatly assists in hooking fast taking fish and small stream trout are fast takers. The tying is quite simple and can use hooks sized 14, 16. The hook shape can vary and in the tying illustrated I have used a traditional up-eyed dry fly hook. Using this shape of hook has the effect of making the pattern sit almost horizontal in the water surface. The body is pulled down into the surface of the water by the weight of the hook bend and imitates the shuck. The hackle imitates the actual fly almost free of the shuck. I have located the post, in this particular tying, directly behind the hook eye, thereby doing away with any head and the pattern is tied off between the body and hackle. As normal I prefer to use a gallows tool for the tying of this pattern.

Moorland stream

Tying the Black Gnat Paraloop

Materials Required

Hook   Up-eyed dry fly. Partridge Captain Hamilton.

Hackle   Quality dyed black cock.

Body   Black polypropylene floss.

Thorax   Fine black polypropylene dubbing.

Post   GSP or alternative.

Thread   Of personal choice 8/0.

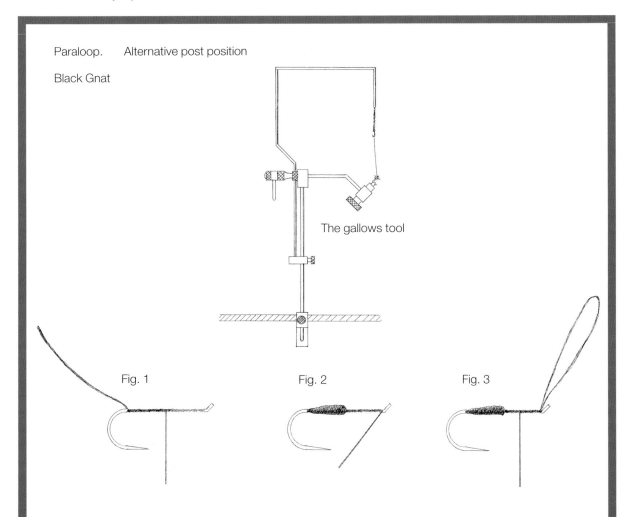

Paraloop.   Alternative post position

Black Gnat

The gallows tool

Fig. 1

Fig. 2

Fig. 3

Fig. 1 Place the hook in the jaws of the vice and test the hook for soundness. Attach the waxed thread and wind using flat turns of thread to the start of the hook bend. Tie in the black body floss, using the 'loop over the thread' method and wind the tying thread to the halfway point along the hook shank, tying in the body floss as you go. There should be no need to cut off any excess hackle as this can be pulled back to the right length when first tied in.

Fig. 2 Remove any twist within the body floss and wind on flat to the halfway point along the hook shank, forming a shaped body. Tie in the body floss on to the underside of the hook shank and cut off the excess floss. Now wind the thread to directly behind the hook eye.

Fig. 3 Take 4 or 5 in (10 or 13 cm) of the post material and form a loop. Tie the loop by the loose ends on to the top of the hook shank so that it extends by the hook eye.

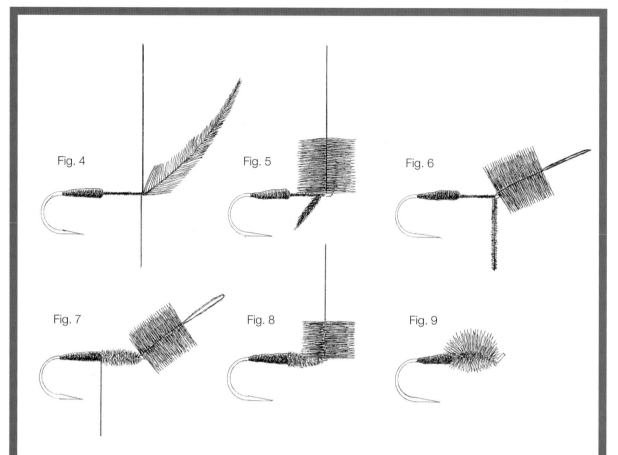

Fig. 4 Tie in the prepared black hackle directly at the base of the post loop, the hackle should extend over the front of the hook and the good side should be facing you but leaning slightly upward.

Fig. 5 Attach the post loop to the gallows tool ensuring that it is held taut. Now wind the hackle first up the post and then down through the previously wound hackle and tie off on to the section of the hook shank to the left of the post.

Fig. 6 Complete the tying in of the hackle and cut off the excess hackle. Remove the post loop from the gallows tool and pull the completed hackle over the front of the hook, this gives access to the thorax area. Wind the tying thread back to the base of the post and dub the thread using the fine black polypropylene dubbing.

Fig. 7 Wind on the dubbed tying thread to the start of the body forming a shaped thorax as you go. The thorax should be thicker in the middle than at either end.

Fig. 8 Now reattach the post loop to the gallows tool and then **compact the hackle** slightly by gently pulling apart the two sides of the loop post above the hackle. Then **double the hackle** so that the hackle fibres will not be crushed against the thorax when the hackle brush is pulled over. This is achieved by gently brushing the hackle fibres towards the front of the hook.

Fig. 9 Remove the post loop from the gallows tool and pull the hackle brush over the top of the thorax. The hackle brush should extend to where the body meets the thorax. If it is too long then just compact the hackle again. Tie in the post loop exactly at the point where the floss body meets the dubbed thorax and complete with a whip finish. Cut off the tying thread.

That completes the Black Gnat to be used as an emerging black midge pattern.

As the season develops and the air and water temperature increases, midge flies of different body colours begin to show themselves and red, green, grey are amongst the many shades that can be found on the water. The same tying sequence as the Black Gnat can be used with only the body shade changing and the hackle used being a light blue dun to imitate more accurately the natural flies. A black body with light blue dun hackle makes for a first class alternative for the Black Midge. These fly patterns can be fished up, across or down stream, but allowance must always be made for the tendency of the line to drag the fly in the current. The use of mends in the line or loose line casts will help to minimize this. I find this fly pattern works best when fishing the larger pools, with back eddies and areas of relatively still water, especially if the bottom is muddy and silted.

The midges (*Chironomids*) are the adult of what, in the UK, have commonly become known as buzzers, the buzzer being the pupa of the fly. Originally the title buzzer referred to the buzzing noise of the adult fly, the name is now almost always applied to the pupa only, pre-emerging or emerging. Buzzer fishing has been one of the UK's faster growth areas of fly fishing in recent years, the methods used having evolved to a highly sophisticated degree. Most of this growth in buzzer fishing has taken place on still waters. What is not always understood or appreciated is the importance of buzzers when fishing rivers and small streams. Midges are wholly opportunistic and any bit of suitable water will be utilized for the laying of eggs and as a nursery for the larva. Take a look at that old bucket in the garden, or anything else that sits holding water. The chances are it will hold midge larvae and pupae. Most small streams have some suitable water, as such the buzzer should never be underestimated as a fly of choice, either in the form of the emerging fly or the pupa. I cannot say that I have ever used a midge larva imitation when fishing small streams. Thinking about it there is probably no good reason why I don't use such patterns, especially if the water conditions are right, but I have never got around to it to date.

The buzzer tied so as to imitate the emerging fly can use many fly tying techniques to achieve the required positioning and shape of the fly pattern in or on the water. There is no doubt in my mind that many patterns tied to traditional dry fly recipes sit on or in the water more as an emerging fly than a true dry fly. This, however, is

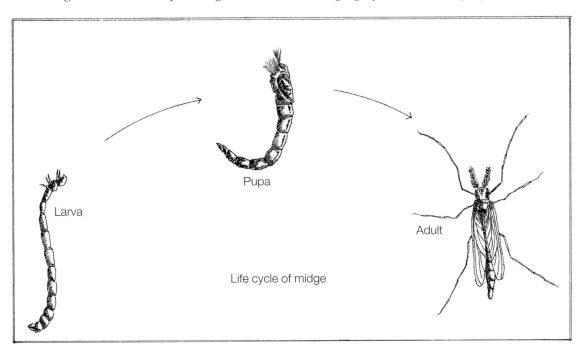

Larva

Pupa

Adult

Life cycle of midge

The life cycle of the midge, from larva to adult.

Tying the CDC suspender buzzer.

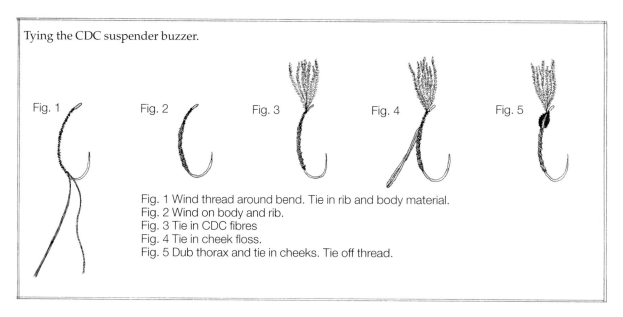

Fig. 1 Fig. 2 Fig. 3 Fig. 4 Fig. 5

Fig. 1 Wind thread around bend. Tie in rib and body material.
Fig. 2 Wind on body and rib.
Fig. 3 Tie in CDC fibres
Fig. 4 Tie in cheek floss.
Fig. 5 Dub thorax and tie in cheeks. Tie off thread.

more accidental than a deliberate imitative technique and is due to the materials used in construction and the actual shape of the fly pattern. One of the most important factors when imitating the emerging fly is the choice of hook. As mentioned previously in this book, continuous bend hooks are more flexible in being able to give the impression of the newly emerging fly climbing out of the skin of the pupa than traditional dry fly hooks. The reason for this is that the rear part of the fly is under water sitting in a more vertical position. This can give a very good impression of the emerging fly and of the pupa prior to it going into full emerging mode. When fishing an emerging midge pattern in a small stream, I will often use cul de canard feather fibres or boot-lace fibres to hold the fly in the surface. Doing this allows the rear of the fly to sit below the surface of the water in the manner referred to as suspended. This can also be achieved successfully using the Parachute and Paraloop methods of adding a hackle. When using the Parachute method fly patterns tied using the Klinkhamar style of tying are ideal. When using the Paraloop method of adding the hackle the open loop method is best employed.

The illustration entitled 'Tying the CDC suspender buzzer' describes how to tie such a fly pattern. The suggested materials are as follows and apply to tying an olive buzzer, but

any number of different materials can be used to tie such flies.

Materials Suggested

Hook	Continuous bend hook. Kamasan B100, size depending on the insect being imitated.
Body	Olive floss wound flat.
Suspension	Bunch of CDC feather fibres.
Thorax	Fine olive polypropylene dubbing, this is dubbed on to the tying thread.
Cheeks	Orange floss formed into a loop. This is tied in with one of the loose ends tied on the near side of the hook shank and the other loose end on to the far side of the hook shank. This allows the loop of floss to be pulled over the front of the hook and tied in to form the cheeks.
Rib	Brown Flexifloss.
Thread	Own choice 8/0.

The Open Loop Paraloop is described in the next illustration and I have used the Green Midge to explain the method. The illustration explains the tying sequence. The basis of the 'Open Loop' method is that the hackle brush is longer in length than the section of the fly pattern it is intended to cover. The result of this is

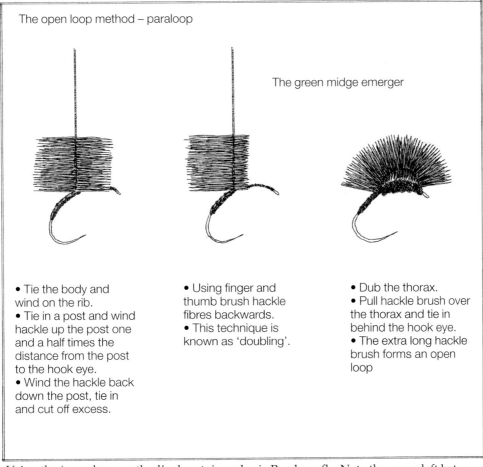

The open loop method – paraloop

The green midge emerger

- Tie the body and wind on the rib.
- Tie in a post and wind hackle up the post one and a half times the distance from the post to the hook eye.
- Wind the hackle back down the post, tie in and cut off excess.

- Using finger and thumb brush hackle fibres backwards.
- This technique is known as 'doubling'.

- Dub the thorax.
- Pull hackle brush over the thorax and tie in behind the hook eye.
- The extra long hackle brush forms an open loop

Using the 'open loop method' when tying a basic Paraloop fly. Note the space left between the post of the hackle brush and the top of the thorax.

that when the hackle brush is tied in it forms an open loop, hence the name.

Materials Used

Hook   Continuous bend hook. Kamasan B100.

Hackle Medium blue dun cock hackle.

Body   Green floss.

Thorax Fine green polypropylene dubbing.

Rib   Dark green tying thread waxed with dark cobbler's wax.

Details on doubling can be found on page 21.

When imitating the midge pupa, prior to the emerging of the adult fly and the pupa entering the emergence mode, the epoxy or varnished buzzer is a pattern to be relied upon to generate

A Klinkhamar style fly pattern.

success. Fished as a single fly or as a team, sport can be fast and furious in the relatively shallow waters of a small stream. Tying the epoxy or varnished buzzer could not be easier. This ease of tying in no way reflects their ability to attract fish, proving, as they have on so many occasions for me, to be one of the most successful fly patterns available. This fly pattern has gained the name Epoxy Buzzer, but as far as I am concerned the use of epoxy resin is messy and unnecessary. When tying these fly patterns, if tying is the right word, I only ever use varnish. The varnish is applied in three or four coats. Using varnish is far easier and just as effective, if not more so, than using epoxy resin. When the fly is completed, fix it in a block of foam and give the fly a coat of varnish, just enough to cover the fly and for it not to gather as a blob on the underside of the fly. Repeat the varnishing every hour or two until a sufficient depth of coating is obtained. I use Sally Hanson's Hard as Nails and the result is perfect. The tying of a varnished buzzer/midge pupa is described in the section entitled 'Nymphs, Larvae and Pupae 2' on page 141.

As with the adult imitation these can be tied in different sizes and colours to imitate those flies present in your own particular water. A little observation will soon indicate which sizes and colours should produce regular results.

The Sedge or Caddis Fly

When the sedge fly (also known as caddis fly) is on the air you know it is time to set up your rod and tie on a fly pattern. These flies are one of the trout's favourite foods, giving a good mouthful and hatching in abundance. For me the sedge is a fly of the late spring and summer evenings, especially summer evenings, although I see it regularly as late as autumn and even late autumn. When the air is warm and the sound of splashing rises from the trout indicate the sedge flies are on the rise. Sedge fly fishing is not finicky or fiddly fishing, rather it is a whole hearted, full bodied and bold affair, with fly patterns tied on hooks up to a size 8. Hatches of sedges can occur at almost any time of the day, but I find mid to late morning and evening into the dark the best times. Fishing a dry fly is my

preferred method, using patterns tied with spun deer hair, to patterns tied using full length body hackled Paraloops. I have found one of the most effective patterns to be what I call the 'Bomb'. It is effective both for its ability to float and for attracting fish. I call it the 'Bomb' because it is a classic Bomber pattern without a wing and tail. Although the pattern, in its bomber form, is more associated as a dry fly for salmon fishing, its effectiveness as a trout fly cannot be denied and I have regularly seen it catch more fish than all other imitations put together, including more realistic patterns of the caddis. My favourite uses spun natural deer hair, palmered with a doubled grizzle hackle, dyed hot orange. Don't ask me why it is so effective it just is. I use it tied on hooks from size 16 to size 10 depending on the size of the flies on the water.

Here is how to tie the medium brown sedge using the Bomb. There is nothing innovative, about the tying, as methods used are very well established. The resulting fly pattern is one I would recommend to anyone. It will fish well in still or slow moving water and equally as well in fast running water. I particularly like to use it when the stream is fast flowing especially in the neck and tails of pools. This pattern can be allowed to drag over the surface of the water, to imitate a skimming sedge fly attempting to take to the wing. I find allowing the pattern to drag gets the best results in the evening as the light starts to fade. If sea trout are in the stream that I am fishing, I am never surprised if a sedge pattern skimmed across the surface of the water entices one to take a lunge. If I am lucky maybe I will hook up with a sea-going brown trout, that is an event that has the potential of being the highlight of any season.

Tying the Medium Brown Sedge Bomb

Materials Required

Hook	Dry fly, Partridge Captain Hamilton size 12.
Body	Natural deer hair.
Hackle	Grizzle cock dyed hot orange.
Thread	Unwaxed of own choice, but perhaps a little stronger than normal for spinning the deer hair.

Photograph 1 Place the hook in the jaws of the vice and test the hook for soundness. Wind the **unwaxed** thread to the start of the hook bend using flat thread and tie in the hackle by the tip. Return the thread to the start of the hook bend.

Photograph 2 Double the hackle using the method described earlier in this book (Air's Apparent II). I find it best to double the hackle at this stage as opposed to after the body has been applied to the hook, just in case the hackle breaks during doubling. It can always be retied in at this stage without too much disruption.

Photograph 3 With the tying thread at the start of the hook bend, offer a generous bunch of deer hair to the hook shank. The bunch of deer hair should be positioned on the top of the hook shank with the tying thread in the centre.

Photograph 4 Now make two turns of unwaxed tying thread around the hook shank and the centre of the bunch of deer hair, pulling the thread as you wind. The deer hair will flare and spin around the hook shank.

Photograph 5 I like to compact the deer hair by placing my finger and thumb at the rear of the spun hair and pushing a blunt nosed empty pen case along the hook shank and against the spun deer hair. Now bring the tying thread to directly in front of the spun deer hair. Push the deer hair fibres back to the rear of the hook and offer another bunch of deer hair to the hook shank as in photograph 3.

Photograph 6 Now repeat the procedure described in photographs 4 and 5 until the whole of the hook shank is covered in compressed deer hair. Complete a whip finish behind the hook eye but leave the thread attached.

Photograph 7 Using scissors, shape the deer hair body taking care not to cut off the hackle during the process. The shape should be like a stumpy cigar.

Photograph 8 Now wind the doubled hackle along the body, palmer style and tie in behind the hook eye. Cut off the excess hackle and form a small head with the tying thread. Complete the fly pattern with a whip finish.

Photograph 9 The completed fly.

This pattern is an excellent sedge imitation and I have found little which can match it as a successful fish catcher when the sedge/caddis are on the water. It will fish well in slow moving and fast water.

The Upwinged Flies

Like the sedge the upwinged flies are loved by the trout and as a result also by the fly fisher. There is something romantic about the mayflies, olives and other flies included in this family and some of the most enjoyable fishing I have experienced has been a result of the enthusiasm of the fish for these flies. Almost any classic imitation will be effective but I often like to use flies tied using the Devaux style funnel method of hackling. The French fly tyer and fly designer Amie Devaux devised this technique and it is just another example of his original and unique approach to fly tying. I use fly patterns tied this way to fish the faster waters, the hackle allowing the pattern to float well while letting the hook point sit low in the water. This fly pattern gives, I believe, a very good impression of an emerging fly caught up in fast flowing water and is always tied on my leader with confidence. Fishing it in the neck and tail of a pool has given me my greatest success when using it, although it is useful when searching out fast flowing and pocket water. My best results have been when the fly has been fished on a relatively slack line allowing the water current to carry it as naturally as possible. The following illustration describes how to tie the fly.

Tying a Devaux Style Mayfly Pattern

Materials Required

Hook	Dry fly up eyed. Partridge Captain Hamilton or similar.
Hackle	Light ginger cock with a skirt of natural partridge.
Body	Cream floss.
Rib	Brown tying thread waxed.
Tail	A small bunch of pheasant tail fibres – long.
Thread	Of personal choice 8/0.

Upland stream

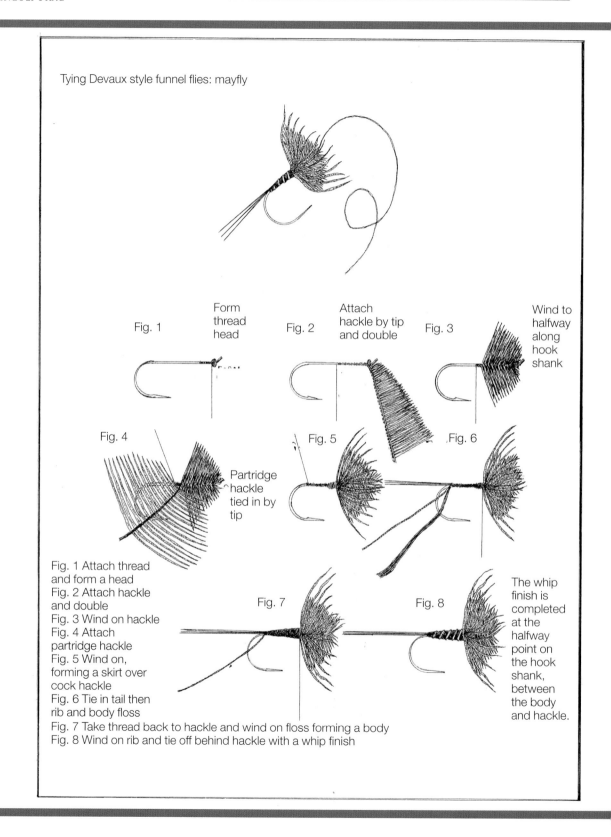

Tying Devaux style funnel flies: mayfly

Fig. 1 Form thread head

Fig. 2 Attach hackle by tip and double

Fig. 3 Wind to halfway along hook shank

Fig. 4 Partridge hackle tied in by tip

Fig. 5

Fig. 6

Fig. 7

Fig. 8 The whip finish is completed at the halfway point on the hook shank, between the body and hackle.

Fig. 1 Attach thread and form a head
Fig. 2 Attach hackle and double
Fig. 3 Wind on hackle
Fig. 4 Attach partridge hackle
Fig. 5 Wind on, forming a skirt over cock hackle
Fig. 6 Tie in tail then rib and body floss
Fig. 7 Take thread back to hackle and wind on floss forming a body
Fig. 8 Wind on rib and tie off behind hackle with a whip finish

Fig. 1 Place the hook into the jaws of the vice and test the hook for soundness. Attach the thread to the hook shank and lay a short base of flat thread. Return the thread to immediately behind the hook eye and form a small head shape using the tying thread.

Fig. 2 Attach the cock hackle by the tip immediately behind the head and double it using the method previously described. Cut off any excess hackle tip. Wind the tying thread to just short of the halfway position along the hook shank.

Fig. 3 Now wind the doubled hackle along the hook shank to just short of the halfway point. Ensure that the hackle fibres are leaning towards the front of the hook. Tie in the hackle and cut off any excess

Fig. 4 Attach the partridge hackle by the tip, immediately behind the wound cock hackle. The fibres of the partridge hackle should be considerably longer than fibres of the cock hackle. Cut off any excess tip.

Fig. 5 Wind on the partridge hackle, two complete winds will be sufficient, so that the fibres skirt the cock hackle fibres. Tie in the hackle and cut off the excess. Now wind the tying thread tight against the partridge hackle forcing the fibres forward. Wind the thread to start of the hook bend.

Fig. 6 Tie in the pheasant tail fibres as a bunch to form the tail. Then tie in the thread rib followed immediately by the body floss, use the 'loop over the thread' method to tie in the rib and body floss. Wind the thread to immediately behind the hackle tying in the ends of the rib and body floss as you go.

Fig. 7 Wind on the body floss forming a tapered body shape and tie in immediately behind the hackle. Cut off the excess floss.

Fig. 8 Now wind on the thread rib and tie in between the body and the hackle. Cut off the excess thread rib. Now complete a whip finish between the body and the hackle, ideally tightening the thread so that it disappears between the body and hackle. Cut off the tying thread.

That completes the tying of a Devaux style mayfly. Again this method of tying can be used to imitate many flies and a little experimentation will reap rewards. Changing hook sizes and the colours of materials allows most emerging flies to be successfully tied.

Unlike the midges and sedge flies, which have three aquatic stages to their life cycle, egg, larva and pupa, the upwinged flies have only two, the egg and nymph. They do have, however, two stages in their adult form. When first emerged the fly is known as the dun (*sub imago*), it is from the dun that the fully developed adult emerges, this is known as the spinner (*imago*)

There are few experiences finer than fishing during a hatch of olives and most small streams will have spasmodic if not regular rises of such flies. I am aware that not everyone appreciates the beauty of flies and admittedly some flies do not appeal to my sense of what is aesthetically pleasing. The olives, however, are without question one of the most beautiful flies on our waters and from a proportion point of view, I believe, even more appealing than the mayflies.

The Blue Winged Olive epitomizes the qualities of these flies. When tying patterns of the adult fly it is important to look at what is required. Most small streams are fairly turbulent so floatability is an important factor. Having to dry a particular fly pattern after every other cast does not endear me to it and whilst floatants are to some extent useful I prefer not to use them when on the water. The best solution is to tie the fly pattern so it can float and continue to float

The mayfly dun floating on the surface of the water before taking to the air.

after being used for some time. To do this, materials must be chosen carefully and light wire hooks are also an advantage. Polypropylene and foam are ideal to mix with traditional materials, sometimes producing patterns that it is just about impossible to sink, patterns that can be fished with for hours without having to resort to the amadou, drying cloth or changing the fly. The following fly pattern comes into this category incorporating both polypropylene and foam. The fly has never failed when I have fished small streams, even when there are no flies hatching, the opportunistic nature of the fish make it successful. The pattern is fairly simple to tie but includes various interesting techniques, as such it is a satisfying fly to tie and even more so to fish. The following tying sequence is of a BWO, the methods can be applied to any number of flies.

I am grateful to Oliver Edwards for bringing this method to my notice through the pages of *Fly-Fishing and Fly Tying* magazine. Mr Edwards had in turn been shown the method by a young Scandinavian fly tyer and had been suitably impressed to write an article on its use. In the article he maintained that the advantage of the method was to keep the hackle sitting correctly. Whilst this is true it is not, in my opinion, the real advantage. The main benefit of this method is the inclusion of foam, which forms a suitable thorax around the hook shank. This greatly assists the floatability of the pattern when fishing. The look of the fly pattern is, again in my opinion, enhanced greatly by the foam thorax. The tying does not exactly mirror Mr Edwards' tying, but the basic principle is the same

Tying the Blue Winged Olive Parachute style using a foam post

Materials Required

Hook Dry fly up eyed preferably e.g. partridge Captain Hamilton.
Hackle Light blue dun cock hackle.
Tail Pheasant tail feather fibres.
Body Fine fibre olive polypropylene dubbing.
Post Thin strip of flexible green foam.

Fig. 1 Place the hook into the jaws of the vice and test the hook for soundness. Attach the thread and, using flat thread, wind to the halfway point along the hook shank and then back again to where the thread was first attached. This lays down a bed of thread to act as a firm foundation for the other materials.

Fig. 2 Tie in the prepared hackle by the base and cut off the excess hackle stalk.

Fig. 3 Take the strip of foam and place it around the hook shank as shown in the diagram. Make sure that the thread butts up to where the foam is placed on the hook shank.

Fig. 4 Now take the thread through the centre of the foam. The thread should now be facing over the hook eye.

Fig. 5 Start to wind the thread in a counterclockwise direction around the foam directly above the hook shank. The turns should be made tight so that the foam grips the hook shank and forms the post, around which the hackle will be wound. Make sure that plenty of space is left behind the hook eye.

Fig. 6 Make six tight turns of thread around the post and then return the thread back between the foam.

Fig. 7 Wind the thread back along the hook shank to the start of the hook bend and tie in the pheasant tail fibres. Make the length of the tail long. Return the tying thread to the start of the hook bend and dub the thread with the polypropylene dubbing. Now wind on the dubbed thread, forming a shaped tapered body. The body should butt right up to the foam post. Take the thread back through the foam post.

Fig. 8 Wind the hackle around the post, two or three windings are enough. The first winding should be the highest winding up the post, the subsequent windings are below the first. Tie the hackle in on the hook shank behind the hook eye and cut off the excess hackle.

Fig. 9 Build a small head with the tying thread and complete a whip finish. Cut off the tying thread and prune down the foam post.

The Blue Winged Olive parachute style

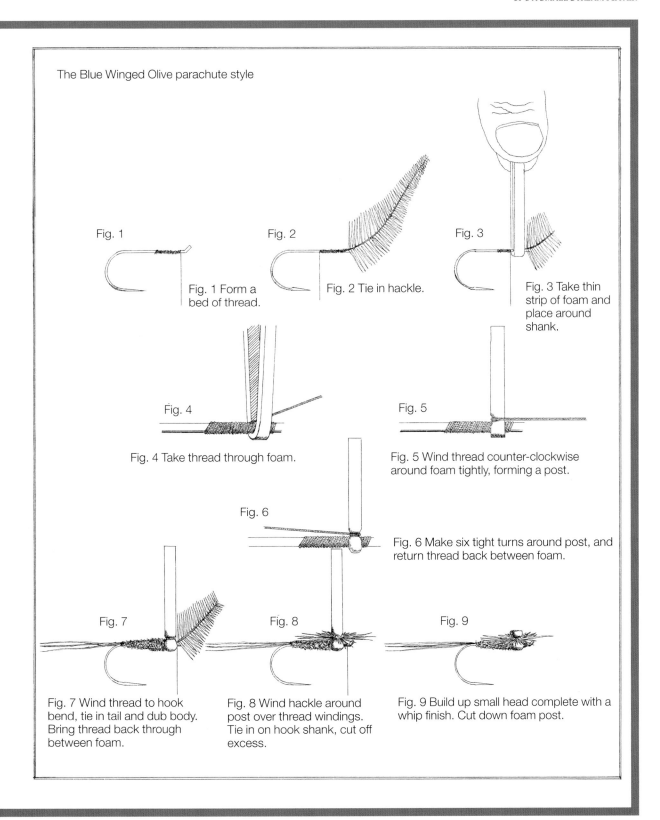

Fig. 1

Fig. 1 Form a bed of thread.

Fig. 2

Fig. 2 Tie in hackle.

Fig. 3

Fig. 3 Take thin strip of foam and place around shank.

Fig. 4

Fig. 4 Take thread through foam.

Fig. 5

Fig. 5 Wind thread counter-clockwise around foam tightly, forming a post.

Fig. 6

Fig. 6 Make six tight turns around post, and return thread back between foam.

Fig. 7

Fig. 7 Wind thread to hook bend, tie in tail and dub body. Bring thread back through between foam.

Fig. 8

Fig. 8 Wind hackle around post over thread windings. Tie in on hook shank, cut off excess.

Fig. 9

Fig. 9 Build up small head complete with a whip finish. Cut down foam post.

The tying of the Blue Winged Olive with a foam post is now complete. This fly pattern is greatly enhanced by the use of the foam post. I have come across foam posts before, but never one formed by bringing the foam strip around the hook shank. This not only provides an excellent post, but also provides an attractive thorax. I really like this tying and the fly patterns, that I have applied the technique to, have all proved excellent.

The moments of the adult upwinged flies are numbered once mating has taken place and the eggs have been deposited. The flies soon begin to die, becoming known as the spent fly. The spent fly is one of those important times in the life cycle of the natural fly that the fly fisher on small streams neglects at their peril. Often ignored in preference to the early adult fly, either in the form of the dun or spinner, the time of spent fly is when the pickings are easy for the fish. Spent flies are going nowhere, other than where the current of the stream takes them, they are dead or dying. Any fall of spent fly is an exciting time on the stream, the fish often forgetting all caution in their enthusiasm to feast. It is a time when fish appear out of nowhere. What earlier in the day may have appeared to be a stretch of water practically devoid of fish, will suddenly become a relative Piccadilly Circus of a stream, with trout rising everywhere. Sometimes the frenzy of feeding will not last long, so I find that it is a good idea to be prepared for a fall of spent flies with suitable fly patterns readily available. The following pattern is one I have used for a few years and I am sure it will continue to play a role for many years to come. Like the previous BWO pattern, it incorporates two of my favourite materials, polypropylene and foam, as such it can be used for as long as it effectively attracts the fish without resorting to drying or changing the fly. The wing is really a Detached Perfect Furled Hackle that is flattened and tied in Paraloop style with a wing case pulled over. This has the effect of creating two hackle wings ideally placed to imitate the spent fly. The position of the fly on the water is very much more imitative than traditionally hackled flies. Like all the flies highlighted the methods used can be applied to many different species of fly, here I have used a Medium Olive, as it is a fly found on many of the streams I fish.

The tying is fairly straightforward, it is, however, best to choose a hackle with fibres longer than those usually used for the selected hook size and the hackle should be very closely wound making the hackle very dense. The detached perfect furled hackle must be prepared before tying in and this is achieved by using the first fingers and the thumbs of both hands to flatten the section of the detached hackle being tied in. The result of this process should be a flat hackle with an equal number of fibres at either side.

The body and thorax of this tying uses a fine natural dubbing dyed reddish brown. The best dubbing material for this particular fly that I have ever used is the brushed fur from Birman Cats dyed. This is extremely fine fur, so fine that individual fibres float in the air. It makes very fine nymph dubbing as its fineness allows water to be absorbed quickly. The females of the medium olive, lay their eggs by climbing down under the water using fence posts, walls and any other convenient items and as such do not break through the water's surface when they are spent. The use of the absorbent dyed Birman fur in conjunction with the hackle and foam wing case creates a fly pattern that sits very low in the surface of the water or just under the surface of the water. I am aware that not every tyer will have access to Birman fur and there is a supplier named in the appendix. A dyed soft underfur from a rabbit will stand as an alternative.

Tying the Medium Olive Spent Spinner

Materials Required

Hook	Dry fly hook. Partridge Captain Hamilton.
Hackle	Light blue dun cock. Detached perfect furled hackle flattened.
Body	Birman cat fur dyed reddish brown or suitable alternative.
Tail	Two micro-fibbetts.
Thorax	As per the body.
Wing Cover	Brown flexible foam.

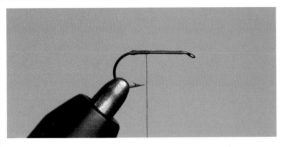

Photograph 1 Fix the hook in the jaws of the vice and test the hook for soundness. Attach the waxed thread and wind to the start of the hook bend. Form a small ball of thread at the start of the hook bend and the wind the tying thread a little way back along the hook shank.

Photograph 2 Tie the two micro-fibbetts on to the top of the hook shank. Now holding the fibbetts in position where one sits to the near side of the thread ball and the other on the far side of the thread ball, wind the thread back to the ball of thread, tying the fibbetts into position as you go. This will split the fibbetts forming two tails. The tails should not be too long in the case of this particular fly pattern, the length of the hook will be suffice. The tails should sink and being shorter than the tails I normally add to spinner patterns, they break through the surface of the water easier. Cut off excess fibbett material.

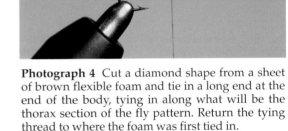

Photograph 3 Dub the tying thread with the body dubbing and wind two thirds of the way back along the hook shank, forming a tapered body as you go.

Photograph 4 Cut a diamond shape from a sheet of brown flexible foam and tie in a long end at the end of the body, tying in along what will be the thorax section of the fly pattern. Return the tying thread to where the foam was first tied in.

Photograph 5 Take the prepared detached perfect furled hackle and tie it in with the hackle extending over the rear of the hook. Return the thread to where the hackle was first tied in

Photograph 6 Dub the tying thread with the thorax dubbing and wind on forming a shaped thorax, thicker in the middle than at the ends. Leave plenty of space behind the hook eye to tie in the remaining materials and form a small head.

Photograph 7 Pull the hackle over the centre of the thorax. Tie in the hackle behind the hook eye and cut off the remaining detached hackle. Lock the ends of the removed hackle with hackle pliers to make sure it does not unwind.

Photograph 8 Pull the foam wing case over the thorax and hackle and tie in behind the hook eye. Stretch the foam and cut off the excess. Now form a small head and complete the fly pattern with a whip finish, cut off the tying thread.

That completes the spent medium olive designed to float just under the surface of the water

Photograph 9 The completed fly.

Stoneflies

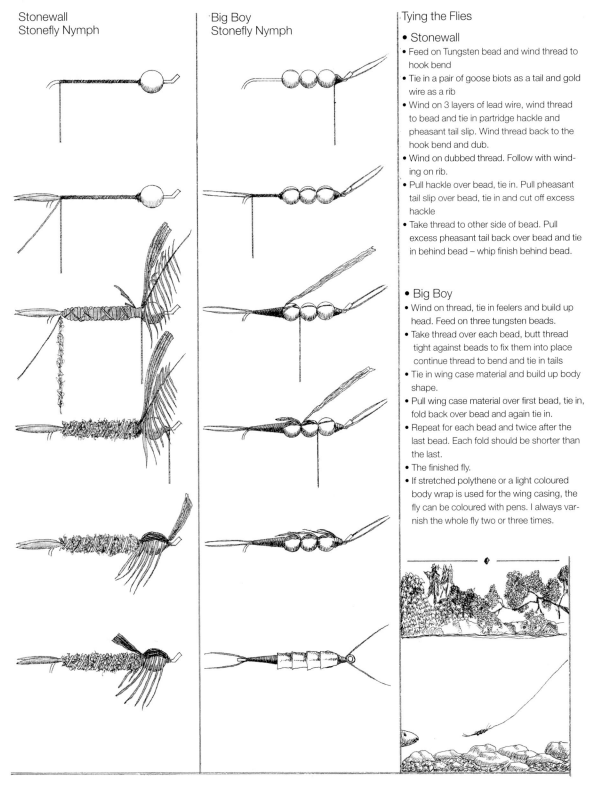

Stonewall
Stonefly Nymph

Big Boy
Stonefly Nymph

Tying the Flies

• Stonewall

- Feed on Tungsten bead and wind thread to hook bend
- Tie in a pair of goose biots as a tail and gold wire as a rib
- Wind on 3 layers of lead wire, wind thread to bead and tie in partridge hackle and pheasant tail slip. Wind thread back to the hook bend and dub.
- Wind on dubbed thread. Follow with winding on rib.
- Pull hackle over bead, tie in. Pull pheasant tail slip over bead, tie in and cut off excess hackle
- Take thread to other side of bead. Pull excess pheasant tail back over bead and tie in behind bead – whip finish behind bead.

• Big Boy

- Wind on thread, tie in feelers and build up head. Feed on three tungsten beads.
- Take thread over each bead, butt thread tight against beads to fix them into place continue thread to bend and tie in tails
- Tie in wing case material and build up body shape.
- Pull wing case material over first bead, tie in, fold back over bead and again tie in.
- Repeat for each bead and twice after the last bead. Each fold should be shorter than the last.
- The finished fly.
- If stretched polythene or a light coloured body wrap is used for the wing casing, the fly can be coloured with pens. I always varnish the whole fly two or three times.

Trout can go nuts over stoneflies and, although the hatches are not prolific on the small streams I fish there is a steady supply and consequently the fish are well acquainted with them. I almost believe that the stonefly nymph is the favourite food of the fish, they accept them so willingly. There is a tradition in Scotland, where the large nymphs are known as 'gadgers', of fishing using the live nymph. These are collected from under stones just prior to the fishing. As I said previously when it comes to fishing the stonefly I prefer to use the nymph rather than the adult fly. A traditional style nymph tied, as per a Pheasant Tail Nymph, is more than adequate although there are many suitable patterns designed as specific stonefly imitations. The use of such flies can be essential when fishing deeper pools and runs where the fly needs to get right down to the stream bed to be effective. Introducing weight to the fly in the form of lead and or tungsten assists greatly. These flies need to be fished on a relatively short line and contact with the fly maintained at all times. The effort is well worth it as they often produce the best fish from a swim. The illustration on page 167 outlines the tying of various patterns. Don't be put off by the amount of weight in the form of lead and tungsten suggested for the patterns, to get the fly down to where the fish are, this amount of weight is sometimes essential, in fact there are many instances where more is required. When using these heavy flies casting is not as we normally know it, rather it is a lift and throw forward, remembering that the line should always be kept relatively short.

The illustration describes the tying of two such stonefly nymphs, the Stonewall and the Big Boy. Both fly patterns are effective in small streams and there have been times when I have used either fly and have taken an unseen fish with every cast.

The Terrestrials

The terrestrial flies are those flies that do not spend any part of their life cycle in the water. These flies are very important for small stream fishing, as many such waters are often not fertile in terms of their insect life, especially the upland streams. For large parts of the year one of the main sources of food for fish comes from terrestrial flies blown on to the water by the wind. Although such flies do not live any part of their lives in the water, there can be little doubt that they are often attracted to water and the surrounding plant and tree life. For the streams I fish the following terrestrial flies are common and all are readily taken by trout: the daddy-longlegs (Crane fly), Hawthorn Fly, Heather Fly, Black Gnat, Cow Dung Fly, and Smuts. Each of these flies has its season and, although they can be found outwith these times, it is during the time when they are most prolific that their use as artificial flies is most effective.

Fishing the stream below Grasholme Reservoir in County Durham one day a few years ago with my friend Eddy Hope, we were baffled at how we could get the rising fish to accept our flies, nothing we presented seemed to have any effect. Eddy went up on the grass slopes above the water and started to kick through the grass. A few minutes later the fish started rising in greater numbers than before and it was clear they were taking flies blown off the grass on to the water. When Eddy returned he had the culprit in his hand, an orange brown Cow Dung Fly. Switching to a suitable pattern saw the first success of the day, a success that continued until we left to go home. The illustration explains how to tie an effective Cow Dung Fly and I would recommend its use whenever these flies are rising around your feet as you walk along the banks of a stream. This fly will float forever without resorting to applying flotant, the occasional squeezing of the fly between tissue paper being sufficient to keep it floating all day, as such it is a favourite of mine. Even when saturated the fly will hover just under the surface of the water. The first time I tried this fly two trout were taken in the first three casts, the fly being allowed to float downstream under a lone rhododendron bush with branches hanging over the water. The following day it was used with equal success on a small stillwater where the fish were rising freely but other anglers were failing to inspire a trout to take. The fly is fished static on still water no retrieve should be used, let the fish find the fly but cover any rises. I named this fly pattern after my friend Eddy, whose surname seemed ideally fitting for a fly fisher.

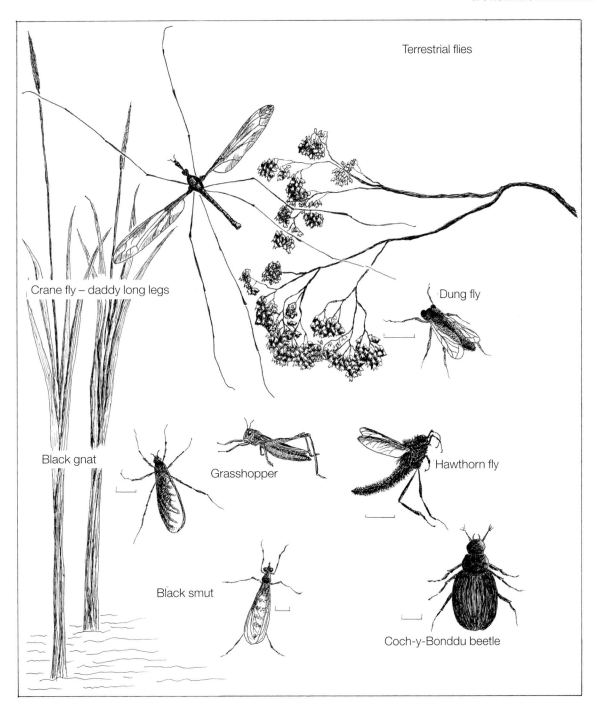

Terrestrial flies

Crane fly – daddy long legs

Dung fly

Black gnat

Grasshopper

Hawthorn fly

Black smut

Coch-y-Bonddu beetle

Tying Eddy's Hope – Cow Dung Fly

Materials Required

Hook	Dry fly up-eye. Partridge Captain Hamilton.	**Body**	Orange polypropylene dubbing.
Underbody	Tying thread and foam.	**Hackle**	Light honey dun or light ginger cock hackle.
		Wing	Foam pulled over.

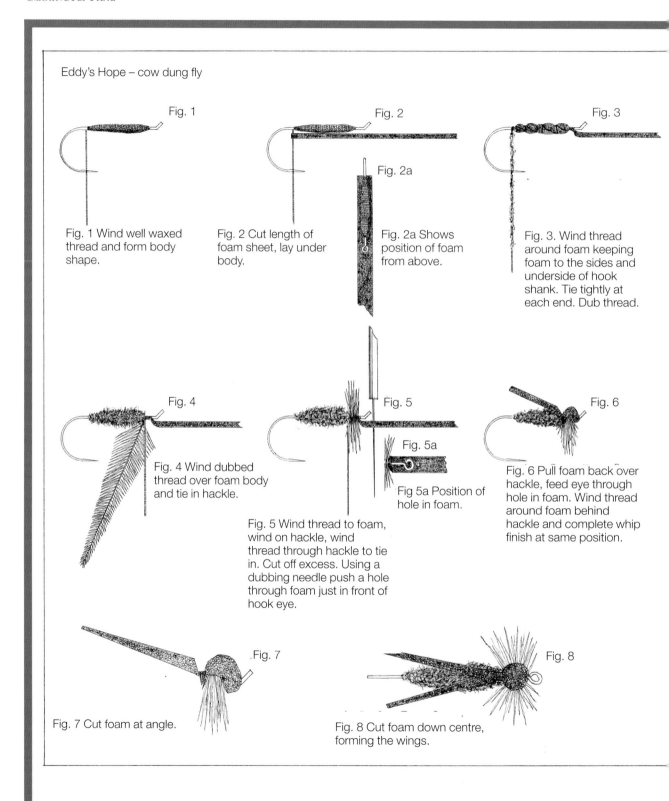

Eddy's Hope – cow dung fly

Fig. 1

Fig. 1 Wind well waxed thread and form body shape.

Fig. 2

Fig. 2a

Fig. 2 Cut length of foam sheet, lay under body.

Fig. 2a Shows position of foam from above.

Fig. 3

Fig. 3. Wind thread around foam keeping foam to the sides and underside of hook shank. Tie tightly at each end. Dub thread.

Fig. 4

Fig. 4 Wind dubbed thread over foam body and tie in hackle.

Fig. 5

Fig. 5a

Fig. 5a Position of hole in foam.

Fig. 5 Wind thread to foam, wind on hackle, wind thread through hackle to tie in. Cut off excess. Using a dubbing needle push a hole through foam just in front of hook eye.

Fig. 6

Fig. 6 Pull foam back over hackle, feed eye through hole in foam. Wind thread around foam behind hackle and complete whip finish at same position.

Fig. 7

Fig. 7 Cut foam at angle.

Fig. 8

Fig. 8 Cut foam down centre, forming the wings.

Fig. 1 Fix the hook in the jaws of the vice and test the hook for soundness. Attach the waxed thread and wind along the hook shank to the start of the hook bend. Then form a shaped underbody as per the diagram. Finish with the thread at the start of the hook bend. Leave some clear space on the hook shank directly behind the hook eye.

Fig. 2 Cut a length of foam strip and lay under the body.

Fig. 3 Wind the tying thread fairly randomly and well spaced around the hook shank and the foam strip. Keep the foam to the underside and sides of the hook shank and do not wind the thread over the foam too tightly, let the foam keep some of its shape. Tie the hook bend end and the section behind the hook eye of the foam very tightly. The space between the hook eye and the start of the body should be enough to make at least eight turns of hackle and a little bit extra. Take the thread back to the start of the hook bend and dub the tying thread with the orange polypropylene body dubbing.

Fig. 4 Wind the dubbed tying thread in close turns around the body and tie in the prepared hackle at the end of the body. Cut off the excess hackle stalk.

Fig. 5 Wind the thread forward towards the hook eye stopping at where the thread tying the foam ends. Wind on the hackle making about seven or eight touching turns. Then wind the tying thread back through the hackle towards the body, tying in the hackle as you go. Ensure the end of the hackle is securely tied, then cut off the excess hackle. The thread should now be at the point where the hackle meets the body. Using a sharp dubbing needle push a hole through the foam at a position centred in the foam strip and a little in front of the hook eye.

Fig. 6 Pull the foam strip back over the hackle and force the hook eye through the hole made using the dubbing needle. Now wind the tying thread using very tight turns around the hook shank and the foam, ensuring the foam stays on the topside of the fly pattern. The turns of thread are made between the hackle and the start of the body. Complete a whip finish at the same position and cut off the tying thread. Ensure that the foam strip wing extends just beyond the end of the body and no further. If it is longer, cut it back to the right length.

Figs. 7 and 8 The next part of the process is optional. Cut the foam at an angle as in Fig. 7 and then cut the foam down the centre of the strip to form two wings.

That completes the tying of Eddy's Hope – Cow Dung Fly. Given the right conditions at the relevant time of year and a little wind, this fly will prove itself over and over again.

There are times when the air is filled with drifting black flies with trailing black legs. These flies, commonly known as Hawthorn Flies, seem to float on the air and are easy victims of any gusts of wind. When they are present they are usually present in large numbers drifting over the water in slow moving clouds. Trout go mad on them and it is only sensible to use a suitable imitation when they are being blown on to the water. The pattern illustrated is one that can be used whenever these flies are on offer to the trout. It is a pattern that can be relied upon to produce a result if it is used at the right time. An imitation of the heather fly can use the same tying substituting legs dyed red in place of black.

The following tying is not in any way innovative but it is very effective when the Hawthorn Flies are being blown or drifting down upon the water.

Tying the Hawthorn Fly

Materials Required

Hook Dry fly size 16. Partridge Captain Hamilton.
Hackle Black cock hackle.
Body Fine black polypropylene floss – double furled extended
Thorax Fine black polypropylene dubbing.
Legs 2 knotted double pheasant tail fibres dyed black and kept fairly short.
Thread Of own choice 8/0.

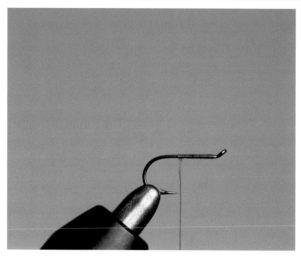

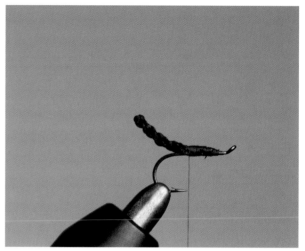

Photograph 1 Place the hook in the jaws of the vice and test for soundness. Attach the tying thread and wind to just past the halfway position on the hook shank, using flat thread.

Photograph 2 Take the black polypropylene floss and furl it once and then repeat and furl it again. This can easily be done just using your fingers. Offer the furled floss to the top of the hook at the thread position. The body should extend a little bit beyond the hook bend and be angled slightly upwards. Tie in the body on to the top of the hook shank, by winding the thread to towards the hook eye. Stop well short of the hook eye and cut off the excess body material. Now wind the thread back to where the body was first tied in.

Photograph 3 Lightly dub the tying thread with a little thorax dubbing and wind on three or four turns towards the hook eye.

Photograph 4 Tie in the legs one on each side of the thorax, the ends of the legs should be pointing downward. Cut off the excess leg material and return the thread to where the legs were first tied in.

Photograph 5 Tie in the prepared hackle, cut off the excess stalk and return the thread to where the hackle was first tied in.

Photograph 6 Dub the tying thread with the thorax dubbing and wind on forming a wide stubby thorax. Leave a little space behind the hook eye. Remove any excess dubbing from the tying thread.

Photograph 7 Wind the hackle using just three or four turns over the thorax and tie in behind the hook eye. Cut off the excess hackle. Form a fairly large thread head and complete the fly pattern with a whip finish.

That completes the tying of the Hawthorn Fly. To tie the Heather Fly just substitute knotted red pheasant tail fibre legs in place of the black in photograph 4.

Photograph 8 The completed fly.

Spider Patterns

Finally I would like to look at that most traditional of all wet flies the spider patterns. These
flies are as effective today as they were when first
devised and for traditional 'across and down'
fishing hard to beat. It is this effectiveness that

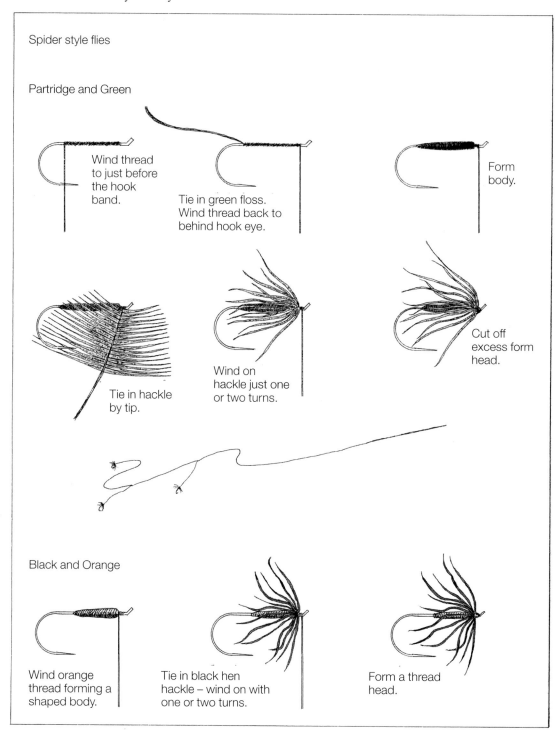

Spider style flies

Partridge and Green

Wind thread
to just before
the hook
band.

Tie in green floss.
Wind thread back to
behind hook eye.

Form
body.

Tie in hackle
by tip.

Wind on
hackle just one
or two turns.

Cut off
excess form
head.

Black and Orange

Wind orange
thread forming a
shaped body.

Tie in black hen
hackle – wind on with
one or two turns.

Form a thread
head.

warrants they have a special mention in any writing describing small stream fly fishing. What do they imitate? Well I think that depends on the size and colours used. Personally I think they can be used to imitate just about any hatching fly caught in the current and any nymph or pupa. I usually fish Spider patterns as a team of two, three or four flies. The tying of such flies could not be easier as can be seen by the illustration. Game bird feathers and hen feathers make better spider hackles than cock hackle due to the softness of the hackle fibres, giving the impression of life when caught up in the current of the stream.

There are a few different ways in which spider patterns can be tied. I describe an old River Tweed technique in the section entitled Drowned Spent Spinner in the chapter 'Legends of the Falls II', where it is described as a sparse palmered hackle. I also give examples of spider patterns tied using this method. The two fly patterns illustrated, the Partridge and Green and the Black and Orange are very typical spider patterns tied in the manner that most fly tyers and fly fishers are familiar with. These are simple fly patterns, but they are no less effective for their simplicity. Rather the opposite, they can always be relied on to give a good chance of connecting with a fish. Just about any combination of colours can be used. Find out what natural flies are emerging, or what nymphs are abundant in the water and choose a spider pattern to suit. Although, out of the water, spider patterns do not resemble any particular natural fly, in the water it is a different matter and I would far rather have a spider pattern tied on my line than any of the realistic patterns that I see around today.

One of the elements of small stream fishing, which seems to take by surprise those anglers new to fishing such water, is the realization that the fish are wild. These fish may not, on the whole, be large but they have not spent the greater part of their lives in a hatchery environment being fed at regular intervals by humans. As such they are completely unaccustomed to the sight of people and caution is the natural response to any person intruding into their space. It is for this reason that I view fishing small streams as trout hunting. Each step must be thought through and taken carefully and each cast made to count. Often you will only get one chance to cover a seen fish or a promising lie, pocket of water or run. Blow that chance by a careless approach or inept cast and you won't get another chance on that bit of water for some

Long hackled spider pattern

A good lie.

time, it's best to move on and try your hand else-where. The biggest trout are also the most wary. I have watched pools on streams where the water is so clear it is almost as if it wasn't there and the fish are swimming through empty space. If time is taken to watch the behaviour of fish in such waters it soon becomes obvious that the larger fish take no chances. They are the ones that at the slightest disturbance dash to some previously located shelter, staying there until the coast is well and truly clear before venturing out again.

The smaller fish tend on the whole to react less to any disturbance, settling back to feeding far sooner than their larger friends. So if you want to catch the bigger fish you must fish accordingly. The larger fish normally occupy the best feeding stations on the stream, but when disturbed their place will be instantly taken over by small trout or parr, eager to snap up any offerings in their absence. If you disturb the water you will probably only catch small fish, if you catch anything at all.

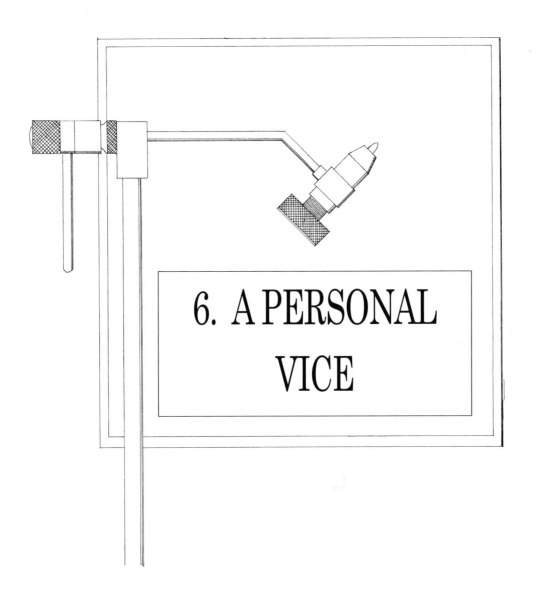

6. A PERSONAL VICE

Part I

My relationships with fly tying vices have followed a very similar course to my relations with people, especially those relationships often referred to as being of an intimate nature. Some have been of a fleeting acquaintance, a brief encounter, a taster and then, for whatever reason, they are lost barely remaining a memory. Others have remained a vital part of my life for years, familiar to such an extent that it is difficult to imagine a time when they were not present. Even in these circumstances time nudges and entices in other directions and before you know it, some other is clamped firmly upon the table.

My first encounter was as a boy, I must have been aged twelve or thirteen years old. My desires at this time were fishing, girls from afar and how to tie fishing flies. In many ways tying flies was a surprising aspiration given that nobody I knew tied flies and I'd never seen a book on fly tying, but there was no doubt tying flies was what I wanted to do. Somewhere or another, most probably in a fishing magazine or tackle catalogue, there must have been a photograph or illustration of a fly tying vice and it was this that I wanted to make in the Thursday morning metalwork class at Wilmslow Grammar School.

I had taken the time to work out how the vice would operate and a design was finalized, complete with detailed drawings. My teacher appeared less than impressed, he maintained that the proposed project was far too complicated for me to attempt and he suggested a far simpler design. Suggesting is not the correct word, implying, as it does, some element of choice. There was no choice, the suggested alternative would be constructed or no fly vice would be made at all.

This arrangement had one major drawback, of which the teacher appeared to be completely oblivious. My original design would have worked well, whilst the alternative was rubbish. So my fate was to spend each session making a vice, which would not do the job required. It is a heart defeating task to spend hours on a project that you know in the end will come to nothing, the only benefit being it kept an occasionally unruly boy occupied for the required period of time.

The major fault with the alternative suggestion was it would not and could not hold a hook, which is, as I am sure you can imagine, a fairly major flaw when it comes down to fly vice design. To make matters worse the vice failed to fix firmly on a table. I realize that this additional shortcoming would not make a jot of difference, the vice would have remained completely useless, it would, however, have given some satisfaction if the series of metalwork lessons had produced something successful at least in part.

Trying to explain these shortcomings to my teacher was a hopeless task, what a young boy had to say being of little interest and no importance to him. That teacher may have had a lot to answer for, with nearly twenty long years passing by before I finally fulfilled my wish. It had remained throughout this time, hidden and quiet in some recess of my being, hibernating awaiting the right conditions to emerge. When it eventually showed itself in its true colours, knocking off the years of slumber with a single shake of its head, it did so with a vengeance.

When I wasn't on the water I was tying flies. Every book was read and studied, each technique practised, until its use was second nature. No stone was left unturned and no brain unpicked in my desire to become a proficient fly tyer. Flies were everywhere, there was no space available for storage that didn't contain tins, boxes, film cases and wallets all full of flies of every description. That was then, now I probably have the worst stocked fly boxes around, in fact it is hard for me to find any fly box that comprises a reasonable selection of usable flies, which I can turn to at a moment's notice. The exception to this is a

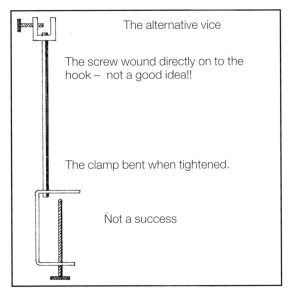

The alternative vice

The screw wound directly on to the hook – not a good idea!!

The clamp bent when tightened.

Not a success

small collection kept stuck in foam above my tying table for use on local waters.

These days I like to tie flies for a specific trip, each fly a part of the pleasure and anticipation experienced. A small tying kit is perfect for travelling, allowing flies to be tied to order. The other method is to raid other fishers' fly boxes. Many a fine fly has been pirated away from box to my pocket, usually, but not always, with the blessing of the owner. This is an especially good method of fly supply when fishing new waters and some time spent chatting up the locals can be beneficial, the natural generosity of some fishermen helping to fill the empty spaces in my box. Don't get me wrong, the main reason my boxes are often poorly stocked is that the contents are given away freely to all and sundry. The acceptance of flies from other anglers feels like a natural part of that process.

When I do tie flies they are of my own design, particular or peculiar to the situation I find myself in. They are on the whole bastard flies, with no given name. The exception to this is when for publication or other purposes, it is deemed necessary to baptize them. In this case names are chosen on a fairly random basis and forgotten as quickly as they are christened. They return to the preferred and I believe more meaningful titles along the lines of 'Light Olive good on Tweed in June', 'Sedge Emerger successful on the Wharfe around Wetherby' and 'Derwent in

May, took the big trout under the bank'. Encouraged by the excesses of modern times and probably wishing to be seen as a 'being on the ball', 'finger on the pulse' sort of guy, it seemed a good idea to use acronyms for these flies, a decisive sound bite appearing preferable to the more descriptive but long winded names being used. This proved, however, to be fruitless and in practise, highly unattractive, the above flies translating into the 'Logotij', 'Sesowaw' and 'Dimttbtutb', respectively. So I now stick to the old more meaningful method.

Some artificial flies readily accept and sit comfortably with a name given at the time of their creation and for some, especially imitative patterns, this name can be quite straight forward. Imitations of flies like the sedge or olive can quite simply be called Sedge or Olive, this does nothing, however, to help identify the exact pattern, which Sedge or which Olive? It's a bit like trying to identify someone called Smith or Brown, the name tells you nothing about the person or which Smith or Brown is being referred to. Because of this it is perhaps necessary to provide a unique name to each original fly. I'm not saying that my long-winded method is the best, far from it, it suits me but few others. What I am saying is that each successful fly should have its own name to identify it from all others so allowing easy recognition.

My first working vice was inexpensive and if I thought about it and rummaged around a bit, I could probably find it stashed safely away somewhere, faithfully ready and waiting for the day when all my other vices cease to offer service. It may have been bought for only a few pounds but the pleasure I derived from its use far outweighed any links to the cost. It did everything I could ask of it, holding the hook firmly, it was easy to tighten and release and unlike the original alternative, clamped firmly to the tying bench. This was the vice I learned to tie flies on. It was also the vice I was using when I discovered that although you never stop learning about fly tying, on the whole the basics are simple and relatively easy to master. This is one of the things I like about it, just about everyone can do it, if there was ever an equal opportunity pursuit, fly tying is it.

Using that first vice the flies I tied would never have won any prizes for aesthetics, saying that neither would the ones I tie today, but they did catch fish and it was this that provided a deep satisfaction and a sense of fulfilment. That a natural fly could be observed being taken by a trout on the water, then hatch the match on the vice, albeit crudely and then use the imitation to catch a fish completed the circle, providing what has, in these modern days, become a rare whole experience. It was to this that my addiction became hopeless. I look on it as a jigsaw puzzle, put all the pieces in place and what is being depicted becomes clear, leave any pieces out and you can still make out the picture, but it is not complete. Seeing a fish take a fly, imitating that fly and catching a fish on that fly makes the picture whole.

I was faithful to my first usable vice for quite sometime, resisting the more sophisticated models, which called out for my attention. It got to the stage, however, where whenever a tackle shop was entered I found myself surrounded by 'fancy a good time' vices and I am a little ashamed of having eventually succumbed to their promises of pleasures unfulfilled. The inevitable is exactly that, inevitable and my loyal and trusty third hand was consigned to the ignominy of a dusty drawer for no fault of its own, but purely my unbridled lust and the fickle nature of the human heart. Its place was taken by a single action, rotating head device whose bold, shiny brassy finish appeared fitting attire for a usurper.

This new model of vice, in one incarnation or another, remained tightly clamped to my tying desk for a good few years. Admittedly the jaw tips cracked on a couple of occasions leaving me with no option but to replace the whole vice, but the same model was used as a replacement each time. This vice was of the type that has sprung jaws and a handle, which when squeezed opened them up to accept the fly, without squeezing the handle the jaws remained permanently closed. The era of this particular vice saw the flies tied within its jaws extending from trout flies into traditional salmon patterns, particularly those of the fully dressed variety. This tool and I got on well, we never argued and, except for the couple of times the jaws cracked, I was well content and happy. The understanding that the same model was used as a replacement when the jaws cracked gave the overall impression that the vice never changed throughout this period.

Tying large salmon flies demands a vice that can hold a big hook without any give whatsoever. The leverage exerted on the jaws of a vice by a 3 in (8 cm) hook is considerably greater than that applied by the average trout fly. This vice proved to be up to the job. The only gripe I had with it was that the fly was not rotated on a flat plane. This meant that when tying the underside of some complicated Victorian feather eater, it was necessary to readjust the hook position, a small but sometimes irritating shortcoming. But to the greater extent we lived in harmony. That is until I found myself demonstrating tying flies on a fairly regular basis. Demonstrating tying flies awakened a discontent within my soul and once more my eyes began to wander. The catwalk model vices displayed elegantly in certain shops once again started to turn my head. Soon the look turned to enquiry, from that point in time I was fated to again disrupt the harmony of my tying bench by introducing a newcomer.

From this time until now I have collected various forms of fly vice, most of them fairly efficient and easy to use. In the end some flaw in their design would have me looking to see what else might be on offer. Today I have some really fancy vices carrying names like Renzetti and Dyna King, all of which do the job of holding a hook look easy. Besides this prime requirement they come under the category of 'all singing all dancing' models, with accessory lists sometimes running into pages. I like these vices and they should last me until my hands can no longer wind the thread. Do I tie better flies on these tools than on my original working vice? The answer to that is no, do I tie them quicker? The answer to that is also no. Do I enjoy using them more than my less sophisticated vices? The answer to that is yes, the quality of design and manufacture make them a joy to use. None of them resemble my original rejected design, although the principle is the same. Looking at them with a more experienced eye, maybe my old teacher was right, it was too complicated for a thirteen year old boy to attempt to make such a device in his first term of metalwork, but then again who knows.

Part II

Of all the equipment that surrounds me when I sit down at my fly tying bench, the two vices have gained my affection to a far greater degree than any other tool that I use when tying fly patterns. I do have a few bits and bobs that I like immensely, an example would be the empty pen case I picked up many years ago that I use for half-hitches. Its value in monetary terms is nothing, but I would be most upset if I were ever to lose it, for all the other half-hitch tools I have worked with are poor performers, paling into insignificance, when compared to this supreme empty pen case.

I am quite fond of two particular pairs of scissors and a hair stacker that I use regularly, but on the whole the greater part of my affection for the inanimate is given to my vices. This, I would like to emphasize, is not a fly by night affection, but an affection built up over many years. The vices I use, do what they said they would do and, what is more, they do it well and with that most rare of attributes, style.

As explained in part one of this chapter, the path I have walked to what appears to be vice satisfaction, is littered by abandoned devices, most of which served me well, but in the end failed to inspire my ongoing loyalty. While I accept that this probably says more about my own character than I would perhaps like to think, it has given me an insight into the many different vices available and their good, not so good and, at times awful attributes.

What should a fly tying vice be capable of?

In my opinion a good vice should have many qualities, each of which will make tying fly patterns more enjoyable. A reasonably good vice will be blessed with most of these required qualities, while a bad vice will have very few, if any. It is a fact of life that the very best vices will always have a price tag to match their efficiency and high standard of design and manufacture. But a reasonably good vice need not cost an arm, a leg and a portion of torso; in fact they are often

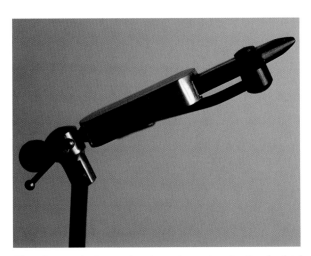 

The above photographs show two vices both of which perform very well. The vice on the left is an inexpensive Regal vice, whilst on the right a top of the range Renzetti is shown. The major practical difference between them is that the Renzetti is true rotary whilst the Regal is only pseudo-rotary.

inexpensive. The very worst vices on the market can have a price tag equivalent to the very best and most expensive, down to a cost whereby their sole attribute is that they are cheap. The fact that a vice costs slightly less than the defence budget does not always ensure that it was designed by someone who really knew what they were doing. I suspect some vices have been designed by engineers looking for an extra income and whose only real experience of flies and fly tying is scraping the casualties off the windscreens of their cars.

What are the qualities that make a good vice? What should a good vice be capable of? After giving this matter some considerable thought I have come up with the following list of eight points that I believe to be important. Not all these points are totally practical, in respect of them being necessary for a vice to perform well and some readers may think my consideration of how a vice looks and feels is unimportant. However, some points are there solely to increase the pleasure experienced when using a vice, which, at least to my way of thinking, is reason enough for me to include them. I start the list with the more obvious and purely practical attributes.

1 Hook Hold It is essential that a vice grips and holds the hook firmly, maintaining such a hold no matter what pressure is applied when tying. This hold must be consistent whatever the size of hook you are using. There are some vices that are excellent when it comes to tying small flies, but fail when a large hook is used. It is important that a vice is capable of gripping all the different sizes of hook you are going to use. I have a vice that I love; it is used for tying most of the smaller patterns I use. As soon as a hook larger than a 6 is applied to the jaws I start to lose confidence in its abilities and change to the other vice I use for larger patterns. The pressure applied when tying on a hook of say size 16, is as nothing compared to tying on a size 2/0. I have also found that the best jaws are serrated or grooved where they grip the hook.

2 Ease of Use It must be easy to fix and remove a hook from the jaws of a vice. Over the years I have come across a couple of vices that require much unnecessary fiddling to fix the hook securely and to remove the hook quickly. In my opinion this is bad design. The process of fixing and removing a hook should be almost as simple as flicking a switch, anything more is a step too far. I accept that small adjustments may need to be made for hooks of a different size, but this procedure should be equally simple.

3 Access This seems too obvious to include, but having experienced using a few vices that appear designed to obstruct the tyer, it is one of the most important matters to be considered. The jaws of a good vice will be free of any impediments to ease of access and manipulation of materials. It is for this reason that I do not like to see large adjusting screws and other such extras on the jaws' mount-

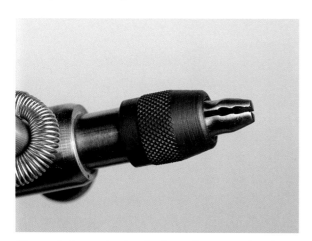

These photographs clearly show the grooved and serrated jaws. Jaws designed this way allow greater grip of the hook especially when using hooks of a larger size.

ing. Another general rule is that no part of the vice should be very much higher than the vice jaws, a few millimetres makes no difference, but anything more is not necessary and, in my eyes, not good design.

4 Solid Base The vice itself must be able to be fixed securely wherever and whenever it is going to be put to use. No matter if a clamp or a pedestal base is used it must hold the vice solidly.

5 Position Adjustments A good vice will allow the height of the actual jaws to be adjusted. Not all tables are the same height and being able to adjust the vice will allow comfortable tying with the vice at a height you are used to. It is also desirable that the vice is not fixed permanently to a clamp so that it can be turned to different positions. Some cheaper vices will not allow height adjustments or for the vice to be turned in any direction. This is due to the clamp being fixed permanently to the vice support. Such vices in my opinion should be avoided.

6 Rotation While not essential for all fly tying, it is to be preferred and is at times highly desirable and convenient if the jaws of the vice can be rotated. There are two types of rotating jaws, the first I refer to as 'true rotary'. A true rotary vice

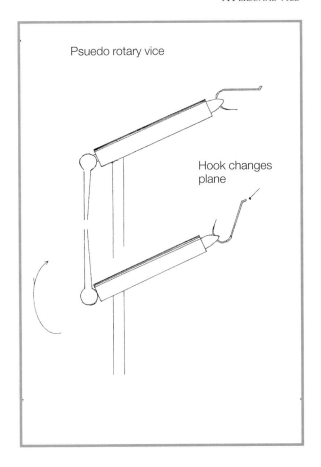

Psuedo rotary vice

Hook changes plane

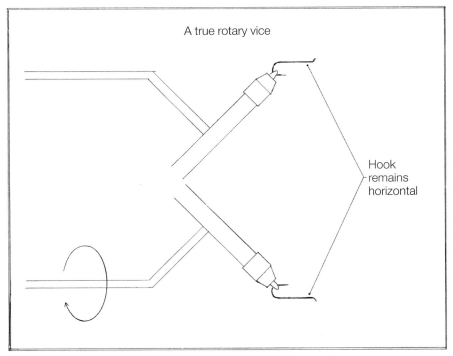

A true rotary vice

Hook remains horizontal

allows the jaws to be spun, while maintaining the hook on the same plane and at the same height. The second type of rotary vice is what I refer to as 'pseudo rotary'. In this case the vice jaws can be rotated but they do not keep the hook sitting on the same plane, or at the same height. The illustration of the two different types of vice describes this better than words. While it is possible to readjust the hook in the pseudo rotary vice, there seems little point in them being able to rotate at all, as the hook will need to be released from the jaws to be reset anyway. The convenience of the true rotary version makes it the far better option if, when tying, it is necessary to rotate the hook. The procedure for rotating the hook should be very simple and should not involve more than one or two adjustments.

7 Quality of Manufacture It is essential that the quality standards employed by the manufacturer are high, this applies to the choice of materials used in construction, all the way to the final finish. Quality materials are a must if the vice is to withstand the rigours of fly tying. Each part of the vice should be made from the most suitable metals and, while being robust, ideally the vice should not be over heavy. I think the best way to look at it is to ask, will the vice become an heirloom? Will it stand up to a lifetime of use and more and, importantly, does it feel like you would want it to. There may be readers who will think I am being pedantic on this point and they are probably right, but the pleasure I derive from using a piece of equipment that is designed and constructed properly, makes it important. I have always had a feeling for objects that are engineered to a high standard. A quality reel is a joy to handle, as well as being reliable in use, the same applies to vices. I dislike vices constructed from materials other than metals. While there are arguments that some other materials, such as composites, do the job, I am afraid I am not convinced. The use of such materials is primarily motivated by cost and does not improve a vice in any way at all, rather, at least in my opinion, they cheapen the look and feel of the tool.

8 The Look Is the vice pleasing to the eye? A tool that is designed well, in my experience, always looks good. A badly designed vice will never look good, just badly designed. I lay a lot of emphasis on the overall shape of a vice, it says a lot about how it will perform when used.

This guide gives an idea of what I look for in a vice. There are other factors, such as: are different types of jaws available and are parts readily available if something goes wrong? But the eight points cover what I see as the important factors when choosing a vice.

A good vice need not include all the eight points, but it should cover most of them. A good vice also need not be expensive. For example, over many years I used a vice that goes under the name of the Regal. This was a simple uncomplicated tool, the jaws of which were permanently closed, except when the lever mechanism was squeezed, to allow a hook to be placed in, or removed from, the jaws. I used two versions over the years, fixed jaws and rotating jaws. The ability to rotate the jaws was on the pseudo basis and as such was pretty meaningless, as the hook would need to be removed so that its position could be reset, a procedure that could just as easily have been performed with the fixed jaws version. That said all the other points were covered up to a certain point and so the vice was a pleasure to use. The quality of the metal used in the jaws was at times suspect, but overall and for a small cost the vice proved itself a worthy third hand.

An excellent vice will include all the above points and, as such, the cost will reflect the quality. Cost alone though is not the guarantee of an excellent vice. There are vices that pretend to high status but have their clamps firmly fixed amidst the dross and care must be taken that all the eight points are fulfilled in case you end up purchasing what will prove to be a waste of time, effort and money.

As you may have gathered from the above, I like fly tying vices, or, to be precise I like good fly tying vices. In fact I like most things that are well designed and engineered, it just so happens that some vices come into that category. As I mentioned before, in many ways vices are like reels. A good solid reel can be purchased for a fairly low price, just so long as it is reasonably basic and does not try to imitate a top of the range model. Such reels can provide years of service and pleasure and, if looked after properly, can be left to some deserving soul in your will.

Cheap reels that attempt to imitate their more expensive betters are invariably a disappointment. Such reels should be passed on to somebody that you do not particularly like, well before the Grim Reaper has reaped your mortal coil. In fact passing them on to someone non-deserving as quickly as possible is the trick, just put the purchase down to experience and over-enthusiasm when in the tackle shop, which is something no angler should ever be ashamed of.

On the whole vices are the same as reels. A simple, well designed, inexpensive vice will serve you well, while those cheap vices that strive to emulate their betters, should be left well alone.

To summarize the above: in my opinion when buying a vice the choice should be either a simple, solid affair at a cost that will hardly be noticed, or a top model from a respected manufacturer. The difference in price will be a minor king's ransom, but both will do what is required and they will do it honestly. Those vices that profess to provide all the features and qualities of a top model at a price nearer a cheap model, do not in my opinion and experience fulfil their promises. They should be treated as Pinocchio vices, the jaws of which grow longer with every sales line that accompanies their promotion.

METHODS AND TECHNIQUES USED IN THIS BOOK

The methods and techniques used in this book are all relatively easy to perform and indeed to master. While some may require a little bit of practice to become proficient in their use, there are none that should prove particularly demanding. In this section I have outlined each method and technique used and provide comments on how their use can be improved and tips, where possible, on how to make applying them easy.

• 'Loop over the thread' method

This is one of those techniques that I wish I had been aware of when I first started fly tying. It was, however, many years before I became aware of it. I was first introduced to this method of applying materials to the fly pattern, through a video given to me by Ken Smith the Nottingham based instructor. The video was of Poul Jorgensen and he uses the method throughout the demonstration he gives on the video.

Two similar hackles with the one on the left doubled and the one on the right as normal.

Despite its simplicity, it is one of my favourite techniques and is the best way I know of applying floss, wire, tinsel or other similar materials to the fly pattern, while maintaining complete control of their placement. The details regarding this method are described on page 68.

• 'Loop under the hook bend' method

This is the method I use exclusively these days when splitting tails on upwinged fly imitations. It is simple and straightforward and allows complete control on the angle of split. The method can be used, equally effectively, for positioning two or three tails. The thread I use for forming the loop is thin, very thin down to size 17/0 is my preference. Using thread this thin adds no discernable bulk to the rear of the body and splits the tails equally as effectively as thicker, more bulky thread. I use Uni-Thread 17/0 Trico for the loop. The details regarding this method are described on page 95.

• 'Doubling the hackle'

This technique is not to be confused with doubling the hackle on Paraloop hackle brushes. Doubling the hackle can be, at least in my opinion, the difference between a fly pattern tied well and one that is excellent. The method is best performed on palmered hackles and on the hackles of wet flies. Effectively doubling resets the hackle fibres from projecting from the side of the hackle stalk to projecting to the rear of the stalk. When the fibres from both the left and right side of the stalk are reset they effectively become a single set of fibres all pointing in approximately the same direction. There are various methods that can be used to achieve this, but the method

A Paraloop hackle from above with the hackle fibres brushed forward with the fingers so that they are predominantly facing forward on the hook. This process is known as 'Doubling Paraloop Style'.

Two examples of furled floss often used for the bodies on Mayflies etc. On the right is a single furling and on the left a double furling. I prefer my furled bodies to be double furled.

described on page 21 is the method I now use, as it is quick, extremely effective and with a little practice makes all other methods cumbersome.

• 'Doubling the hackle' Paraloop Style

While the result of this technique is similar to 'doubling the hackle' in that it resets the hackle fibres so that they are pointing away from their original position that is where any similarity ends. The method is used on a formed Paraloop hackle brush and is designed to prevent any hackle fibres being caught between the core of the hackle brush and the hook shank, when the Paraloop is pulled over the top of the hook. This is an essential method to use when tying Paraloop flies and like the normal method of 'Doubling the hackle' can be that extra something that makes a fly tying excellent.

• Compacting the Hackle

Again this is a technique that has been developed for use when tying Paraloop fly patterns. Prior to the hackle brush being pulled over and tied in, the loop is opened up above the hackle brush, by gently pulling the two sides of the loop apart with your fingers. This will have the effect of compacting the hackle brush. To maximize compaction a dubbing needle can be inserted into opened loop and the side of the dubbing needle can be used to push the hackle brush

downward, this will reduce the height of the hackle brush by compacting it to the limit.

• Furling

Furling is for me one of those magical techniques that can be applied in many different ways. Not all materials can be furled, but I am happy to say most can be. I say happy because I love furling and the results achieved make it one of the most interesting of fly tying techniques. The method can be used to form a body as described on page 81, or to create the detached furled hackles described in 'Air's Apparent II' starting on page 17. Furling is one area of fly tying that I believe has much to offer, a lot of which has, as yet, not really been developed fully.

• Open Loop / Loose Loop method

This is, without doubt, one of the most important techniques used in fly tying. It is important in that it allows the materials being offered to the fly to be placed where they are required to be tied in, without being pulled out of place by the tightening tying thread. It is to be assumed that all fly tyers are familiar with this technique.

• Pre-Formed Foam Underbodies

Pre-formed foam underbodies allow bulk to be added to the fly pattern without reducing its ability to float. Bulk can also be added to a pattern without running the risk of increasing the

Various preformed detached hackles. (*left to right*) Crumpled Furled, Perfect Furled, Crumpled Furled and deer hair hackle.

Flex and Foam - this shows how the Flexifloss/Supafloss, or any other name this product goes under, is fed through the slice of foam cylinder.

water absorption of the fly pattern. Bulk can also be added without significantly increasing the weight of the fly pattern. One of the important factors to consider when using pre-formed foam underbodies, is that the foam itself does not have to give, on its own, the fly pattern the ability to float. Rather it is the combination of all the materials applied that allow the fly pattern to float efficiently. This being the case, the amount of foam applied to a fly pattern need not be enough to make the hook float, it is just one of a combination of materials that produce the floatability. The details regarding Pre-Formed Foam Underbodies are described on page 46.

• Pre-Formed Detached Hackles

Pre-formed detached hackles are an excellent alternative to more traditional methods of providing a hackle on a fly pattern. Personally I think this is a growth area and one that we will see a lot of development in in the future. My contribution to this development are the Perfect Furled Hackle and the Crumpled Furled Hackle, both described in detail on pages 23 and 30 respectively. While forming a detached hackle may, initially, appear complicated and time consuming, the fact that each hackle formed can provide the hackling on many fly patterns more than makes up for the time spent in forming them.

• Flex and Foam

The Flex and Foam method allows the application of foam to a fly pattern in ways that are not possible using other methods. The method uses standard foam (e.g. Plastazote) readily available from fly tying materials outlets and stretchable lycra floss, going under various trade names like Super Floss, Flexifloss, Supafloss and many others. These two products form what I see to be a perfect marriage and as such can be used together in many different ways. The basic Flex and Foam method allows a piece of foam to be applied to a fly pattern without the tying thread being applied to the actual foam, the Flexifloss effectively pulls the foam onto the fly pattern. This is a method that I believe has tremendous potential. To date I have only applied it to Parachute flies and with these it has proved invaluable. The details regarding this method are described on page 52.

• The Under Thorax Method

I think this technique is one of the most important I have ever used when creating my dry fly patterns and it presents a footprint on the water to be coveted. The method is so simple I have to kick myself that I did not think of it before. Probably someone else has already used this method, but I have never seen it except on my own tyings. Simple, yet so effective, easy to apply and giving almost complete control over the shape of the hackle, I feel that a complete book could be written about this one technique alone. The details regarding the application of this method are described on page 65. Give this one a try – it will not disappoint you.

• The Under and Over Thorax Method

This method is a development of the Under Thorax method. In the case of the Under and Over Thorax the technique is applied, like the name suggests, to under the thorax and over the thorax. For this reason it is ideal for forming wings on spent spinners, as the hackle can be changed into a relatively flat wing. The details of how to utilize this technique can be found on page 93.

• Thread Management

There is often a reference, during the tying instructions within this book, to winding the thread flat or spinning the thread tight. Both these instructions refer to the way in which the thread is wound on to the hook or around materials applied to a hook. To wind thread flat, the thread must first be spun counter to the twist applied during manufacture, doing so allows the thread to be wound flat, whereby each turn of thread applies less bulk to any one point, spreading the thread over a wider area. Spinning the thread tight has the opposite effect. When wound upon a hook shank, more thread is applied over a given distance, when compared to using normal or flat thread, therefore increasing the bulk, but also making the turns of thread more cutting, allowing more tension and grip to be applied at any one point.

• Sparse Palmered Hackling

This is an old traditional method of hackling a fly pattern that you seldom, if ever see in modern tyings. It should, however, be better known and more widely used as it is extremely effective. The best way to describe such patterns incorporating this form of hackle is, 'Spider patterns with the hackle wound along the hook shank'. I find three complete turns of hackle along the hook shank to

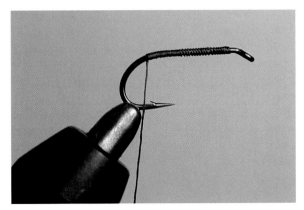

Thread management - The difference between tight wound thread and unwound thread. The windings on the half of the hook shank closest to the hook eye are tight wound and the windings on the hook bend side are unwound. Unwinding the thread allows less thread material to be added to the hook at any one point.

be just right. Tie the hackle on to the hook at the end of the body using the tip of the hackle. See page 103.

• Applying Wings

The important factor when applying just about any wing to a pattern is that the material used must be applied accurately upon the hook shank. In the case of dry fly feather slips wings, not only must the feather slips be place accurately upon the hook shank, but when the thread is tightened, it is absolutely essential that the tying thread pulls the feather fibres directly down upon each other and that the fibres are not pulled over to the side by the tying thread. To do this the loose loop/open loop method must be used, with the finger and thumb holding the materials tightly in place while the turns of tying thread pull the feather fibres downward on top of each other, during the tying in process. In the case of hackle tip and hair wings the same method is used to ensure correct placement of materials.

• Locking Turns for Hair Wings

This method is like a pet of which I am particularly fond. The technique I use differs from that which is normally advised and is of particular interest to anyone who ties using hard hair, for example Squirrel Tail. Usual wisdom recommends that when tying in hard hair, the tying thread should be wound tight so as to give a deeper more penetrating grip. This makes sense but is only part of the story. By spinning the thread tight a more penetrating grip can be achieved but the area of tying thread gripping the hair is significantly reduced. When tying in hard hair this factor is extremely important if the fly patterns tied are to remain durable and not suffer from premature baldness. The method I use requires the thread to be first wound around the hair using **flat** waxed thread and then the thread is spun tight and the **tight spun** thread wound tightly around the previously wound flat thread. Using this method both the area of thread actually in contact with the hair is increased considerably and the thread spun tight provides the final lock.

• Flattened Lead Underbodies

Again this is a very simple but extremely effective technique, which in its own right results in a very acceptable nymph pattern. Principally, however, it is used to provide an underbody on nymph patterns, creating a shaped foundation on to which the other material can be built. The result of using this method allows significant weight to be added to a fly pattern, while at the same time maintaining a fairly streamlined profile. The details on how to form flattened lead underbodies are described on page 123.

• Woven Bodies

Weaving the body of a fly or nymph pattern is a well-established method and there are many different methods of weaving used. In my own case I use a very basic technique that fulfils all my requirements regarding woven bodies and yet it is simple to both learn and perform. Waxing the materials to be woven as well as the underbody, makes weaving a body so much easier when compared with using unwaxed materials on an unwaxed body. The reason for this is grip, the waxed materials grip each other with far more vigour than unwaxed materials. So if you are new to weaving or normally cannot be bothered making the effort, then wax up the materials and give it a go. The beauty of weaving, at least in my opinion, lies in the ability of the technique to form a body where the topside is a different colour to the underside. This colour difference is to be found on many insects and as such weaving can be considered a good technique for tying imitative patterns. The procedure for creating a simple woven body is described in detail on page 131.

• Front and Rear Emergers

Most emerger patterns have a rear shuck, a pseudo tail designed to represent the shuck of the insect. Front and Rear Emergers are fly patterns tied to imitate the emerging fly, however, in their case the shuck is visible at both the rear of the hook and at the front of the hook. This more

Flattened Lead Underbodies —The above photograph shows the effect of flattening the lead underbody. From above the body is wide, while the side is thin and streamlined.

Another example of a woven body.

accurately imitates the natural emerging fly. The main body of the fly pattern is formed in the centre of the hook shank with the materials used to imitate the shuck being applied at both ends of the hook. I prefer to use a continuous bend hook when tying this type of emerger pattern. This is because, with the body of the fly tied in the centre of the hook shank, both ends of the hook can be submerged and contribute towards imitating the shuck prior to it being wholly discarded by the emerged fly. The method used to create such fly patterns can be found on page 42.

• Paraloop Hackle

The Paraloop hackle is, as far as I am concerned, one of the most useful ways in which a hackle can be applied to a fly pattern. There are countless ways to apply a Paraloop hackle, such is its versatility, but each method involves pulling a hackle, wound around some form of post, over the top of the fly pattern. In my opinion the Paraloop is a natural development of the parachute fly, but offers far more options on how the hackle can be applied and the resulting profile, when compared to the parachute method. The Paraloop hackle is used, in one form or another on various patterns in the book, including using pre-formed detached hackles and as will be clear it can be added to a fly pattern in many ways. The hackle can be pulled forward over the hook shank or formed behind the hook eye and pulled

back over the hook shank. A short hackle or a hackle extending the full length of the hook shank and all points between, can be used, it all depends on how the completed fly pattern is meant to act when on the water.

A description and procedure for tying the basic Paraloop can be found on page 151. On page 23 you will find a description of how to apply a detached hackle as a Paraloop and on page 36 the different ways in which the basic hackle can be applied is explained.

• Parachute Hackle

Just about every fly tyer will be familiar with the parachute technique of providing a hackle on a fly pattern. The method was originally developed in the tying shop of Alex Martin's of Glasgow and Edinburgh, Scotland in the early part of the nineteen hundreds and I believe some gentleman tried to patent the idea in the USA in the nineteen thirties. Originally Alex Martin's had the copyright on the name 'Parachute' and, as such, different names were devised by other fly tying companies to describe the technique when marketing their own fly patterns. Just like the Paraloop, the parachute hackle uses a post to wind the hackle around and in the case of the parachute fly described in this book the post is a strip of foam looped around the hook shank. When tying parachute flies it is best to make the first wind of hackle the highest up the post and

A Paraloop hackle prior to tying in.

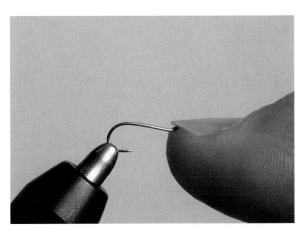

Testing the hook for soundness by springing it with your thumb nail. It is also wise to check that the hook eye is well formed and that the barb is not over-deeply cut.

the following windings should be below the first winding. There are numerous methods of tying in the wound hackle, including tying in on the actual post, it is normally possible to tie in the hackle, after winding, on to the hook shank. The details of the use of a parachute tying are described on page 162.

• The Whip finish

The whip finish is the final locking of the tying thread before it is cut from the completed fly pattern. I prefer just to use my fingers, rather than a whip-finish tool, but that is a matter of choice. No matter what method you use the whipping turns must progress towards the hook eye with each turn of thread. If this is not the case then there is no point in completing a whip finish, as the thread will not be truly locked.

• Testing the hook for soundness

Every pattern starts with this instruction because it is important. Place the hook in the vice jaws and first look to see if there is any impairment. For example is the cut for the barb over deep, is the eye formed correctly or are there any sharp imperfections? After checking the hook for such problems, then twang the hook hard with your finger. Does the hook bend too easily or does it break? By doing the above tests prior to starting to tie a fly pattern, time is not wasted by the hook proving to be sub-standard, just as you come to complete the whip-finish.

MATERIALS
USED IN THIS BOOK

Every material is required to do its duty and to fulfil what is expected of it.
No material is required to do that which it cannot be expected to do.

This section describes all the materials used when tying the fly patterns described in this book. The materials I recommend are those that I believe to be the best for the purpose they are used for. Saying that, I do not wish to imply that they are the only materials to use when tying the fly patterns described, try out other materials, they may well be an improvement on the materials I have chosen. I can, however, vouch for those materials I have recommended, they will do all that is expected of them. I am a great believer in quality and this is, while not quite so important with most of the manmade materials (there are notable exceptions to this), no more important than when using natural materials, hackles and furs etc. Many of the problems encountered by tyers can be isolated to the materials being used. Poor quality hackles will cause problems and, even if the problems are resolved, will still result in second rate tyings. My basic philosophy regarding materials is to acquire the best you can and beware of false economy. What may appear to be an expensive material will often, in the longer term, be the most cost effective. The materials listed below have all been used in my own tyings over a reasonable period of time and have each proved to be up to the job in hand. When I specify a particular brand, it is because I believe that particular brand to be the best for the specific purpose for which it is to be applied. An example of this is polypropylene floss, of which there are many different brands available. They are, however, not all the same, some are good, some are not so good and some are excellent. My requirements when using this material are fineness of fibre and floatability and although I know of a few very good products, the best in my opinion is Tiemco Aero Dry Wing. This floss is fine, very fine when compared to other polypropylene floss, it also has three holes running through the centre of each fibre making it the front runner in floatability. The same applies to polypropylene dubbing, and I have found no better selection of colours or fineness of fibre than Fly-Rite's poly dubbing and so that is what I use and recommend.

I must take the opportunity to emphasize that I have no connection with any fly tying material manufacturer or distributor and, as such, my comments regarding the materials recommended are straightforward and based on my personal experience and not by some other form of incentive.

The Materials
Antron Dubbing

This material has been around for many years and is manufactured by Dupont. It is available in a vast selection of colours. I like to use it on the bodies of patterns that sit low or under the surface of the water. It dubs on to a thread with ease and can be mixed with other dubbing materials such as Lite Brite. I have always liked Antron, if used correctly it can add an impression of life to a fly pattern by adding a little reflectivity and translucence, without being too showy. Antron is available from most good fly tying material suppliers.

Birman Cat Hair

This is one of my favourite materials for forming nymph bodies or the bodies of fly patterns that are required to sit low in the water supported by some other material e.g. foam applied to another part of the pattern. The fibres are extra fine and can be dubbed on to a thread easily. It is possible to form dubbing ropes from this material without using a thread. There is a problem and that is obtaining supplies of it. The Birman cat is the sacred cat of Burma and is one of the most popular breeds of pedigree cat, so they are not so rare as you may think. There are Birman Cat clubs around the world and a local diplomatic approach may produce a result. The hair is a result of brushing the cat and a little will go a long way. There is one supplier of the hair for fly tying and that is The Craftye Fisherman in Edinburgh, Scotland. The address can be found in the section on suppliers.

Body Wrap

There are many forms of body wraps available for tying flies. I have found that all do the job well, no matter what name is used to market the product. I also make use of the plastic material used in the manufacturing of some plastic bags. The bags used by the fly tying material distributor Veniard's are ideal. This plastic can be cut into strips, permanently stretched and then applied to the fly pattern. Of the materials produced specifically for this purpose the following products all work well; Bodi-Stretch, Body Stretch and Body-Flex. There are plenty of other products available, including Latex. The materials are available either in sheets and can be cut into strips, or they are available as strips. It is fairly transparent, flexible and stretchable. Products are readily available from fly tying material shops and mail order companies.

CDC

Cul de canard feathers come from around the preen gland of a duck. The fibres are extremely fine and it is this that allows it to float so well. If you know a friendly hunter then you will have as much of this material as you need. Failing that, the CDC sold under the names of Benecchi 'Devaux' and Marc Petit-Jean are excellent, with each feather having been selected for its quality.

Cobblers' Wax

Dark cobblers' wax is my preferred wax and I would not be without it. Some fly tying outlets sell it. Traditional cobblers will often be able to provide a supply if approached. It is not as easy to get hold of today as it was in the past. If cobblers' wax is proving hard to find then beeswax or any of the lighter coloured hard wax sold for fly tying will do. I have to say though

The Birman cat will provide wonderful fur for nymph bodies, a quick brushing will provide enough material to tie many fly patterns.

Coq de Leon tailing feathers. The feather to the left is of one colour and known as Indios, the feather on the right is speckled or mottled and is know as Pardo. These provide excellent fibres for both tails and wings.

that dark cobblers' wax is the best at least in my opinion.

Cock Capes

Always buy the best cock capes that your budget can stretch to, in the longer term this will prove good economics. Purchase half-capes if the cost is prohibitive to buy the whole thing. Capes, either the neck or saddle, are best when the cocks providing the product have been genetically bred and selected for the attributes useful for fly tying and names like Whiting Farms and Metz come immediately to mind. My favourite cock capes come from Whiting Farms, the consistency and length of useful hackle, on occasion, has to be seen to be believed. I have had single hackles from Whiting saddle capes that are more than capable of tying a dozen dry flies.

Coq de Leon Feathers

I love the feathers that are provided from this cock. Whilst the capes can be excellent, in this book I only use the feathers that are suitable for tailing and it is in providing these feathers that the Coq de Leon is in a class of its own. The feather fibres are very long and lacking in web, making them ideal for tying long tails. There are two types of feather available, those that are speckled, known as Pardo and feathers that are a flat colour, known as Indios. It is only recently

that the fly tying community as a whole has appreciated the value of these feathers, although many individual tyers have long been fans of them. This appreciation has resulted in the feathers being more readily available. I have feathers supplied by Whiting Farms and Ellis Slater. Although not used as such within this book, Coq de Leon feathers make fantastic wings.

Deer Hair

The deer hair used in this book is limited to the Bomb. Any deer hair that flares easily and is not over-coarse is ideal. Deer hair, has quite rightly become a popular and extremely useful material. The relative hollow nature of some deer hair gives it the ability to flare when it is applied to a hook and the thread is tightened. This is a great gift to fly tyers. Suitable deer hair is now available from all the good fly tying material suppliers that I know of.

Flexifloss

This is one of those products that is marketed under many different names, in fact just about every wholesale supplier has their own name for this useful product, another name is Supa-Floss. The product is made from Lycra, it is highly stretchable, expanding to around six times its resting length and it has no memory. Flexifloss is available in many different colours and it will

Deer Hair.

Flexifloss, Flex-Floss, Supafloss or any number of different names. This Lycra-based product is extremely versatile and ideal when used with foam products, as in the Flex and Foam Method.

happily accept a dye. This product is very useful and can be applied in many different ways. It is found in most fly tying material outlets.

Foam

Hunt for your own or buy it from the fly tying material dealer. Expanded polystyrene cups and polystyrene food containers are easily sourced. The flexible foams are probably best bought from a fly tying material supplier. Plastazote is one of my favourite materials and is available in sheets of varying thickness.

GSP

Gel Spun Polypropylene, halleluya for such a great material! Strong, very strong, flexible and thin, this product is great for such things as hackle posts and tying in materials where extra pressure needs to be applied without the material breaking. I love GSP. It is not always easy to get hold of and a little detective work may be required, but it will be time well spent. Using the flame from a cigarette lighter can melt GSP, this makes it my preferred core for many of the different detached hackles I use.

Hen Hackles

Personally I do not think it is so important to use hackles taken from genetically selected birds, when using hen hackles, as compared to when using cock hackles. On the whole the requirements for the use of the hen hackle is less exacting than those required when using cock hackles. Saying that I prefer to use high quality hen hackles in my own tyings. They are far easier to use than those capes of a lesser quality and more consistent in the resulting hackle. As such I tend to use the capes provided by Whiting Farms. The selection of natural coloured capes is fairly comprehensive and capes dyed to a specified colour are also available.

Holographic Tinsel

Holographic tinsel is available either in hanks or wound on bobbins and comes in varying widths. There is a wide colour selection. Holographic

Various hen hackles, natural and dyed. The hen hackle is softer than the cock hackle and as such is ideal when movement of hackle is required.

tinsel adds a sparkle to the fly in a way that no other material can, reflecting many different colours. I like to use it sparingly, usually as a rib or wing, but sometimes as a body material, especially on buzzers or emerging upwinged fly patterns. A little bit of holographic material will go a long way when applied to imitative fly patterns. This material has, in recent years, become readily available through most fly tying material outlets, both retail and mail order.

Holographic tinsel in shank form. It is available on a bobbin.

Kevlar Thread

I use Kevlar thread as an alternative to GSP for providing posts around which hackles are wound, when tying Paraloop or parachute fly patterns. It is strong, but in my opinion not as useful a material as GSP. It will not melt when a flame is applied to it, so it cannot be bonded together easily. Saying that I know a lot of good tyers who use it regularly. Kevlar is sold by most fly tying material suppliers.

Lead Wire

Lead wire of varying thickness is available from most fly tying material outlets. Care should be taken when winding lead wire to prevent it from breaking. Normally I use lead wire as an underbody on nymphs, lures or wet fly patterns, where the lead is wound over a foundation layer of tying thread on the hook shank and then wrapped in fairly random turns of thread to bind it firmly in place. A drop or two of fast drying glue e.g. superglue or Zap a Gap finalizes the job.

Lite Brite

Used in small amounts, Lite Brite is a wonderful material to add to imitative fly patterns. A little added to a dubbing provides an impression of translucence and life. Lite Brite is a fine fibre dubbing that puts a sparkle into a fly pattern like no other material can and I just love it. Just a touch added to an imitative fly pattern, either mixed with a dubbing or as a wing, is all that is

ever needed. The material comes in a wide selection of colours, but for me the pearl version provides everything I need. Lite Brite is available from most dealers and I cannot sing its praises enough, but only so long as it is applied to imitative patterns judiciously and sparingly.

Metal beads

I usually use two types of metal bead, gold coloured and tungsten. The best beads are those that are counter-sunk on one side of the drilled hole, this allows the bead to be fed onto the hook easily. The counter-sunk side should face to the rear of the hook when the bead is in place on the hook shank. For general purposes the normal metal beads are adequate, but where extra weight is required then tungsten beads are extremely useful. These beads are heavy, very heavy and they are also expensive, they do the job of adding weight to a fly pattern, very well. Both types of beads are widely available and come in packs of varying numbers.

Metal Wires

Standard stainless steel wire is used in a couple of the tyings in this book. It is available in different thicknesses from most fly tying material suppliers.

Micro-fibetts

Fine tapered nylon filaments that were first popularized in fly tying circles by John Betts. Micro-fibetts provide fine tails on upwinged fly

A selection of gold metal beads.

Micro-fibbets as used for tailing.

patterns. I prefer to use them on spent spinner patterns rather than anything else. They can easily be coloured, although they are supplied in various shades. I recommend that they only be used as split tails, two or three and never as a bunch. Widely available.

Partridge Hackle

I prefer to buy the whole skin when using bird feathers and the Grey or English partridge is my preferred choice. Invariably the feathers sold in packets lack consistent quality. At least if you have the whole bird skin you have a choice of which feathers to use. The grey breast feathers and the brown back feathers are the ones I use the most, normally tied in on the hook by the tip and slightly doubled before winding on. These feathers are ideal if the impression of movement is required, as they are soft and relatively long. Like most feathers partridge dyes well. Available in good fly tying material outlets.

Pheasant Tail Fibres

The pheasant tail provides tails, bodies and legs on fly patterns as well as wings and probably many other things that don't come to my mind at this time. This is one of the most useful of all feather fibres. Dyes easily and is widely available. In this book it is used as tailing material and as legs. When used as legs the individual fibres are knotted giving the impression of the leg joint and allowing the leg to be angled.

Pheasant tail fibres are a most useful material. Here the fibres have been knotted to provide legs for fly patterns.

Polypropylene Dubbing

The only polypropylene dubbing that I know of that is truly worth its salt, is that supplied by Fly Rite Inc. This product is of the finest fibre and has the widest range of colours of any other suppliers of polypropylene dubbing that I am aware of. Put simply it is the best available and I for one would not be without it. It dubs on to a thread very easily and a little goes a long way. Available in the USA from Fly Rite Inc and in the UK from Niche Products, the addresses of both suppliers are available in the list of suppliers.

Partridge hackle.

Fly Rite dubbing material comes in many colours and colour mixes and is my favourite polypropylene by far. This is a well thought out and presented product.

Tiemco Aero Dry Wing—this product is my favourite polypropylene floss. The fibres are very fine and each fibre has three channels running through it. A wonderful product.

Polypropylene Floss

There are many suppliers of polypropylene floss, on the whole most of the products available are fairly indifferent, tending to be fairly coarse in the fibre and limited in colours. The main exception to this is the excellent Tiemco Aero Dry Wing. This product is first class, not only is it lighter than water, but there are three hollow channels running through each individual fibre, making it the ultimate floating fibre.

Rayon Floss

Standard rayon floss is useful when there is no requirement for the material to assist in floating, as such I tend to use it on bodies that sink or cut through the surface of the water. The fibres can be very fine and as such very smooth bodies can be formed when using it. This product is widely available in many colours and thicknesses.

Superglue and Zap a Gap

I use a drop of glue for securing underbodies and, on occasion, when the fly is completed at the tail end with a whip finish, in this case a tiny drop is all that is required.

Thread

The thread I use in most of my tyings is a natural looking coloured thread (slightly yellow), when waxed, using cobblers' wax, it takes on a slightly darker colour. The thread is about 8/0 and is very strong compared to other similar looking threads. It is manufactured in the UK by Gutemann, code number U151 SKALA and is a multistrand polyester thread. The thread is marketed by The Craftye Fisherman under the name 'Microthread'. I have used hundreds of different threads over the years, but it is this one that I prefer.

Varnish

When varnish is required I use Sally Hanson's Hard as Nails. It is excellent and does everything I require from a varnish. It is available from some enlightened fly tying suppliers or from chemists or beauty product shops. I love the look on the shop assistant's faces when some of my fishing friends pluck up the courage to buy some from a beauty product supplier. I am sure some of these big guys take a week or two just building up to the time when they have to go in to stock up on varnish.

I usually only use one type of thread—a polyester micro-thread marketed by the Craftye Fisherman in Edinburgh. It offers everything I want from a tying thread. I rarely use any other colour than the one shown.

Hooks

Wet Fly Hook

I use the standard Partridge or Kamasan wet fly hook. Most manufacturers or distributors can provide a suitable equivalent.

Continuous Bend Hook

The Kamasan B100 is the hook I use when I want the fly pattern to stay on or in the surface of the water. For sinking fly patterns the heavier wire Kamasan B110 is ideal. Again there are many suitable alternatives.

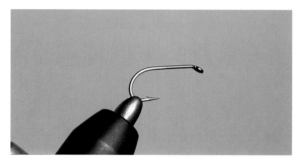

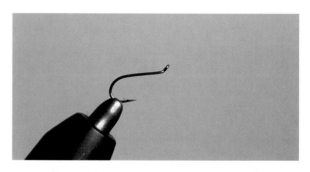

Short Shank Wet Fly

The Kamasan B160 is the hook used for the patterns contained in this book where a short shank wet fly hook is required.

Dry Fly Hook

All fly hook manufacturers produce a dry fly hook, I use Captain Hamilton dry fly hooks manufactured by Partridge.

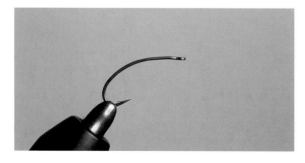

The photographs show each of the hooks I use in this book and it will assist readers in identifying suitable alternatives.

Klinkhamar Style Hook

The Partridge Klinkhamar hook is the one I use. There are suitable alternatives available from different manufacturers

THE GALLERY

The fly patterns in this section are a collection that use the techniques and methods described previously. Each pattern is illustrated, the materials required listed and methods used highlighted. The gallery provides a hint of the variation of fly patterns that it is possible to tie using the techniques described in this book.

1. Wulff Pattern
with foam underbody

Materials Required

Hook	Dry fly hook e.g. Partridge Captain Hamilton.
Thread	Own choice size 8/0.
Body	A shaped polystyrene under body, over-wound with a single layer of fine polypropylene dubbing.
Hackle	Grizzle cock.
Tail	Deer hair.
Wing	Deer hair.

Special Instructions

I have tied this pattern using deer hair for the tail and wing. To stop the deer hair from over flaring it is necessary to loop the thread directly around the bunched deer hair without taking the thread around the hook shank prior to finally tying in. Wulff patterns are ideal candidates for the use of polystyrene underbodies, with the relatively thick body the use of an underbody minimizes water absorption into the body material.

2. Mayfly Spinner
using the over and under thorax method

Materials Required

Hook	Dry fly hook e.g. Partridge Captain Hamilton.
Thread	Own choice 8/0.
Body	Fine ivory polypropylene floss.
Hackle	Grizzle cock.
Tail	Coq de Leon dark blue dun.
Rib	The tying thread coloured orange with permanent marker pen.

Special Instructions

This pattern uses the technique of locking the thread between the hackle and body and then using the thread to form the rib. The thread is tied off at the end of the body where the tail is tied in. In this case the thread is coloured prior to winding on as the rib by using an orange permanent marker pen

3. Drowned Spent Spinner
double furled body and foam over thorax

Materials Required

Hook	Dry fly hook e.g. Partridge Captain Hamilton.
Thread	Own choice 8/0.
Body	Double furled cream polypropylene floss with a light brown thread included in the furling.
Wing	Blue dun hackle points.
Thorax	Fiery brown polypropylene dubbing with foam over-thorax.

Special Instructions
Furl and tie in the body first, then prepare and tie in the wings so they are pointing out over the eye of the hook. Tie in the foam over-thorax at the point the body starts and then dub thorax. Pull the foam over the top of the dubbed thorax and tie in behind the hook eye. Now pull the wings back and when forming the head fix them into position with the tying thread. Ideally the wings should not be symmetrical.

4. Large Olive Emerger
crumpled furled hackle over foam thorax

Materials Required

Hook	Klinkhamar Style.
Thread	Own choice 8/0.
Body	Off-white polypropylene dubbing mixed with Lite Brite.
Hackle	Dark olive cock 'crumpled furled'.
Thorax	Light olive polypropylene dubbing with foam over-thorax.

Special Instructions
This pattern is tied off between the body and the thorax. First tie in the crumpled furled hackle directly behind the hook eye with the hackle facing over the hook eye. Then tie in the foam over-thorax. Now dub the thorax with the dubbing. Pull the foam over the dubbed thorax and tie in, cut off excess. Pull hackle over the foam and tie in, again cut off excess. Dub the thread and complete the body, tying off with a whip finish between the body and the thorax. Brush out fibres.

5. Spider Pattern
sparse palmered hackle

Materials Required

Hook	Wet fly hook.
Thread	Own choice 8/0.
Body	Black thread.
Hackle	Light blue dun cock.

Special Instructions
Wind tying thread to the start of the hook bend and tie in the hackle by the tip, now double the hackle. Tie in the black body thread and wind the tying thread back to behind the hook eye. Wind on the black thread to form the body and tie in behind the hook eye, cut off excess. Now wind the hackle forward, using only three turns to cover the body and tie in behind the hook eye, cut off excess and form a small head.

6. General Emerger
flex and foam on swimming nymph hook

Materials Required

Hook	Swimming nymph hook used upside down.
Thread	Own choice 8/0.
Body	Fine cream sparkling dubbing (SLF).
Hackle	Light blue dun cock.
Thorax	Fiery brown polypropylene dubbing.
Post	Superfloss/Flexifloss with foam addition.

Special Instructions
The swimming nymph hook is a great hook for parachute emerger patterns, with the hackle sited on the flat section of shank directly behind the hook eye. Using the hook in this way provides a very useful profile for imitating the emerging fly.

7. Yellow May Dun
sub emerger

Materials Required

Hook	Short shank heavy wire hook. In this tying I have used a carp hook.
Thread	Own choice 8/0.
Body	Rear of body four or five windings of lead wire. Bright yellow dubbing.
Hackle	Yellow hen or cock, long in fibre.
Front Hackle	Partridge dyed yellow or very light olive.

Special Instructions
Tying exactly as example on page 53 in chapter 'Airs Apparent II'.

8. Sedge Emerger
polystyrene foam under body

Materials Required

Hook	Kamasan B100.
Thread	Own choice 8/0.
Body	Polystyrene underbody over-wound with brown polypropylene dubbing mixed with Lite Brite.
Hackle	Red cock.
Thorax	Fine dark brown polypropylene dubbing.

Special Instructions
Wind the thread around hook bend and tie in underbody. Dub thread generously with body dubbing and wind one layer over the underbody. Tie in hackle at start of thorax section then dub thread with thorax dubbing. Wind dubbed thread to behind hook eye and then wind hackle over the dubbed thorax. Tie in hackle and form a small head.

9. Light Olive Emerger
crumpled furled hackle

Materials Required

Hook	Dry Fly Partridge Captain Hamilton.
Thread	Light yellow 8/0.
Body	Fine white polypropylene dubbing mixed with a little Lite Brite.
Hackle	Light Blue dun cock 'crumple furled'.

Special Instructions
In this fly pattern the crumple furled hackle is tied in directly behind the hook eye, with the body of the hackle point out over the hook eye. The body is then formed using the mixed polypropylene and Lite Brite mix, the shape of the body is pronouncably cigar shaped, the length of the body is the distance from the hook eye to the start of the hook bend. The hackle is pulled over the whole of the body and tied in at the start of the hook bend. The excess is cut off and the thread extended around the hook bend and then completed with a whip finish.

10. Large Spurwing Spinner
poly wings crumpled furled hackle

Materials Required

Hook	Dry Fly Partridge Captain Hamilton.
Thread	Own choice.
Body	Light coloured fine polypropylene dubbing.
Hackle	Light blue dun.
Tail	2 micro-fibbets.
Wing	Light blue or light grey fine poly floss.
Thorax	Darker dubbing than the body dubbing.

Special Instructions
Wind the thread to the start of the hook bend and form a small bulge of thread to force the micro-fibbets apart, tie in micro-fibbets to form tail, allowing the bulge of thread to place each tail correctly. Dub the tying thread with the body dubbing and wind along the hook shank forming a shaped body. Tie in the crumpled furled hackle with the body of the hackle facing over the back of the hook, cut off excess and return thread to where the hackle was first tied in. Take the thread to the centre of the thorax section and tie in the poly floss wing using figure of eight turns of thread. Return thread to where hackle was tied in and dub with thorax dubbing. Form a thorax, wind the dubbed thread around the poly wings in figure of eight turns. Pull the hackle over the thorax making sure that it is loose and not stretched tight. Now tie in the hackle, cut off the excess and form a small head.

11. Light Midge Emerger
flex and foam – front and rear emerger

Materials Required

Hook	Kamasan B170.
Thread	Own choice.
Body	Fine ivory polypropylene dubbing.
Hackle	Natural white cock.
Post	Superfloss/Flexifloss.

Special Instructions
 Basic Flex and Foam tying placing the post in the centre of a continuous bend hook to allow it to present the shuck at the front and rear.

12. Olive Dun
under thorax method

Materials Required

Hook	Dry Fly Hook Partridge Captain Hamilton.
Thread	Own choice.
Body	Dark olive floss.
Hackle	Olive cock.
Tail	Olive cock as per hackle.
Wing	Medium blue dun cock hackle tips.
Under-Thorax	Single strand of olive coloured thread.

Special Instructions
Tie in tail, form body, tie in under-thorax thread. Then tie in hackle and wind on, tying in behind hook eye, cut off excess. Pull under-thorax thread through the underside of the hackle and tie in with the thread very tight. Form a small head, complete with a whip finish.

13. Mayfly Spent Spinner
wound crumpled furled hackle

Materials Required

Hook	Dry fly hook Partridge Captain Hamilton.
Thread	Own choice.
Body	Cream and ivory polypropylene dubbing.
Hackle	Medium blue dun crumple furled.
Tail	Coq de Leon.
Wing	Fine light grey/blue poly floss.

Special Instructions

This tying is quite simple but utilizes the crumpled furled hackle in another way to that described previously. In this tying the tail is tied in followed by the body, then the crumpled furled hackle is tied in at the same place that the normal hackle would be tied in. The poly wings are added, halfway along the thorax section using figure of eight winds of tying thread. The hackle is then wound around the shank behind and in front of the wing. This provides a messy hackle, which I find very attractive and has proven itself to be a real fish catcher.

14. Eddy's Hope - Cow Dung Fly

Materials Required

Hook	Dry fly hook Partridge Captain Hamilton.
Thread	Own choice 8/0.
Body	Underbody foam, gold brown polypropylene dubbing wound over.
Hackle	Red cock.
Wing	Same foam as body.
Thorax	Body foam pulled over eye.

Special Instructions
As per tying described on page 169.

15. Big Boy

Materials Required

Hook	Heavy nymph hook.
Thread	Own choice.
Body	3 metal beads (Tungsten).
Tail	2 feather fibres.
Rib	Wire.
Body cover and Thorax	Body stretch or body wrap.

Special Instructions
As per tying on page 167

16. Spent Spinner
perfect furled hackle

Materials Required

Hook	Dry Fly Partridge Captain Hamilton.
Thread	Own choice 8/0.
Body	Reddish brown polypropylene dubbing.
Hackle	Ginger cock perfect furled hackle.
Tail	3 micro-fibbets.
Thorax	Fiery brown polypropylene dubbing.

Special Instructions
Tie in perfect furled hackle directly behind hook eye with the hackle extending over the hook eye. Form the thorax from the dubbed thread. Pull hackle over the thorax and tie in, cut off excess. Tie in tails and separate. Dub thread and form body, tying off with a whip finish between the body and hackle.

17. Olive Dun
under thorax, front and rear

Materials Required

Hook	Dry Fly Partridge Captain Hamilton.
Thread	Own choice 8/0.
Body	Light olive polypropylene dubbing.
Hackle	Front medium blue dun cock. Rear grizzle cock.
Tail	3 micro-fibbets.
Under Body and Under Thorax	A single strand of light brown thread.

Special Instructions

Tie in tails first and split using 'thread under the hook bend' method, then tie in under thorax/under body thread. Tie in and wind on rear hackle. Dub the thread and form body. Tie in and wind on front hackle. Pull under thorax/under body thread directly along the underside of the hook shank working it through the rear and front hackles, then tie in behind hook eye, form a small head and complete with a whip finish.

18. General Spent Spinner
wound crumpled furled hackle

Materials Required

Hook	Dry Fly Partridge Captain Hamilton.
Thread	Own choice 8/0.
Body	Brown polypropylene dubbing.
Hackle	Medium blue dun cock crumple furled.
Tail	Brown poly floss.
Wing	Brown poly floss.

Special Instructions

Tie in tail and split into two (or three if required), dub thread and form a tapered body. Tie in the crumple furled hackle where a normal hackle would be tied in. Tie in wing using figure of eight turns of thread into the middle of the thorax section. Wind the hackle towards the hook eye and tie in, form a small head and complete with a whip finish.

19. Midge Emerger
perfect furled hackle

Materials Required

Hook	Kamasan B170.
Thread	Own choice 8/0.
Body	Light brown and ivory polypropylene dubbing.
Hackle	Light blue dun cock.
Shucks	Holographic Tinsel.

Special Instructions

Wind the thread around the hook bend as in the photograph and tie in the holographic tinsel, wind the thread back to where the body will start. Wind tinsel to thread and tie in, cut off excess. Tie in perfect furled hackle with the body of the hackle facing over the rear of the hook. Dub the thread with the body dubbing and form a chunky body. Pull hackle over the body and tie in, cut off excess. Tie in holographic tinsel and wind to hook eye and then back to body, tie in at this point, complete with a whip finish.

20. General Emerger
perfect furled hackle

Materials Required

Hook	Dry fly Partridge Captain Hamilton.
Thread	Own choice 8/0.
Body	Fiery brown polypropylene dubbing.
Hackle	Furnace cock perfect furled.

Special Instructions

A little different this one in that the hackle is allowed to loosen from the core slightly prior to finally tying in. This does not form the most durable of fly patterns, but it is extremely effective, with a lot of movement and one that I would use when I was a little unsure of what to tie on my tippet.

SUPPLIERS

Most of the materials used in this book are readily available and as such there is no need to specify suppliers. There are some, however, that can prove difficult to find and as such the following may be of some assistance.

Birman Cat Fur
The only supplier of this material that I know of is the Craftye Fisherman
13 Montagu Terrace
Edinburgh EH3 5QX Scotland.
Tel: 0131 551 1224 Fax: 0131 551 1226

Tiemco Aero Dry Wing
In the UK
Farlows/Sportfish
Winforton,
Hereford HR3 6SP
Tel: 01544 327111 Fax: 01544 327093
Web site: www.sportfish.co.uk
email: sportfish@sportfish.co.uk

In the USA
Umpqua Feather Merchants
17537 N. Umpqua Highway.
PO. Box 700.
Glide, OR 97443
Tel: 503-496-3512   Fax: 503-496-0150
Web site: www.umpqua.com
email: umpqua@umpqua.com

Fly-Rite Polypropylene Dubbing
In the UK
Niche Products
1 White Mead,
Broomfield,
Chelmsford,
Essex CM1 7YB
Tel/Fax: 01245 442041
Web site: www.nicheflytying.com
email: niche.fly@virgin.net

In the USA
Fly Rite Inc.
7421 S. Beyer,
Dept.FT,
Frankenmuth,
MI 48734
Tel: 517-652-9869   Fax: 517-652-2996

All the other products specified are to be found in most fly tying material suppliers or mail order catalogues.

The tail of the pool

INDEX